Patterns of Linguistic Variation in American Legal English

ŁÓDŹ
STUDIES IN LANGUAGE

Edited by
Barbara Lewandowska-Tomaszczyk

Vol. 22

PETER LANG
Frankfurt am Main · Berlin · Bern · Bruxelles · New York · Oxford · Wien

Stanisław Goźdź-Roszkowski

Patterns of Linguistic Variation in American Legal English

A Corpus-Based Study

PETER LANG
Internationaler Verlag der Wissenschaften

Bibliographic Information published by the Deutsche Nationalbibliothek
The Deutsche Nationalbibliothek lists this publication in the Deutsche Nationalbibliografie; detailed bibliographic data is available in the internet at http://dnb.d-nb.de.

ISSN 1437-5281
ISBN 978-3-631-61581-2

www.peterlang.de

TABLE OF CONTENTS

PREFACE AND ACKNOWLEDGEMENTS

This book was envisaged as an attempt to look from a new angle at some linguistic aspects of what has been commonly referred to as legal English. Even though legal language has been studied from a multitude of perspectives and by a great number of scholars, I still find certain areas related to the linguistic description of this phenomenon inadequately covered. In particular, there are scarcely any studies explicitly addressing linguistic variation in legal English from the genre perspective and in terms of recurrent linguistic patterns. Thus, this work focuses on the description of variation in legal English in terms of preferred arrangement of lexical items into larger strings of units in individual legal genres.

The research presented in this volume was inspired by recent developments in corpus linguistics, especially those exploring the lexis-grammar interface. This book aims to account for some phenomena inherent in legal language in the framework of this relatively recent linguistic approach.

The research that led to this volume was facilitated by the Fulbright Scholarship Program in which I participated in 2007 at the University of Northern Arizona, USA. I am grateful to professor Douglas Biber and professor Randi Reppen for their encouragement and support during my stay in Arizona.

During the preparation of this volume, some findings were presented to a number of colleagues at different conferences and meetings in Poland and abroad. I am thankful to them for their comments and criticisms. I have been particularly fortunate in having professor Barbara Lewandowska-Tomaszczyk as my boss and mentor, who provided me with invaluable advice and guidance making sure I stayed focused on finishing the book. Her help is greatly appreciated. I would also like to thank my colleagues at the University of Łódź for their insightful comments and perspectives on many of the ideas in the book when these were still in the process of development.

I owe a special debt of gratitude to professor Douglas Biber and professor Leszek Berezowski for reading through the draft version and for giving comments on it.

My special thanks are also due to Michał Kornacki for proofreading and editing this volume.

And last but not least, I am grateful to Ania, Kasia and Kuba for being very supportive of my work and putting up with my tedious schedule for so many years.

CHAPTER I: INTRODUCTION

1.1. Variation in legal discourse

Translators, linguists, law students or other individuals who begin to deal with legal language in their university studies or in the course of their professional work face a bewildering variety of legal writings. In fact, they quickly discover that what is routinely referred to simply as "legal language", represents an extremely complex discourse embedded in the highly varied institutional space of a particular legal system and its respective legal culture. The designation "legal language" tends to emphasize the subject matter, the domain in which language is used, i.e. law, at the expense of the linguistic element. Still, it is generally acknowledged that law does not exist without language. Legal rules and regulations are coded in language. Legal concepts and legal processes are accessible only through language. If a legal text is criticised for being abstruse and incomprehensible to the general public, the problem most probably lies with the language. The expression "legal language" hides a multitude of specific classes of texts (genres) employed by various professional groups working in different legal contexts. Legal discourse spans a continuum from legislation enacted at different levels (e.g. state, federal), judicial decisions (judgments, decrees or orders), law reports, briefs, various contractual instruments, wills, power of attorney, etc., academic writing (e.g. journals, textbooks), through oral genres such as, for example, witness examination, jury summation, judge's summing-up, etc. to various statements on law reproduced in the media and any fictional representation of the foregoing. This list is by no means exhaustive. It merely indicates the extraordinary diversity of legal discourse.

The major goal of this book is to demonstrate that the universe of legal texts involves not only different situational characteristics of legal genres, such as different modes (speech, writing) and different production circumstances in which legal genres are created, different participants and the relations among them, or different communicative purposes, but that legal texts differ dramatically in terms of their linguistic characteristics. Important linguistic differences among legal texts can be found even in texts which have been created in the same mode, i.e. written, and which deal with roughly the same topic. For example, the language of Text Excerpt 1.1 from a textbook appears 'normal' in that it is written in standard academic English. It uses several legal terms to clarify the nuances of meaning involved in a legal issue related to contract law. The text employs complex syntax carefully crafted and edited in the form of four sentences cohesively tied and resulting in impersonal and highly nominal style.

Text Excerpt 1.1. *Textbook: Unfair Contract Terms Act*

Controls were likewise imposed on guarantees and indemnity clauses. In the former case, it was rendered impossible, without any possible recourse to the test of reasonableness, for guarantees to exclude negligence liability where the loss or damage arose from the use of goods by a consumer. As far as indemnity clauses were concerned, they could not impose any liability on one person to indemnify another for that other's negligence or breach of contract, if the term did not first satisfy the test of reasonableness.
There was a further extension of control in that the Unfair Contract Terms Act also subjected to the test of reasonableness exclusion clauses where they appeared in contracts for the transfer of ownership or possession of goods where the law relating to the sale or hire-purchase of goods did not apply.

The following excerpt from a contract deals with a related concept of indemnification. However, despite the apparent similarity, the contract illustrates strikingly different linguistic characteristics:

Text Excerpt 1.2. *Registration Rights Agreement: "Indemnification"*

The Company shall indemnify Holder, each of the Holder's officers and directors, and each person controlling such Holder, with respect to such registration or qualification effected pursuant to this Agreement, and each underwriter, if any, and each person who controls any underwriter of the Registrable Securities held by or issuable to Holder, against all claims, losses, damages, and liabilities(or actions in respect thereto) arising out of or based on any untrue statement or alleged untrue statement of a material fact ("Untrue Statement") contained in any prospectus, offering circular or other document (including any related registration statement, notification or the like) incident to any such registrations or qualification, or based on any omission or alleged omission to state therein a material fact required to be stated therein or necessary to make the statements therein not misleading ("Omission"), and shall reimburse Holder, each of the Holder's officers and directors, and each person controlling Holder, each such underwriter and each person who controls any such underwriter, for any legal and any other expenses reasonably incurred in connection with investigating or defending any such claim, loss, damage, liability or action.

Excerpt 1.2 illustrates many of the characteristics typically associated with "legalese", i.e. type of legal language that favours long, convoluted sentences (in fact, this excerpt contains only one sentence which consists of as many as 186 words), impersonal constructions, conjoined phrases and lists of words (usually nouns) resulting in an exceptionally dense use of technical vocabulary (e.g., *claim, loss, damage, liability or action*), multiple negation, the use of *shall,* etc. In comparison with the previous excerpt, the contractual provision is marked by relatively few verb phrases and a heavy reliance on phrasal syntax. Unlike in the textbook, cohesion in this contract is ensured through repetition of lexical items (e.g. Holder). The sheer length of Text Excerpt 1.2 is attributable to the extremely frequent use of phrasal coordination and past participle forms placed in post-nominal positions (e.g., *registration or qualification effected pursuant to ...*). These two excerpts come from different legal genres representing different levels of specialist communication and different goals. Linguistic characteristics highlighted above reflect those differences. For example, the heavy use of coordination and the determiner *any* is intended to allow for all conceivable contingencies in contractual provisions.

The primary goal of this book is to identify and describe linguistic differences of the type signalled above. The following chapters demonstrate the there are many ways in which legal genres differ. The analyses involve comparing a number of legal genres at different levels, ranging from vocabulary and multi-word expressions to co-occurrence patterns of multiple linguistic features.

1.2. Previous research on legal language and linguistic variation

It is no exaggeration to say that the last two decades have seen a veritable explosion of interest in studying the relationships between law and language. The complexity of this area is reflected in the multitude of perspectives from which research has been carried out. These range from genre and discourse analysis (Bhatia, 1983, 1993; Conley and O'Barr, 1998; Danet, 1980; Goodrich, 1987; Klinck, 1992; Kurzon, 1994, 1997; Maley, 1985, 1994; Shuy, 2001; Stygall, 1994, 2002; Tiersma, 1999; Trosborg, 1995, 1997), to semiotics (Jackson, 1994, 1995; Kevelson, 1988, 1989; van Schooten, 1999), modality (Bennett, 1989, 1990; Gotti, 2001; Kimble, 1992; Lauridsen, 1992), and forensic linguistics (Berk-Seligson, 2002; Coulthard and Johnson, 2009; Cotterill, 2002; Gibbons, 2003; Hollien, 2001; McMenamin, 1993; Olsson, 2004). The rapidly growing interest in the converging fields of law and language has prompted some scholars to postulate the emergence of a new interdisciplinary field of legal linguistics (cf. French *jurilingustique,* or German *Rechtslinguistik*) covering a range of different, albeit related, areas such as legal terminology and lexicography, legal translation and interpreting, analysis of legal discourse, courtroom discourse, linguistic human rights, language policy and planning, etc. (see, more recently, Šarčević, 2009; Sočanac, Goddard and Kremer, 2009).

However, relatively few major linguistic publications raise the issue of variation in legal language. Early research on the language and law interface dating back to the 1960s and 1970s (e.g. Crystal and Davy, 1969; Gustaffsson, 1975; Spencer, 1975) focused on statistically significant features of lexico-grammar used in a particular type of legal texts. Such analyses belong to the early studies of language variation as "register" (Halliday, McIntosh and Strevens, 1964). In the absence of advanced computational and corpus procedures, they were severely limited to only few significant features. It was simply not feasible to provide a comprehensive description of register variation by considering the full range of texts and linguistic characteristics. The advent of corpora and computational analytical tools has made such analyses possible.

Tiersma in his book *Legal Language* acknowledges the existence of variation in legal language by noting the following: "It should be evident by now that there is great variation in legal language, depending on geographical location, degree of formality, speaking versus writing, and related factors. The language and style of lawyers also differs substantially from one genre of writing to another" (1999: 139). Veda Charrow (1982: 84) notes that the designation "legal language" spans a continuum "from almost "normal" formal usage to highly complex varieties that differ substantially from normal formal usage". Klinck (1992: 134) asks a very pertinent question: "If on the one hand we justify our use of the term "legal language" by saying that it is a distinctive sublanguage of English, and on the other, we recognize further diversity within "legal language" itself, should we not be talking about legal languages?" A similar view is found in Maley (1994) who asserts that "There is not one legal discourse but a set of related legal discourses. Each has a characteristic flavour but each differs according to the situation in which it is used" (Maley, 1994: 13).

This perception of legal language has led to the emergence of different taxonomies and typologies. For example, Danet (1980: 471) proposes a well-known classification based on stylistic categories of degree of formality related to different modes of text production. Thus, in terms of mode, Danet distinguishes between written and oral texts, with the latter subdivided into spoken-composed and spoken-spontaneous. The degree of formality is marked by means of four distinct categories (frozen, formal, consultative and casual). Various legal genres can be thus distinguished and compared according to this set of contextual factors. This important sociolinguistic scheme suggests that legal genres vary depending on the degree of codification, standardisation and predictability of lexico-grammatical structures. For example, genres such as insurance policies, contracts, leases and wills are subsumed under the "frozen" and "written" categories, reserved for texts with highly formal traits and with features typical of the written mode. According to Danet's scheme, other written genres such as statutes, briefs and appellate opinions exhibit a lower degree of formality in comparison with that of witness examinations and motions, which belong to the oral mode (Danet, 1980: 471).

After conceding that legal discourse is expressed in various legal situations, Maley (1994: 13) lists several categories such as judicial discourse, courtroom discourse, the language of legal documents (contracts, regulations, deeds, wills, statutes), the discourse of legal consultation[1]. Tiersma (1999) provides a tripartite division of legal texts into three major categories of *operative* legal documents (those that create or modify legal relations such petitions, statutes, contracts, wills, etc.), *expository* documents (e.g. judicial opinions which analyse objectively legal points and *persuasive* documents (e.g. briefs or memoranda). He concludes by asserting "Clearly, legal language is not monolithic. Even if we limit ourselves to the written variety, there is substantial variation among different genres of documents. Generally speaking, operative documents have by far the most legalese, as compared to persuasive and expository documents" (Tiersma 1999: 141). More recently, Gibbons (2003: 15) reiterates some fundamental and classic distinctions of legal language. One basic dividing line runs along the written vs. spoken mode. Thus, there are written, largely monologic texts of legislation and other legal documents and the spoken more interactive and dynamic texts found in a variety of law-related processes, such as, for instance, courtroom interaction, police investigations, prisons and consultations between lawyers and clients. Another well-known distinction proposed by Trosborg (1995: 32) concerns "language as realized specifically in legal documents, i.e. texts covered by the scope of statute law and common law, namely (i) legislation, and (ii) simple contracts and deeds", referred to as "the language of the law", which should be distinguished from other uses of "legal language".

Despite the recognition that legal language is indeed heterogeneous, most linguistically-oriented studies have so far either treated legal language[2] as a largely monolithic phenomenon (e.g. Mellinkoff, 1963, Crystal and Davy, 1969, Tiersma, 1999[3], Alcaraz and Hughes, 2002) defined largely in terms of several distinctive lexico-grammatical features such as, for example, the excessive use of the passive voice, conditionals, archaic adverbs and prepositional phrases, the use of *shall,* etc.) which should apparently hold true for all types and categories of legal texts, or there have been a number of studies that focus on a single textual category and a limited range of linguistic features (e.g. Gustaffsson, 1975) focused on binomials and multinomials, Finegan (1982) looked at form and function in testament language; more recently Williams (2005) focuses on verbal constructions used in prescriptive legal texts). Either way, research efforts were essentially directed at identifying classes of factors that make legal language distinctive *relative to* general, non-specialized language. However, all the statements cited above as related to the issue of variation in legal language have

1 Maley (1994:16) also provides a classification of legal discourse reflecting the consecutive stages of a "conflict resolution scheme".

2 It should be noted that the appropriateness of using the designation "legal language" has been the subject of much debate. Klinck 1992 contains a detailed discussion of various perspectives adopted with respect to this issue. See also Mattila (2006).

3 While acknowledging the existence of variation in legal English, the book focuses on providing a general description of legal language disregarding the genre/register perspective.

not been followed up by empirically-grounded research practice which would document with reasonable accuracy the many different ways in which legal texts are different or similar. A case in point is Mattila (2006). This study acknowledges that legal language varies according to a particular genre or discourse community. As a result, one can talk about "the language of *legal authors, legislators* (laws and regulations), *judges* and *administrators,* as well as *advocates*" (2006: 4). Then, the description of a given "language" is worded in extremely broad terms:

> "The language of legal authors is characterised by greater freedom than the other sub-genres of legal language. At the same time, legal authors employ a good deal of scholarly vocabulary, notably Latin words and sayings. Courtroom language is especially formal, often archaic. It often has a categorical character in that judges use unreserved declarations and peremptory orders" (2006: 4).

It appears that there are virtually no studies that would provide an explicit description of linguistic variation *within* legal language or a description of variation between legal language and other specialised languages. To paraphrase Halliday's introductory comment on the term "scientific English", from his seminal 1988 article "On the language of physical science", the term "legal language" has been all too often used as a convenient label for a generalized functional variety, or register, of the modern English. Unfortunately, such labelling often implied that it was either stationary or homogeneous ignoring a great degree of variability of legal language and its constant evolution.

1.3 Register and genre perspectives on legal language

Previous linguistic investigations of legal language have relied on the concepts of register and genre in the construction of their analytical frameworks. The way these concepts have been understood and used is therefore of fundamental importance in further discussion of variation in legal language. Thus, the next section provides a brief overview of how register, genre and style have been used in previous studies of language variation.

1.3.1 Different perspectives on text varieties: register, genre, style

There is a long and rich tradition of studying variation in language use. Linguistic variation can be approached from at least four major perspectives (see Biber and Conrad, 2009). Each perspective attempts to account for the patterns of linguistic variation by focusing on a different factor. In the first approach, there is a focus on investigating the informational properties of text elements, such as "given" or "new" informational status, "focus", "topic", and the preference to place "heavy" constituents at the end of a clause in English. Such investigations conducted within the field of linguistic pragmatics or functional linguistics study how these factors influence the choice of one linguistic variant over another. In the second, historical linguistics approach, variation in language is examined across time periods. In the third approach, demographic characteristics of a speaker are explored within the realm of dialectal and sociolinguistics studies. Finally, the fourth perspective, adopted in this book, examines the situational context and communicative purpose. It should be pointed out that these approaches differ in terms of how they define linguistic variation.

Atkinson and Biber (1994) and Biber (1995) contain an extensive survey of previous synchronic and diachronic empirical studies of register variation. Most recently, a useful overview of how the concepts of register, genre and style have been used in previous research on language variation can be found in Biber and Conrad (2009). Interestingly, there does not seem to be a general consensus on the exact meaning of such seemingly obvious and related terms. In many studies, one concept is adopted and used exclusively while the others are ignored. For example, in his seminal book *Variation across Speech and Writing*, Biber exclusively uses the concept of genre. The term genre is also employed in the now classic studies done by Bhatia (2002) and Swales (1990). In other studies, however, register is the preferred concept. The following excerpt from Biber's 1995 book *Dimensions of Register Variation* is a good illustration of this perspective (1995: 9-10):

> In my own previous studies, I have used the term *genre* as a general cover term, similar to my use of register in the present book. In Biber (1988: 68), I describe *genres* as "text categorizations made on the basis of external criteria relating to author/speaker purpose" and "the text categories readily distinguished by mature speakers of a language; for example ... novels, newspaper articles, editorials, academic articles, public speeches, radio broadcasts, and everyday conversations. These categories are defined primarily on the basis of external format" (Biber 1989: 5-6). In practical terms, these categories are adopted because of their widespread use in computerized language corpora. The use of the term *register* corresponds closely to *genre* in these earlier studies.

In this approach, register distinctions are defined in non-linguistic terms such as the speaker's purpose in communication, the topic, the relationship between the addressor of a message and its recipient, and the production circumstances. In studying variety across registers, both situational characteristics as well as corresponding important linguistic features are taken into account. Biber uses the term *register* to refer to varieties that other scholars would name genres. Thus, novels, biographies, letters, book reviews, sermons, lectures etc. are all registers. The use of this term is extended to cover language variety at different levels of generality. This applies both to very specialized varieties such as "methodology sections in experimental psychology articles" and fairly general ones as, for instance, "academic prose".

Register can also be discussed in conjunction with another term widely used in sociolinguistic studies, i.e. *style*. To some extent, the two terms overlap. These two words can be used as cover terms for all kinds of situational variation. As a result, Crystal and Davy (1969) use *style* while Biber (1995) and other scholars, particularly those working in the field of language learning and teaching, prefer the term *register* to what is essentially the same type of situational variation. Many sociolinguists, following Trudgill (1983) tend to employ *style* as the more general term, reserving *register* for the specialized language that occurs when certain topics are discussed by people with shared background knowledge and shared assumptions about those topics, particularly when related to their occupation or profession. For example, American lawyers might employ legal register by using the expression "Miranda warning" where laypeople would need to resort to a lengthy explanation to the effect that it is a police warning that is given to people held in police custody or in a custodial situation before they are asked questions relating to the commission of a crime. For some scholars, the term *register* in this sense is primarily a matter of vocabulary, either because of the use of special words or because ordinary words are used in a special sense. Many words associated with a particular register are technical or semi-technical words. Legal register has many words that are used in a technical sense (e.g. *trust, consideration, party*).

There are, however, research studies which distinguish between register and genre (e.g. Ventola, 1984; Martin, 1985; Ferguson, 1994). Such studies are based on Systemic Functional Linguistics which has an extensive theoretical framework associated with these concepts (see Halliday, 1985; Martin, 1985; 1997, 2001; Matthiesen, 1993). Martin argues that register and genre are on different "semiotic planes" (Martin, 1985). Genre is viewed as a social process in which participants belonging to a certain culture use language in predictable sequential structures to fulfil certain communicative purposes. Genres have been also perceived as "conventional instances of organized text" (Couture, 1986: 80). The dynamic and interactive nature of genres as closely involved in human and more specifically professional communication is acknowledged in Swales' definition of genre (1990: 58):

> A genre comprises a class of communicative events, the members of which share some set of communicative purposes. These purposes are recognized by the expert members of the parent discourse community, and thereby constitute the rationale for the genre. This rationale shapes the schematic structure of the discourse and

> influences and constrains choice of content and style. Communicative purpose is both a privileged criterion and one that operates to keep the scope of a genre as here conceived narrowly focused on comparable rhetorical action (1990: 58).

On the other hand, registers have been referred to as the "expression-plane" of genre (Martin, 1985) and they tend to be associated with typical linguistic choices within different genres. The choices are influenced by three contextual variables called field, tenor and mode in Systemic Functional Linguistics.

1.4. Register, discipline, genre and legal language

Despite the absence of a general consensus concerning the use of register, genre and style, research on legal language has been more consistent in their use, probably due to the influence of the conceptualization proposed and popularized by Bhatia for over a decade (see, for example, Bhatia, 1993; 1994; 1997; 2004). Thus, by and large, the term *register* has been used to refer to a general kind of language associated with a domain of use, i.e. law. More recently, Bhatia (2004: 30) insists on distinguishing between register and *discipline* noting that the latter "represents the content", while the former the "language associated with it". On the other hand, the term *genre* has been understood as referring to more specialised varieties, such as brief, statute, contract, judgment, textbook or academic essay. At the same time, genres cut across disciplines. For example, textbooks from different disciplines can all share certain typical generic characteristics attributed to the common communicative purpose of providing students with established, state-of-the-art disciplinary knowledge. Thus, Bhatia contends, textbooks tend to rely on certain shared generic resources, such as typical lexico-grammatical features, rhetorical organization and "the use of multiple modalities to make disciplinary knowledge accessible to the uninitiated readership" (Bhatia, 2004:31). In addition, studies of a legal genre tend to involve considering its communicative purpose(s), the setting(s) or context(s), the social or professional relationship between the participants, the background knowledge of the participants, etc. (Bhatia, 1993: 101).

While this perception of genre is shared in the present study, the concept of legal register is rejected for two reasons. First, it somehow erroneously implies a hierarchical relationship between these two concepts, whereby "legal register" represents some vague superordinate term covering various types of legal texts (genres) and being practically synonymous with the notoriously imprecise notion of 'legal language'. This concern is echoed in Hatim and Mason (1990: 54) who rightly observe:

> [...] We need to beware of positing such unrestricted registers as "commerce" and "journalism". To attempt to quantify the frequency of items of vocabulary and grammar in such wide domains cannot lead to any meaningful characterization of a register.

Second, the use of "genre" and "register" may signal different methodological approaches. The genre perspective usually focuses on issues related to discourse communities, ideology and power, while the register-oriented study tends to deal with characteristic lexico-grammatical linguistic features.

1.5. The concepts of register and genre as used in the present study

After Biber and Conrad (2009), this study uses the concepts of genre and register as different *approaches* or *perspectives* for analyzing legal texts rather than different kinds of *texts* or different *varieties*. Table 1.1 below (adapted from Biber and Conrad 2009:16) summarizes the most important methodological characteristics of registers and genres[4].

Table 1.1. *Methodological characteristics of registers and genres*

Defining characteristic	Register	Genre
Textual focus	sample of text excerpts	complete texts
Linguistic characteristics	any lexico-grammatical feature	specialized expressions, rhetorical organization, formatting
Distribution of linguistic characteristics	frequent and pervasive in texts from the variety	usually once-occurring in the text, in a particular place in the text
Interpretation	features serve important communicative functions in the register	features are conventionally associated with the genre: the expected format, but often not functional

The two perspectives appear to differ in terms of textual focus, linguistic characteristics relied upon in the analysis, distribution of linguistic characteristics and the interpretation. In the register perspective, the analysis is usually based on

4 Biber and Conrad 2009 also include *style* as yet another perspective but since the concept of style is not referred to in this study, it has been dropped from further discussion.

a sample of text excerpts representative of a particular variety and the focus is on lexical and grammatical features which are frequent and which are pervasive (widely distributed) across this variety. Such typical features are then examined according to their function(s) in the situational context of the variety. In contrast, the genre perspective focuses on language characteristics which may occur only once in a text and which are usually located at a specific place in the text. These linguistic characteristics can be specialised, formulaic expressions crucial to the construction of a particular genre. As a result, an analysis is based on complete texts. The language features are conventionally associated with the genre. They conform to the cultural expectations of how a particular genre should be constructed. It should be pointed out that the same texts can be analyzed from both register and genre perspectives. For example, a genre study of a legal document known as *power of attorney* would analyze the expected textual conventions for complete texts of this type of legal documents. These conventions specify that a power of attorney should begin with the date when the document was made, the person who made it (*This Power of Attorney is made this xx day of xx 20xx by me xxx)* and the designation of a person appointed to be the attorney (I/*We hereby appoint Mr/s xxx to be my/our Attorney*)[5]. This type of analysis would result in proposing a macrostructure, i.e. format or organizational outline. A macrostructure in most such documents consists of two major types: *commencement and performative act* and the *operative parts* (see Alcaraz and Hughes 2002: 144-146). A typical power of attorney closes with the so-called testimonium clause (*In witness whereof I have hereunto set my hand this ....[date]*). All these conventional expressions arranged in accordance with a specific organizational format contribute to the creation of what a legal culture recognizes as the genre of power of attorney. From a register perspective, this specialized variety contains a frequent occurrence of *to-infinitive* clauses, prepositional phrases (e.g. *on my behalf, in the name of*), nominal chains (e.g. *any other act matter or thing*), nominalizations, etc. For example, the dense use of nominalization can be attributed to the highly specialist and informational nature of this text variety.

It should be noted that whether a particular text belongs to the category of *legal* texts is not determined solely on the basis of lexico-syntactic or conventional features. Such text must be accepted by the professional community in the course of actual legal proceedings (cf. also Gizbert-Studnicki, 1986; Jopek-Bosiacka, 2006).

The present book combines these two perspectives by treating them as complementary whenever possible. As a result, only complete texts are considered in terms of both important lexico-grammatical features and specialised

5 These examples come from authentic texts published in *Selection of English Documents* by Tepis Publishing House (1998).

expressions. These are identified by means of frequency counts and then analyzed in their immediate co-texts as well as against the overall document macrostructure. In other words, the following chapters show that certain linguistic patterns with a clear functional focus tend to cluster in particular places in the legal texts. Thus, both register and genre perspectives have been integrated into the analytical approach adopted in this book. The object of study are seven written varieties formally recognized in the US legal culture i.e. briefs, academic journals, contracts, opinions, professional articles, legislation, and textbooks. However, instead of focusing on extra-linguistic issues of ideology, power and discourse communities, this book takes a narrower approach by examining the ways in which lexico-grammatical linguistic features are patterned across different legal texts.

The major claim made in this book is that rather than use general, umbrella terms such as "legal language" or "legal register", the complexity and interrelatedness within legal language appear to be best viewed in terms of some sort of grouping of genres yoked together within the same domain. There have been a few interesting concepts proposed which are relevant to legal genres.

Meritorious claims usually cite legal authorities, such as statutory laws or case law, to support their arguments. Undoubtedly, law essentially depends on the two most conventionally standardized disciplinary genres, i.e. legislation and judgments to realize its disciplinary goals (Bhatia, 2004:55). This centrality is reflected in the *intertextual* and *interdiscursive patterning* that these mutually dependent generic constructs display in various forms of legal discourse, including academic journals and textbooks. In fact, all legal genres are intertextually linked to a varying extent. The degree of such interrelatedness depends on how narrowly or broadly a given legal action or professional activity is defined. Using the case of tax accountants, Devitt (1991) proposes the concept of *genre set* to denote a range of written genres that this particular professional group creates in the course of their work. She discusses several distinct but intertextually linked letters, such as an opinion letter to the client, a response letter to the client, a letter to tax authorities, etc. Similarly, Candlin and Bhatia (1998; and more recently Bhatia 2004) demonstrate how this concept could be employed in the case of a solicitor's professional activity. The interaction between a solicitor and a client usually involves completing a set of tasks leading to the production of various documents, such as a client file, a legal brief and a letter of advice. This set of written products can be referred to as a genre set. A genre set is thus a grouping of distinct albeit related generic constructs which are employed within the same, usually narrowly defined professional activity with a clearly designated agent (a professional) who performs this activity.

The concept of genre set has been extended by Bazerman (1994: 97) who proposes the concept of *systems of genres*. While the concept of genre set is somehow one-sided in that it represents the work of one participant to a professional activity, e.g. the solicitor, systems of genres attempt to account for the full range of genres. Bazerman (1994: 97) asserts that:

> The system of genres would be the full set of genres that instantiate the participation of all the parties – that is the full file of letters from and to the client, from and to the government, from and to the accountant. This would be the full interaction, the full event, the set of social relations as it has been enacted

Thus, the concept of systems of genres is broader and more comprehensive than genre set. However, it might still prove to be inadequate in order to capture fully the complexity of legal language. The reason for this is that law involves a range of strictly defined professional activities as well as larger sets of domain-specific generic constructs. Systems of genres as proposed by Bazerman are limited to the description of a particular professional activity.

This book favours a recent concept of domain-specific *disciplinary genres* proposed in Bhatia (2004). It represents the universe of particular systems of genres connected with different professional activities and combined with larger legal genres such as legislation, contracts, legal briefs, etc. In the course of professional activity, its participants need to refer to, interpret and exploit such larger generic constructs in order to achieve their professional objectives. Taken together, all such genres combined form a set of domain-specific disciplinary genres. Worth stressing is that such a set can be found in different configurations depending on the nature of a particular professional legal activity and the extent to which other genres are referred to or relied upon. The perception of legal language as consisting of a multitude of different, albeit related, domain-specific disciplinary genres seems amenable to corpus work in general and this study in particular. While, it is probably not feasible to build an exhaustive collection of all genre sets or genre systems existing in the domain of law, the contemporary corpus resources and tools allow the analyst to compile a dataset encompassing a set of selected domain-specific genres arranged in a particular configuration. Seen against such background, the ALC (The American Law Corpus) contains a set of interrelated disciplinary genres consisting of primary genres (Bhatia, 2006) or constitutive text type (Kjaer, 2000), which — through intertextual links — determine legal practice and target genres (Bhatia, 2006) or reproductive text types (Kjaer, 2000), such as, for instance, contracts.

1.6. Overview of the book

The approach adopted in this book is closely related to the commonly accepted usage-based, context-of-use or inductive stance in linguistics (see e.g. Kemmer and Barlow, 2000; Langacker, 2008, or Tomasello, 2003). Recent contributions in these areas have led to the observation that "human beings construe non-linguistic reality the way they think about themselves or speak and write to others, becoming manifest and accessible predominantly in large computer-readable collections of spoken and written natural texts" (Schulze and Römer, 2009: 2). The present study links up with the extensive evidence on the interrelatedness of vocabulary and syntax provided by corpus linguistics, which has been emerging by means of various theoretical and methodological assumptions, some of which include (and are, in fact directly or indirectly drawn upon in the present analysis) idiom principle (Sinclair, 1991), collocation, colligation, semantic preference, and semantic prosody, the pattern grammar work (Hunston and Francis, 1999), the theory of lexical priming (Hoey, 2005). As previously mentioned, this book makes use of a corpus of seven different disciplinary legal genres, which, until now, appears to be the first to utilise a large-scale collection of annotated data of legal discourse. I explore legal discourse in various types of situations and contexts, e.g. academic, judicial, commercial, providing legal advice, etc. My interest lies with identifying and accounting for lexical, lexico-syntactic and phraseological patterning present in various textual manifestations of contemporary American legal discourse. I follow an empirical research design that relies on a number of analytical approaches including corpus linguistics and genre and register analysis in the sense described in Section 1.4 above. Both quantitative and qualitative examinations are combined in respect of data obtained from corpus and computational methodologies in my investigation of a range of lexico-syntactic features of individual legal genres relative to one another and to other specialist genres.

The central goal pursued in the book is to provide a corpus-based, relatively comprehensive linguistic description of variation among several selected legal genres by surveying the distinctive linguistic characteristics and their co-occurrence within each genre. These linguistic descriptions include vocabulary distribution and use (*keywords*), extended lexical expressions (*lexical bundles*), and lexico-syntactic co-occurrence patterns (*Multi-Dimensional Analysis*). The findings are then interpreted in functional terms in an attempt to provide an overall characterization of the most commonly encountered types of legal language and to describe the extent to which selected legal genres are different or similar linguistically. The claim made in this study is that what is commonly referred to as "legal English" should be more accurately described as a system of related domain-specific genres, which vary widely in terms of patterning, understood here as recurring lexical and lexico-grammatical combinations discernible in large collections of authentic texts by means of quantitative and qualitative analytical techniques. Chapter 2 focuses first on the design and construction of the American Law Corpus and then it moves on to introduce a range of methodologies employed in the analyses provided in this book. Chapters 3-6 explore linguistic patterning at three different levels. Chapter 3 starts with overall patterns of vocabulary use by examining the proportion of the total number of words (tokens) and types (different words) and the distribution of high-frequency words across the legal genres. Thus, this chapter attempts to offer insights into the diversity of lexical choice in legal language. The latter part of Chapter 3 uses the Keyword Analysis to investigate which words are unusually frequent in a particular legal genre relative to the other genres. This quantitative analytical part is followed by an in-depth functional analysis of these words in their relevant contexts culminating in proposing functional categories for the previously selected keywords. Chapter 4 takes us beyond the level of individual words to examine the distribution and functions of multi-word expressions across the different text genres. It starts from the assumption that collocations differ depending on the text type and they thus represent an extremely useful means to discriminate between different legal genres. Chapters 5 and 6 both use Multi-dimensional Analysis, a research technique for studying co-occurrence patterns in a given language variety. The former relies on the 1988 MD model, which enables one to examine variation in legal genres relative to a number of other written genres in English. The latter discusses findings based on a new Multi-dimensional Analysis after carrying out a new factor analysis with a view to identifying co-occurrence patterns unique to the domain of legal texts.

Finally, Chapter 7 will summarize the results of the analysis, offer pedagogical implications and emphasize directions for future research.

CHAPTER II: THE METHODS AND THE CORPUS

2.1. Introduction

The descriptions of legal language provided in this book emerged from different research methodologies applied to examine a multi-genre corpus of legal texts. Much of the published work on legal discourse[6] has focused on the functions of a specific feature (or features) in a particular legal genre or on the analysis of legal discourse in different courtroom situations or other legal contexts, especially in the field of forensic linguistics. The research goal in this book is to provide a comprehensive linguistic description of a range of legal genres based on large authentic data. The data comes from what is probably the largest and most representative corpus of legal discourse. Thus, this chapter first describes the design and construction of the corpus and it demonstrates how individual genres fit in within the larger framework of legal institutions or what could be collectively described as the world of law. The latter part of this chapter introduces different methodologies employed throughout the book.

2.2. Design and construction of the American Law Corpus (ALC)

The collection of texts (hereinafter called the *American Law Corpus* or the ALC) contains over 5,500,000 words and represents seven major genres which are part of the American legal culture and education. Table 2.1 below shows the overall composition of the ALC by genre category.

Table 2.1. *Composition of the American Law corpus*

Genre	# of texts	# of words
Academic journals	71	552,487
Briefs	64	763,222
Contracts	177	1,178,616
Legislation	60	1,178,516
Opinions	114	1,182,246
Professional Articles	100	201,404
Textbooks	104	519,116
Total	**687**	**5,578,393**

6 The term "discourse" is used in this book in the sense of "the study of language use". (See Schiffrin, Tannen, and Hamilton, 2003:1) for a recent survey of the range of definitions given to this term).

The design of a corpus is one of the most important considerations and it certainly occupies the central place in this research approach. The corpus should be representative of the target domain of use. Discussions of issues connected with corpus design and its representativeness can be found in an ever-growing body of corpus-related literature (see, for example, Leech, 1991; Biber, 1993; Hunston, 2002). Generally, corpora must be designed to represent particular registers, dialects, or other domains of use. The representativeness of the corpus affects the kinds of questions that can be addressed and the generalisability of the results of the research. Representativeness is determined by two major considerations: *composition* and *size*. The composition of a corpus refers to the text categories included in the design of the corpus.

Corpus size is routinely measured by the total number of words in the corpus. As Biber (1993) points out, the number of texts is the most important consideration for studies which focus on the text as the basic unit of analysis. But it is equally important to consider the number of texts from different categories, and the number of words in each text. Clearly, if too few but long texts are included, a single text could then adversely affect the outcome of an analysis. Enough texts must be included in each category to capture variation across speakers or authors (see Biber, 1990, 1993). Biber (2001: 108-123) refers to experimental research articles as a good example where the different sections, such as Introduction, Methods, Results and Discussion, have different patterns of language use. In this case, any sampling carried out by the researcher must obviously include all of these sections. Otherwise, the corpus would fail to adequately represent the language patterns found in this register. However, if one expects precise guidelines concerning the number or size of the text samples, then the situation becomes rather complex. In LSP studies, factors such as the needs of a project and the availability of data are of central importance. Certain legal texts, such contracts, deeds or other private law documents may be particularly difficult to collect due to issues of confidentiality and privacy. While "the bigger is always better" rule does not necessarily apply in the case of special-purpose corpora (see Bowker and Pearson, 2002: 45-54 for a more detailed discussion), a corpus of limited size might not include all the relevant terms and linguistic patterns. My experience in compiling a legal corpus suggests that the size of a corpus should be related to the degree of specificity of a particular text category. General categories, such as legislation or contracts, should contain over one million words but more narrowly-defined genres could have only 200,000 words. Of course, any such prescriptive comments should be treated with caution. It is recommended, and such is also the opinion of the author of this book, that specialised corpora should ideally include full-text samples rather than excerpts (see, for instance Bowker and Pearson, 2002: 45-57 and McEnery, Xiao and Tono, 2006)).

The textual (genre) categories selected for the American Law Corpus were randomly sampled from a range of written activities associated with the American legal culture. The depth of sampling for each genre category reflects the present author's assessment of its relative availability and importance. Sixty different statutory instruments comprising almost 1,200,000 words represent the genre of legislation, which forms the ultimate primary mandatory authority in the US legal system (Brostoff and Sinsheimer 2003). The other primary authority texts included in the ALC are the opinions of the Supreme Court of the United States. These two genres were selected since both judge-made law and legislatively-enacted statutes are the primary vehicle through which American law develops (see also Tokarczuk, 1998 and Lee, Hall and Hurley, 1999). The third major and one of the largest corpus sections (1,178,616 words) includes contracts. In fact, this one-word designation hides a bewildering variety of legal instruments ranging from relatively simple and short (often just one-page) documents, such as *Bill of Sale* or *Contractor Agreement* to very complex commercial agreements made between various corporations. This latter type of contracts could run for several pages, as is the case with *Registration Rights Agreement* or *Asset Purchase Agreement.* As a result, three major genres of legislation, opinions and contracts are sized almost identically allowing direct comparison in purely quantitative terms.

Nearly equally-sized are also two genres representing legal academic language, i.e. academic journals and textbooks. In the case of the former, data comes from several different journals published on-line by US Law Schools, such as for instance, University of Virginia School of Law. Recognizing the existence of topic-based variation within this category, the corpus design tried to ensure a wide range of different sub-disciplines without claiming an exhaustive sampling. The areas included in the dataset comprise administrative law, admiralty, agriculture law, bankruptcy law, commercial law, corporation and enterprise law, dispute resolution and arbitration law, environmental law, family law, securities and tax law. Unlike academic journals, textbooks target almost exclusively commercial law and contract law. The other major characteristic for this category is that it consists of text samples rather than full texts. This exception to the general full-text-only principle had to be made given the size of individual textbooks. Data collection focused on capturing ten different samples from ten different undergraduate textbooks on contracts and commercial law. Four samples were taken from one general textbook introducing readers to the general principles of the English law. Each sample contains about 5000 words.

The category of briefs groups appellate briefs written by counsel (lawyers) and required to be filed with appellate court, which in our case is the US Supreme Court. This legal genre represents an interesting combination of operative language structured according to very particular formatting governed by the Rules of Appellate Procedure (Black, 1990) and persuasive language, since the primary goal of briefs is to present the important legal issues of the appeal to the court. The sixty-four documents collected in our dataset date from 2000 and 2007 and this time span corresponds to the period from which Supreme Court opinions were sampled for this study. Extra care was taken to ensure that each brief contains around 11,000 words but, inevitably, some deviation ensued.

Finally, professional articles represent a new type of text available only over the Internet from the well-known law and government website www.findlaw.com. FindLaw.com is a free legal information web portal owned by Thomson Reuters. It was created by Stacy Stern, Martin Roscheisen and Tim Stanley in 1995, and after becoming the highest-trafficked site on the Internet, was acquired by Thomson West in 2001. The site is designed to help consumers, small-business owners, students and legal professionals find answers to everyday legal questions, and to find legal counsel when necessary. The site includes case law, state and federal statutes, the West Legal Directory, legal news and analysis. The articles appear to be intended for different types of audience. They provide free legal information and advice on a wide range of specialist issues ranging from assignee liability, stock options, lease to complex litigation issues. In most cases, the density of specialist terms and level of detail provided suggests that such information is intended for other professionals or for interested lay persons with considerable knowledge of law or some willingness to learn about it. However, there are also (considerably fewer) articles clearly aimed at the general public, as reflected, for example, in the following title *Frequently Asked Questions about Pursuing a Civil Lawsuit.* The articles are authored by practicing lawyers from various law offices. Their limited size (slightly above 2000 words) suggests that an interested reader should contact a lawyer and pursue this matter further aided by a professional.

2.3. Data coding and corpus processing

All the documents were stored as separate files and tagged for parts of speech and semantic categories using the "Biber tagger". The Biber tagger is a computer programme developed by professor Douglas Biber from Northern Arizona University, USA to provide a grammatical 'tag' or annotation for each word in a text file. For example, the following sentence from a Supreme Court opinion:

> *I believe we have an obligation to provide needed clarification concerning an important issue that has generated confusion among the federal courts.*

is transformed into the following tagged version:

I ^pp1a+pp1+++=I
believe ^vb+vprv+tht0++=believe
we ^pp1a+pp1+++=we

have ^vb+hv+vrb++=have
an ^at++++=an
obligation ^nn+nom+++=obligation
to ^to++++=to
provide ^vbi+vsua+++=provide
needed ^vbd+++xvbn+=needed
clarification ^nn+nom+++=clarification
concerning ^in++++=concerning
an ^at++++=an
important ^jj+atrb+++=important
issue ^nn++++=issue
that ^tht+rel+subj++=that
has ^vbz+hvz+aux++=has
generated ^vprf+++xvbnx+=generated
confusion ^nn++++=confusion
among ^in++++=among
the ^ati++++=the
federal ^jj+atrb+++=federal
courts ^nns++++=courts

As can be seen, tags follow every word in the text. The tag symbols and tag fields represent the grammatical and semantic annotation identified by the tagger. For example, the word *believe* in the sample above has a "vb+vprv+tht0" tag which means that it is a private verb followed by *that* deletion. The tagset incorporates an extended version of the CLAWS tagset (see Garside, Leech, and Sampson, 1987). More details about the Biber's tagger can be found in Biber (2006: 28-29). Tagged texts allow easy and immediate processing and counting of the rates of occurrences of linguistic and grammatical features. A complementary "tag-count" programme also created by Biber automatically provides normalized counts per single files of up to 150 different grammatical or semantic features occurring in a corpus. All texts in the corpus are coded with a header to identify content area and genre. The texts were scanned to disk (textbooks) or copied from websites.

Essentially, WordSmith 5.0 (Scott 2006) at http://www.lexically.net/wordsmith/version4 was used to obtain data for the different types of linguistic analyses used in this book. The rates of occurrences of all linguistic features used in the analyses (Chapters 5 and 6) were normalized per 1,000 words. Norming in quantitative research is necessary to compare adequately the distribution of the linguistic features across corpora or corpus components which vary in size (Biber, Conrad and Reppen 1998). Only the occurrences of lexical bundles (Chapter 4) were normalized per 1,000,000 words. The descriptions in this study (Chapters 5 and 6) are based on a wide range of linguistic features. These are described in detail in Section 2.8 below.

2.4. The American Law Corpus and the World of Law

The corpus described in previous sections had been envisaged to reflect the real world of legal discourse and its institutions. Clearly, the focus of the analysis is on textual artefacts, i.e. the genres but these are inevitably embedded in the context of specific institutional and disciplinary practices, procedures and the culture of the American legal system. Legal language analysed in this book is in fact American legal language. Aside from reasons of space, it was the author's intention to preserve the homogeneity of jurisdiction and, consequently, of the legal culture. The system of common law originating in Great Britain has spread to many other countries around the world, notably to the United States, Canada, Australia, New Zealand, South Africa and to India and other countries where English was recognized as one of the official languages. Despite sharing certain basic characteristics, the language and legal institutions in the respective countries have come to differ markedly from one another (Williams, 2005: 31). Indeed, since the United States is a federalist system, the American common law is created at both federal and state levels thus leading to certain inevitable local idiosyncrasies. Further, while there is a central or federal government structure, each state also has corresponding government structures. The federal government has powers which are specifically defined in the United States Constitution. At the same time, the states have all the remaining government powers and functions not specifically reserved from the federal system. In both the state and federal governments, the power within the government is divided into three separate sections or branches, i.e. the judicial, executive and legislative[7]. Importantly, each branch of government provides a source of a different type of law (Brostoff and Sinsheimer, 2003: 43). Similarly, there are two co-existing court systems, the federal courts and the state courts. The jurisdiction of the federal court system is limited in its subject matter. On the other hand, the state courts have broad subject matter jurisdiction. The legislative branch of government enacts statutes as a source of law. The federal and state systems of government have bicameral legislatures.

This brief outline of the US legal system should already signal the presence of complex relationships between the three government sections at the two levels. Given the corpus-based approach of the present study, difficult decisions had to

7 Worth noting is that the term *government* in the United States is not restricted to the executive branch only. Instead, it can refer to the federal government and all its agencies and bureaus (cf. also Black 1990).

be made regarding the choice of corpus material. For reasons of space and homogeneity, the corpus design focused on the federal resources. Equally important was the status and significance of the institutions which appropriate the generic resources in question. For example, collecting the opinions of the US Supreme Court seemed an obvious choice given the significance and the influence this institution has exerted on the American legal system and legal education. Alpheus Thomas Mason (1969) is credited with the following statement about the U.S. Supreme Court: "the American counterpart of the British Crown, but unlike a queen on the throne, the Court has real power. It can bring Congress, President, state governors and legislators to heel" (Abraham, 1998: 35). It is the only court mentioned in Article III or in any other part of the Constitution. All the other federal courts have been created by statute.

Further, the Supreme Court is regarded as the national symbol of justice. It is the highest court in the United States. The Supreme Court consists of the Chief Justice and eight Associate Justices. The U.S. Supreme Court has both original and appellate jurisdiction, but it exercises the former only in rare instances. The primary task of the Court is thus appellate. In that capacity it serves as the final arbiter in the construction of the Constitution of the United States and it provides a uniform interpretation of the law, although its very power to do so also enables it to change its mind from case to case. However, to a large extent, it attempts to adhere to precedent, the well-known doctrine of *stare decisis,* i.e. "let the decision stand". In this way, the precedents are given the authority of established law. It is thus little wonder that learning to read and understand cases, especially those given by the US Supreme Court, is a fundamental task that is mastered in all law schools. The collection of 114 opinions included in the ALC obviously represents but a fraction of the Court's enormous output. Still, this sample should capture the general trends in lexico-syntactic patterning representative for the collective end product of the nine justices. In fact, an opinion is usually written by one judge (technically referred to as "justice") after winning the approval of the majority. The process of opinion writing is frequently a difficult and laborious task, sometimes running into months, occasionally even years. However, the average length of work ranges from thirty-five to fifty-eight days (Abraham, 1998: 143). There is little doubt that, in most cases, an opinion is the collective product of inordinately painstaking labour, long process of persuasion or, maybe more appropriately, bargaining that accompany the drafting of opinions. It is clear that all of the judges, at one time or another, are constrained by group and institutional concerns. It is therefore again worth stressing that many, if not all, of the Court's opinions, although ostensibly the work of one person, are really the product of many minds, in the sense that the judge who writes the opinion often has to add to, delete, or modify the original draft in order to be able to retain the support of his or her colleagues.

The genre of briefs is inextricably linked to the specific institutional framework of the US Supreme Court[8]. In accordance with the appeal procedure, before presenting their oral arguments, counsel for both sides will submit a legal brief summarizing the facts of the case as well as the legal reasoning behind their arguments. There are two types of briefs typically used in proceedings before the Supreme Court: amicus curiae briefs and merit briefs. The former are usually filed in appeals concerning matters of a broad public interest, e.g. civil rights cases. This type of briefs may be filed by private persons, various organizations or the government. The latter (also known as briefs on the merits) refers to briefs on the inherent rights and wrongs of a case, absent from any emotional or technical biases (Black, 1990). Both types of briefs are represented in the dataset, while merit briefs account for 65% of all the briefs collected in the ALC. Of those, 75% are filed by the Solicitor General. The Solicitor General is the third-ranking official in the US Department of Justice, following the Attorney General and the Deputy Attorney General. Due to its special relationship with the Supreme Court, the post of Solicitor General has always enjoyed a high reputation in legal circles. The Solicitor General is in charge of all the government's litigation in the Supreme Court, which constitutes in excess of 50 per cent of the Court's total workload. That official (plus deputies and assistants) argues all of the government's cases before it. The Solicitor's General's office supervises all government briefs filed in the Court, and the Solicitor General must personally approve or disapprove of any case before the government takes it to the Court.

2.5. Research methodologies used in the analyses

Corpus linguistics is rightly viewed as a research approach that has developed over the past 40 years to study language use in large, principled collections of texts. The central goal of corpus-based analysis is to document and interpret generalisable patterns of use. Unlike in other related sub-disciplines of discourse analysis and functional linguistics, corpus linguistic investigations of language use are usually designed as quantitative studies aimed at arriving at some generalisable findings representing some domain of use. Biber, Conrad and Reppen (1998:4) point to four basic characteristics of corpus-based analysis:

- it is empirical, analyzing the actual patterns of use in natural texts;
- it utilizes a large and principled collection of natural texts, known as a "corpus", as the basis for analysis;

8 This section is based on information culled from the official website of the Supreme Court of the United States – http://www.supremecourt.gov/.

- it makes extensive use of computers for analysis, using both automatic and interactive techniques;
- it depends on both quantitative and qualitative analytical techniques.

The descriptions provided in the following chapters were obtained by means of standard procedures of corpus linguistics based on a tagged corpus. However, the analysis of vocabulary features (the KeyWord Analysis) provided in Chapter 3, multi-word expressions (lexical bundles) documented in Chapter 4 and the Multi-Dimensional Analysis reported in Chapters 5 and 6 require additional explanation.

2.6. Methodology in the KeyWord Analysis

The concept of a *keyword* is by no means new. In fact, it has two meanings. The original one is associated with a lexical item which is considered *key* because of its cultural, historical or social importance (see, for example, Williams, 1985). However, in present-day corpus linguistics, a keyword is understood as a statistically significant word form. Keywords have become popularized thanks to the computer software *WordSmith Tools* devised by Mike Scott (1996-2008). Keyword analysis is still a relatively new analytical tool although this seems to be changing. Recently, there have been a number of studies devoted to discourse analysis in which keyword analysis is proving to be extremely useful (see, for instance, Tribble, 2000; Johnson *et al.,* 2003; Baker, 2004; Xiao / McEnery, 2005; Culpeper, 2009)[9]. Generally, it is argued that keyword analysis can reveal not only a great deal about the subject matter, the "aboutness" of a particular text genre, but it can also help specify the salient features which are functionally related to that genre. However, there are relatively few studies which use this analytical tool to examine disciplinary genres – one exception is Cacciani (forthcoming), which treats keywords as cues to knowledge construction in the genre of research articles.

In the help function of *WordSmith Tools 5.0*, Scott (2008) refers to keywords as "those words whose frequency is unusually high in comparison with some norm". Extracting keywords involves comparing two wordlists. One wordlist is based on the words from a particular genre, the other wordlist is a larger reference list[10]. Roughly, keyword analysis consists of two major steps. The first is largely automated and is performed by a computer programme. To that effect, the *KeyWords* facility of the programme *WordSmith Tools 5.0* was used in the present study. The other step is carried out by the researcher and it basically consists of examining the words generated by the programme and determining

9 Comprehensive bibliography on various aspects of keyword analysis can be found at http://www/lexically.net/publications/publications.htm

10 See McEnery *et al.* (2006: 308-312) for a detailed description of the procedure.

their discoursal functions in the relevant contexts. The entire process should not be considered in any way as "mechanical". A lot depends on the type of data that the researcher selects and what parameters he or she adopts for the subsequent analysis. Culpeper (2009: 34-35) has a useful discussion of what decisions need to be made when performing a keyword analysis. He points out that in any keyword analysis, "the choice of data for comparison (the reference corpus) is an issue". In short, the keyword results are bound to be affected by the reference corpus (and its subsets). In the present analysis, a decision was made against comparing the legal data with a large multi-genre corpus, such as the BNC (*British National Corpus*) or the COCA (*Corpus of Contemporary American English*). Comparing a range of specialized genres from the same domain against a general reference corpus would inevitably lead to obtaining findings which may be highly homogeneous and probably valid for legal language in general, but they would not help identify features unique to a particular genre. Consequently, the reference corpus was designed using text files from all legal genres minus the genre under examination. Thus, for instance, the keyword analysis of the academic journals involves comparing a smaller wordlist based on all text files from this category with a reference wordlist consisting of all the other genres *excluding* legal academic journals. It should be then possible to obtain findings which could be interpreted as representative or indicative of the genre in question but *relative to* other legal genres.

There are other parameters available in *WordSmith Tools* that prompt the analyst to make further important decisions before approaching the computer-generated output. One such parameter concerns the so-called minimum "frequency cut-off point". This parameter defines the minimum number of times a word must appear in a dataset to be considered as "key". The frequency cut-off point is a useful parameter which can be adopted to avoid obtaining too much data and it can also minimize the occurrence of highly local or idiosyncratic keywords. The minimum frequency cut-off point should be set bearing in mind the size of one's data. In this analysis, it was set at 25. Another parameter which can be used involves applying tests for statistical significance. Such tests are intended to measure the significance of the unusualness of a keyword and enable the researcher to assess the strength of the differences in frequency of the word from what one might to expect on the basis of the reference corpus. The log likelihood test was selected for this analysis. The analysis was repeated with the chi-square test but almost identical results were obtained, with only some minor differences in the ranking of keywords. The probability value was set at 0.000001 (1 in a million) since my major concern was that of selectivity. As Culpeper (2009: 36) stresses, "manipulating the p value is a useful way of controlling the quantity of keywords derived, and thus the number of keywords a researcher must interpret". Also, it is desirable to provide raw frequencies (as shown in Appendix A) of particular items in keyword lists, because this may be yet another factor helpful in reducing the risk of identifying words which appear locally. Finally, it is advisable to consider *dispersion*. *WordSmith Tools* enable users to generate a dispersion plot for a given item. As Scott (2008) explains in the help function of *WordSmith Tools*: "a dispersion value is the degree to which a set of values are uniformly spread". In the present analysis, this function helps to determine how the occurrences of a particular word are distributed across the dataset. By looking at the plot, it is possible to find out in how many different texts the word has been found and whether it tends to concentrate heavily, for example, at the beginning of a text or at its end, or perhaps in the middle. In the example below (Figure 2.1), the original keyword list for academic journals identified *Alaska* as the seventh keyword. This item had its raw frequency of 626 hits and keyness calculated at 1436.47. It is in fact found in only eight texts and tends to concentrate heavily in only four different documents. The dispersion value provides some mathematical support for this: plot dispersion ranges from 0 to 1, with 0.9 indicative of highly uniform dispersion and 0 or 0.1 of very irregular distribution. In addition, a further restriction was adopted whereby only words which are found in at least ten different texts are considered. As a result, *Alaska* was eventually removed from the list of keywords.

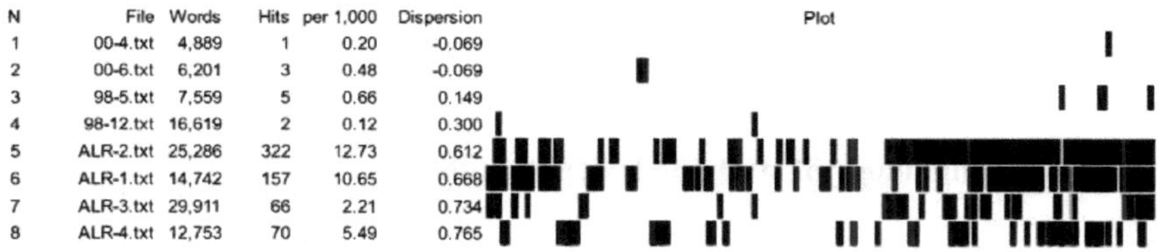

N	File	Words	Hits	per 1,000	Dispersion	Plot
1	00-4.txt	4,889	1	0.20	-0.069	
2	00-6.txt	6,201	3	0.48	-0.069	
3	98-5.txt	7,559	5	0.66	0.149	
4	98-12.txt	16,619	2	0.12	0.300	
5	ALR-2.txt	25,286	322	12.73	0.612	
6	ALR-1.txt	14,742	157	10.65	0.668	
7	ALR-3.txt	29,911	66	2.21	0.734	
8	ALR-4.txt	12,753	70	5.49	0.765	

Figure 2.1. *The dispersion of the word Alaska*

Another example is that of the word *securitization*. It appeared as the ninth keyword in the original keyword list in academic journals, with keyness calculated at 1400.72. Its raw frequency is 310 hits in the academic journals while it was found only once in the reference corpus. However, its distribution turned out to be restricted to only one text! Thus, the word *securitization* was not included in the final version of the keyword list. The scope of this analysis was further limited to one hundred keywords grouped in order of keyness for each genre and listed in Appendix A. As a result, only keywords which were found in at least 10% of the total number of texts in a given genre were retained. In the case of academic articles, this means that a keyword remains 'key' if it is found in at least 10 different texts and their distribution is spread evenly across the texts.

The next step in any KeyWord analysis is to attempt at proposing a classification of the extracted keywords. Scott (2000) maintains that there are essentially three types of keywords: proper words, keywords related to the text's "aboutness" (which corresponds to Halliday's (1994) ideational metafunction) or "content" and finally, keywords which tend to indicate style rather than "aboutness". In the case of legal texts, "aboutness" keywords are terms of art, such as, for instance, *company, agreement, shares* or *partner* in contractual instruments. Regarding key indicators of style, Scott (2000: 143) cites the example of high-frequency words such as *because, shall* or *already* and comments:

> These would not usually be identified by the reader as key [...] But the fact that KeyWords identifies such words should prompt you to go back to the text [...] to investigate why such words have cropped up with unusual frequencies.

As Culpeper (2009) notes, it seems that "aboutness" keywords relate to open class words, i.e. lexical words which are the main carriers of meaning in a text (Biber et al, 1999: 55), while stylistic keywords can be associated with a closed class or closed system of function words. For his analysis of the character-talk of Shakespeare's *Romeo and Juliet*, Culpeper (2009: 39) proposes a three-way categorization of keywords into "ideational keywords", "textual keywords" and "interpersonal keywords". Chapter 3 proposes an extensive classification of keywords identified in the ALC. It emerges that there are different, even genre-specific keywords found in particular legal genres.

2.7. The methodology of studying lexical bundles

The next step in the overall description of linguistic variation in English is to move beyond the level of word patterns by examining how multi-word expressions are utilized in individual legal genres. There are many different approaches and perspectives on this type of linguistic construct so a brief overview is first provided.

2.7.1. Overview of studies devoted to multi-word expressions

Recently, there have been several studies which use multi-word sequences to discriminate between different registers (e.g. Biber et al, 1999, Biber, Conrad and Cortes, 2003), text types (e.g. Stubbs and Barth, 2003) and disciplines (e.g. Groom, 2005; Hyland, 2008). Such studies are the result of extensive work in corpus linguistics and the growing recognition of the central importance of phraseology. Hunston and Francis (1999) propose a theory of language as phraseology which they term *pattern grammar*. Following Sinclair's *idiom principle,* they consider "semi-preconstructed phrases that constitute single choices" (Sinclair, 1991: 110) as the essential unit of linguistic meaning and structure, and as the principal focus of linguistic analysis (for further discussion, see Hunston, 2002; Partington, 1998; Sinclair, 2004; Stubbs, 2001; 2002; 2004). Drawing upon this line of reasoning and assuming that "there is ultimately no distinction between form and meaning" (Sinclair, 1991:7), Groom (2005: 258) formulates an important hypothesis by suggesting:

> (…) we should expect different written and spoken genres and different discourse communitites to select or prioritise different phraseological patterns; the former on the grounds that they serve different communicative and institutional purposes and thus prioritise different rhetorical strategies [..], and the latter on the grounds that they are characterised by different ideational interests and interpersonal practices.

Ultimately, Groom assumes that each disciplinary genre might have its own unique phraseological profile (2005: 258). Groom's observation is highly relevant to the present analysis. The greater part of this chapter is devoted to documenting the extent to which legal genres are similar or different in terms of extended lexical collocations (lexical bundles). At issue is precisely the interplay between different communicative and institutional purposes of the many legal genres and the constraints imposed by the legal community.

2.7.2. Phraseology and multi-word expressions

Before proceeding further, it seems necessary to clarify some terminological issues connected with the notion of phraseology. Gries (2009) notes that the notion of phraseology has become very widespread but many authors tend to use it without providing a clear-cut definition or they have treated phraseology as interchangeable with other terms, such as, for instance *extended lexical unit* (as, for instance in Stubbs, 2001). Indeed, a crucial question should be posed concerning the status of multi-word units as phraseologisms. Gries (2009: 4) pleads for "a rigorous definition of co-occurrence phenomena in general, and phraseology in particular". He offers six criteria useful in defining phraseology: (1) the *nature* of the elements involved in a phraseologism; (2) the *number* of elements involved in a phraseologism; (3) the *number of times* an expression must be observed before it counts as a phraseologism; (4) the permissible *distance* between the elements involved in a phraseologism; (5) the degree of *lexical and syntactic flexibility* of the elements involved; and finally (6) the role that *semantic unity* and *semantic non-compositionality / non-predictability* play in the definition (2009: 4). After discussing each criterion, Gries (2009: 6) proposes what could be considered as probably the broadest definition of a phraseologism: "the co-occurrence of a form or a lemma of a lexical item and one more or additional linguistic elements of various kinds which functions as one semantic unit in a clause or sentence and whose ferquency of co-occurrence is larger than expected on the basis of chance". This definition is worth noting for being explicit with regard to each of the above-mentioned parametres and for extending the range of phenomena regarded as phraseologism. As a consequence, it encourages researchers to define carefully the level at which they examine a potential phraseologism and to decide how many elements a phraseologism is supposed to comprise. It also prompts one to consider many types of multi-word expressions as phraseologisms. Indeed, the term *multi-word expression* or *multi-word unit (MWU)* is used to refer to a broad category encompassing a wide range of different, albeit related, phenomena such as phrasal verbs, nominal compounds, institutionalized phrases, named entities (e.g "United Nations", compound adverbs ("by the way") and many others (cf. Villavicencio et al, 2005).[11] What appears to be common to all these constructs is their high frequency of occurrence in language in order to express concepts or fulfil discoursal functions that cannot be carried out by means of a single word. They differ in terms of their syntactic and semantic properties. The flexibility and variation in their form can range from fixed expressions such as *kith and kin* or *lo and behold* to lexical items displaying some degree of internal variation. Irrespective of the differences, there is a general consensus among linguists that this type of expression represents a significant part of language and the speaker's lexicon.

Further discussion in this chapter is confined to more formulaic, multi-word sequences. Such word combinations have been studied from many perspectives and under different names. Indeed, a bewildering range of terms has been ascribed to this linguistic phenomenon. Biber et al (2003) notes the presence of such terms as "lexical phrases", "formulas", "routines", "fixed expressions", "prefabricated patterns" (or "prefabs"), and "lexical bundles" (p. 71). This list can be extended to include "chains" (Stubbs 2002), "dyads", "tryads", etc. (Piotrowski, 1984:93) "clusters"(Scott, 2008) "statistical phrases"(Strzalkowski, 1998: 14), or "n-grams" (Stubbs, 2007). Such a plethora of terms reflect a multitude of approaches and perspectives from which such expressions can be studied. In fact, it is characteristic of many early studies to focus on the theoretical aspects in order to determine the optimum approach to deal with such units. Examples of such studies include Hakuta (1974), Pawley and Syder (1983), Redeker (1991), Sinclair (1991), Lewis (1993), Weinert (1995), Howarth (1996); 1998a,b), Wray and Perkins (2000), and Yorio (1980). Two basic research questions which emerged at that stage concern the method or methods of defining and identifying such units and analysing their discourse functions (Weinert, 1995: 182). Attempts to identify significant multi-word combinations can be found in Renouf and Sinclair, 1991;

11 See also http://memura2004.di.ubi.pt/description.htm which suggests that MWU is a term preferred in Natural Language Processing. See also Maia et al. 2008 for further discussion.

Kjellmer, 1991; Butler, 1997, 2003; Altenberg, 1993, 1998; Hudson, 1998; de Cock, 1998; Howarth, 1998a,b; Moon, 1998; Gledhill, 2000; Granger, 1998; Francis et al., 1996, 1997, 1998; Hunston and Francis, 1998, 1999; Partington, 1998; Aijmer, 1996; Nattinger and DeCarrico, 1992. The differences between various empirical studies can be best captured in terms of five crucial aspects (adapted after Biber et al., 2003: 72):

1. The research goals of either describing the full range of multi-word sequences in a given variety or describing a small set of 'important' word combinations;
2. The methodological criteria adopted to identify multi-word units: perceptual salience, frequency, etc.;
3. The formal characteristics of the multi-word units studied: continuous sequences, discontinuous frames, or lexico-grammatical patterns; two-word collocations or longer sequences;
4. The issue of representativeness as reflected in the size of corpora ranging from a small corpus of, for instance, 10,000 words to huge national corpora (such as the *British National Corpus* or the *Corpus of Contemporary American English*);
5. The extent to which language varieties (usually use-related as in register or genre) are accounted for in the analysis. Examples of studies include those that ignore this aspect totally, while others set out to explicitly compare multi-word units across different registers (spoken and written).

From the perspective of corpus linguistics, a fundamental distinction should be also made between "corpus-based" and "corpus-driven" approaches (see Tognini-Bonelli, 2001: 84-87). The choice of a particular approach carries implications for the study of formulaic language in large text corpora Biber (2009: 2). In "corpus-based" research, formulaic expressions are pre-selected on the basis of linguistic features derived from accepted linguistic theories. Subsequent corpus analysis consists in examining how these expressions are used (a case in point is Moon, 1998). In contrast, "corpus-driven' research is characterised by making few a priori assumptions. This approach is more inductive and linguistic constructs are expected to emerge from analysis of corpus. Biber stresses that "In its most basic form, corpus-driven analysis assumes only the existence of words; co-occurrence patterns among words, discovered from the corpus analysis, are the basis for subsequent linguistic descriptions" (Biber, 2009: 2). Some researchers combine the two approaches. For example, Renouf and Sinclair (1991) studied multi-word combinations of function words with a variable lexical slot (e.g. *a +? + of* or *be + ? + to*) which they called "collocational frameworks". The collocational frameworks were preselected and resulted from a corpus-based approach, while the lexical fillers were discovered thanks to a corpus-driven analysis. Biber's studies of lexical bundles (see, e.g. Biber et al 1999, Biber et al 2004) represent a more radical corpus-driven approach and this methodology will be discussed in detail in the latter part of this chapter.

Irrespective of methodological differences signalled above, the importance of pre-fabricated multi-word expressions was recognized in view of the evidence that some multi-word combinations are stored in mental lexicons as single units (see Ellis, 1996; Howarth, 1996; Wray and Perkins, 2000). This carries obvious implications for language acquisition studies. The importance of this type of expressions has been noticed in literature dealing with foreign language pedagogy. Information about systematic patterns of use of such lexical units can be used to help learners of English to produce natural idiomatic English. Multi-word expressions are regarded as an indispensable component of fluent linguistic production. Their presence or absence may indicate the lack of fluency or conversely an adequate competence of a member of a particular professional community (see, for instance Cortes, 2004). Most importantly, an awareness of preferred sequences of words is directly related to the control and mastery of a given register or genre. Thus, pedagogically-oriented studies focus on the identification of frequent fixed expressions within a given discipline. Learning such expressions should help newcomers to a given disciplinary community acquire the specific rhetorical practices of their communities.

The correlation between recurrent phrases and disciplinary variation has been more recently explored in Oakey (2002) and Hyland (2008). More specifically, Hyland focuses on the use of extended lexical patterns (lexical bundles) in the context of EAP (English for Academic Purposes). He demonstrates how this type of expression represents a building block in the creation of academic discourse and how bundles can serve as indicators of variation across different academic disciplines (Hyland, 2008).

Recent years saw a similar surge in research on this type of linguistic expression in specialised discourse. Schulze and Römer (2008) in their introduction to the special issue of *International Journal of Corpus Linguistics: Patterns, Meaningful Units and Specialised Discourses* emphasize the inextricable link between the performativity in language and the way "speakers and writers do things by predominantly and unconsciously employing patterns or phraseological items, i.e. strings of words that are highly structured, well-organized and firmly entrenched in the human being's mind" (2008: 1). Studies of specialised language collected in this issue demonstrate how specialised meanings are expressed and encoded by means of phraseological patterns and how they are linked to the particular domains in which they were used. Chapter 4 continues this theme by exploring the use of multi-word expressions (lexical bundles) in the legal domain.

2.7.3. Lexical bundles: the concept, background and previous research

Set against the backdrop outlined above, Biber et al. (1999) research into lexical bundles appears as an innovative and significant step forward in the scrutiny of multi-word patterns. It was one of the first, if not the first, large-scale corpus-based register-oriented analysis of recurrent word combinations. His findings documented in Biber et al. (1999) and Biber et al. (2003) examine conversation and academic prose and are based on substantial language dataset. The corpus material for the spoken part included about 4 million words of British English conversations and about 3 million words of American English conversations. The academic prose corpus comprised both academic research articles (c. 2.7 million words) and advanced academic books (c. 2.6 million words. For more detailed information about the corpus, see Biber et al. (1999:32-34). Frequency was the sole criterion used to identify long multi-word combinations ranging from 4- to 6-word sequences. The term "lexical bundle" was first used by Biber et al. (1999) in the now classic *Longman Grammar of Spoken and Written English.* Chapter 13 documents the study which compares recurrent sequences of words in conversation and academic prose. Biber refers to lexical bundles as 'extended collocation' and defines them as multi-word sequences that occur statistically very frequently in a given language variety. The frequency criterion is approached in a somewhat arbitrary manner by adopting different frequency cut-off points. For example, in Biber et al. (1999) and Biber et al. (2003), this threshold is established at 10 times per million words for four-word sequences but at only 5 times per million words for five and six-word combinations. Varying the frequency criteria can certainly affect any analysis because adopting a lower or higher cut-off point determines its output (the number of identified bundles). In addition, only continuous, uninterrupted sequences are considered as bundles. Shorter bundles are frequently found to be part of a longer combination. A three-word bundles *do you want* can be part of a four-word bundles *do you want me,* which can be part of a five-word bundle *do you want me to* and this sequence could in turn be part of a six-word combination *do you want me to do.* It is also worth bearing in mind that the programme which identifies word combinations reads through each text in the corpus and records a given sequence starting with the first word of the text and moving on one word at a time. Importantly, unlike in other similar approaches to multi-word units such as n-grams or chains or clusters, the occurrences of a given sequence must appear at least in five different texts of a given genre or register. This criterion has been designed to guard against local repetitions and/or individual idiosyncratic styles. Biber emphasizes the distinction between lexical bundles and idioms. While idioms are "relatively invariable expressions with a meaning not derivable from the parts" and are not "necessarily common expressions (…)"., lexical bundles occur very frequently in a given language variety, i.e. register. Biber cites stereotypical idioms such as *kick the bucket* and *slap in the face* as examples of idiomatic expressions which are in fact very rare. They can be found infrequently in fiction (with less than five occurrences per million words) but hardly ever in other registers. On the other hand, lexical bundles can be extremely frequent with over 400 hundred occurrences per million words (e.g. certain three-word bundles such as *I don't think* or *do you want*; see Biber et al, 1999: 994). This clearly suggests a strong correlation between the size of a bundle and its frequency. As can be seen on the basis of a few examples demonstrated above, lexical bundles are not complete structural units. In sum, the lexical bundle methodology is characterized by three defining features of corpus-driven research. It focuses on analysis of the actual word forms identified in the corpus rather than lemmas; it is based on analysis of sequences of word forms without taking into account grammatical/syntactic status of those words, and finally, it employs "frequency information derived from the corpus as the primary evidence to be used in the analysis" (Biber, 2009: 7).

The same analytical framework was used in several subsequent studies of spoken and written academic genres (e.g. Biber et al, 2003; Biber et al, 2004; Biber, 2006: Chapter 6), in history and biology academic writing (Cortes, 2004), in political discourse (Partington and Morley, 2004), and in a range of academic disciplines and genres (Hyland, 2008). The analysis included in Chapter 4 synthesizes findings reported in earlier studies of lexical bundles in British judgments (Goźdź-Roszkowski, 2006a) and in contractual instruments (Goźdź-Roszkowski, 2006b). Now, it extends these findings to cover other legal genres (legislation, opinions, briefs, academic journals, professional articles and textbooks).

2.8. Overview of methodology in the Multi-Dimensional approach

Finally, this chapter introduces the methodology of Multi-Dimensional analysis, which has been followed in Chapters 5 and 6. It is the first time that this analytical tool has been utilized to study dimensions of variation between genres and other specialised and non-specialised genres (Chapter 5). More importantly, there have been no Multi-Dimensional studies of variation within a single-discourse domain (Chapter 6).

The concept of Multi-Dimensional analysis (MD) has been extensively discussed in Biber (1988, 1995), White (1994), and Conrad and Biber (2001). An overview of the essential characteristics of this methodology is provided below. The MD analysis was first introduced by Biber over twenty-five years ago (Biber, 1984, 1985, 1986) and then applied in the analysis of a range of spoken and written registers and genres (e.g. Biber, 1995; Precht, 2000; Atkinson, 2001; Conrad, 2001; Quaglio, 2004). MD data is derived from Factor Analysis (FA) which considers the sequential, partial, and observed correlations of a wide-range of variables producing groups of occurring factors or dimensions. According to Tabachnick and Fidell (2001), FA is employed to summarize patterns of correlations among variables, to reduce a large number of observed variables to a smaller number of factors or dimensions, and to provide an operational definition (a regression equation) for an underlying process by using these observed variables. The purposes of FA support the overall focus of corpus-based MD analysis which aims to describe statistically correlating linguistic features and group them into interpretable sets of linguistic dimensions. The patterning of linguistic features in a corpus creates linguistic dimensions which correspond to salient functional distinctions within a register or genre, and allows comparison between different language varieties. It is then further developed to identify salient linguistic co-occurrence patterns in a language using empirical/quantitative terms and to compare spoken and written registers in the linguistic space defined by those co-occurrence patterns. The notion of linguistic co-occurrence was accorded formal status in the MD approach, in that different co-occurrence patterns are analyzed as underlying dimensions of variation. Its significance has been noticed and stressed in many linguistic publications. Brown and Fraser (1979: 38-39) note that it can be "misleading to concentrate on specific, isolated [linguistic] markers without taking into account systematic variations which involve the co-occurrence of sets of markers". Hymes (1974) identifies "speech styles" as varieties that are defined by a shared set of co-occurring linguistic features. Halliday (1988:162) defines register as a "cluster of associated features having a greater-than-random… tendency to co-occur".

It is worth emphasizing that the MD analysis does not stop at using quantitative techniques. In fact, qualitative techniques are necessary to interpret the functional bases underlying each set of co-occurring linguistic features. The dimensions of variation have both linguistic and functional content. The linguistic content or level consists in a group of linguistic features (for example, nominalizations, prepositional phrases, attributive adjectives) that co-occur with a high frequency in texts. Based on the assumptions that co-occurrence reflects shared function, these co-occurrence patterns are interpreted in terms of the situational, social, and cognitive functions most widely shared by the linguistic features. In other words, linguistic features co-occur in texts because they reflect shared functions. A simple example cited in Conrad and Biber (2001: 6) is the way in which first and second person pronouns, direct questions, and imperatives are related to interactiveness. Contractions, false starts, and generalized content words (for example, *thing*) are all related to the constraints imposed by real-time production. However, many co-occurrence patterns are often not immediately transparent, so there is a need to employ a careful qualitative analysis focused on a particular stretch of text.

2.8.1. Steps in MD analysis

This section describes the MD analytical procedure (based on Biber, 1988) followed in the present study. Initial data processing for FA required a manual segmentation of individual texts into genre categories in order to analyze each legal genre separately. The segmented texts were tagged for parts-of-speech and semantic categories using Biber's tagging programme. Then, the tagged features in the corpus were counted and normalized per 1,000 words by a tag-count programme also developed by Biber. At this stage, it should be pointed out that there are two different types of MD analysis. One involves carrying out a full MD analysis based on a new factor analysis (hence it is often referred to as "new" MD analysis) and the other uses previously identified dimensions to study new areas of research (frequently referred to as the 1988 MD model). The dimensions identified in Biber's now classic *Variation across Speech and Writing* have been often used as a convenient point of reference to describe and compare additional registers or genres in the context of those already explored in Biber 1988 (cf. Part II of Conrad and Biber, 2001). When applying the 1988 MD model, there is no need to carry out a separate factor analysis because the linguistic features relevant to the study have already been identified. Chapter 5 explores variation among legal genres applying the 1988 model of variation, while Chapter 6 is based on a full MD analysis. The analysis reported in the former relies on 67 linguistic features used originally in Biber 1988 and organized according to 16 major grammatical and functional categories:[12]

1. Tense and aspect markers
2. Place and time adverbials
3. Pronouns and pro-verbs
4. Questions
5. Nominal forms
6. Passives
7. Stative forms (*be* as main verb, existential *there*)
8. Subordination features (e.g. *that* verb complements, present participial adverbial clauses, past participial postnominal (reduced relative) clauses, etc.)
9. Prepositional phrases, adjectives, and adverbs
10. Lexical specificity (type/token ration, mean word length)
11. Lexical classes (e.g. conjuncts, downtoners, hedges, amplifiers, emphatics, etc.)
12. Modals

12 Fuller linguistic descriptions of these features can be found in Biber (1988: Appendix II)

13. Specialised verb classes (public verbs, private verbs, suasive verbs, *seem* and *appear*)
14. Reduced forms and dispreferred structures (contractions, complementizer *that* deletion, stranded prepositions, split infinitives, split auxiliaries)
15. Coordination (phrasal coordination, independent clause coordination)
16. Negation (synthetic negation, analytic negation)

However, the full MD analysis the findings of which are provided in Chapter 5, was carried on a much larger set of 129 linguistic features. There was a need to run several FAs piloting various combinations of the tag-counted features in order to finalize the list of items comprising the dataset. Linguistic features that correlated below .15 in communality values after extraction and did not load in any of the factors were excluded. After a series of tests, 42 lexical and syntactic features (shown in Table 2.2) were retained because they had been found in statistically significant co-occurrence patterns.

Table 2.2. *Linguistic features used in the new full MD analysis*

No.	Linguistic features	Description/Example
1	Type/Token ratio	Number of words occurring in the first 400 words of texts
2	Word Length	Mean length of words in a texts
3	Present Tense Verbs	All present tense verbs identified by the tagging programme
4	Second Person Pronouns	*you, your, yours, yourself*
5	Demonstrative Pronouns	*that, those, this, these*
6	Pronoun *It*	Instances of pronoun *It*
7	BE as main verb	Forms of *Be* verb
8	Adverbial subordinator: causative	*because*
9	Indefinite pronouns	e.g. *anyone, everybody, nothing*
10	Possibility modals	*can, could, may, might*
11	Nouns	All nouns identified by the programme
12	Prepositions	All prepositions identified by the programme
13	Attributive Adjectives	e.g. the small room
14	Past Tense	Past tense verbs identified by the tagging programme
15	Third Person Pronouns	*he, him, himself, she, her, herself, they, them,* etc.
16	Perfect Aspect Verbs	Verbs in perfect aspect construction
17	Phrasal Coordination	Noun and noun; adj and adj; verb and verb; adv and adv
18	Nominalizations	Words ending in –tion, - ment, - ness, or –ity (and

		plurals)
19	Predictive Modals	*will, would, shall*
20	Adverbial subordinator: condition	*unless, if*
21	Necessity Modals	*must, ought, should*
22	Agentless Passives	passive forms of verbs where the agent is left unexpressed
23	*By*-passives	passive forms of verbs where the agent is expressed by in a *by*-phrase
24	Postnominal Passives	Passive forms of verbs in postmodifying participle clauses
25	Adv. Subordinator: other	*as, except, until*
26	Downtoners	e.g. *barely, nearly, slightly*
27	Predicative Adjective	e.g. *the room is small*
28	Conjuncts	e.g. *alternatively, nevertheless, therefore*
29	WH Clauses	Clauses with WH (*what, which, who*) head
30	THAT relatives	*that* relative clauses on subject and object positions
31	THAT cl. with non-factive verb	*that*-clauses which co-occur with non-factive verbs, such as *believe*
32	THAT cl. with factive verb	*that*-clauses which co-occur with verbs that assert the truth value of the propositional content of a clause, e.g. *know*
33	THAT cl. with likelihood verb	*that*-clauses with *seem* and *appear*
34	TO cl. with desire/intent/decision verb	*to*-clauses occurring with *desire, intend, decide*
35	THAT cl. with all adjectives	*that*-complement clauses controlled by adjectival predicates
36	THAT cl. with all nouns	*that*-complement clauses controlled by nouns
37	Stance Adverbs	e.g. undoubtedly, evidently, truthfully, wisely (certainty, likelihood, style, attitude)
38	Cognitive Nouns	Nouns related to mental/cognitive processes or perceptions, e.g. assumption, belief, opinion, notion, etc.
39	Quantity Nouns	Nouns specifying a quantity, amount, or duration
40	Activity Verbs	"primarily denote actions and events that could be associated with choice, and so take a subject with the semantic role of an agent (LGSWE, pp. 361-362, 367-368, 370) e.g. apply, control provide, sell, share,
41	Communication Verbs	"a special subcategory of activity verbs that involve communication activities (speaking, writing)" (LGSWE, pp. 362, 368, 370) e.g. claim, propose, quote, etc

42	Mental verbs	"denote a wide range of activities and states experienced by humans; they do not involve physical action and do not necessarily entail volition. Their subject often has a semantic role of a recipient (LGSWE, pp. 362-363, 368-369, 370) e.g. believe, know, think

The considerable reduction in the number of relevant linguistic features may be ascribed to the highly specialist nature of legal texts, the sublanguage property whereby only a limited (in comparison with natural general language) number of linguistic features is actually and meaningfully employed. This term, as defined in (Kittredge and Lehrberger 1982), carries with it the idea that sublanguage is a subset, or part of the language as a whole. In the next section, more details are given about the new factor analysis used for the present analysis.

After features have been tagged, other computer programmes calculate frequency counts of each features in each text. These counts are then normalized to a common basis to enable comparison across the texts. In both types of MD analysis, counts are normed to their frequency per 1,000 words of text[13]. Each and every linguistic feature has a certain amount of variability across the total number of texts in a corpus. This means that a given feature can be quite frequent in some texts but relatively infrequent in others.

Table 2.3. *Descriptive statistics for three linguistic features (per 1,000) in contracts*

Linguistic feature	Mean	Minimum value	Maximum value	Standard deviation
Nouns	312.4	215.1	405.6	28.8
Paste tense	4.7	0.0	25.0	4.4
3rd person pronouns	4.2	0.0	27.4	4.7

For example, Table 2.3 shows that nouns in English contracts range from a minimum of 215.1 occurrences per 1,000 words in some documents to a maximum of 405.6 occurrences per 1,000 words in other texts. The variance of a feature's distribution measures the extent of dispersion of values across the total range of variation. For some features, most values can be found in the proximity of the mean score (which is 312.4 for nouns), with only a few values near the minimum and maximum. Other features could have their scores widely scattered

13 The normalization procedure is discussed in detail in Biber 1988:75-76 and in Biber, Conrad, and Reppen, 1998: Methodology Box 6)

reflecting the fact that many texts have values near the minimum and maximum. The programme (statistical software SAS) used in the MD analysis is capable of determining the extent of shared variance among the features. A high amount of shared variance occurs when two features are found at similarly frequent levels in some texts and equally low levels in other texts. In that case, shared variance is directly linked to co-occurrence. Factor analysis is used precisely for the purpose of determining the shared variance among features. In doing so, multiple factors are extracted, "where each factor represents the maximum amount of shared variance that can be accounted for out of the pool of variance remaining at that point" (Contrad and Biber, 2001: 20). The strength of the relation between each linguistic feature and each factor is indicated by means of "factor loading". The factor loading shows the amount of variance for a particular feature with respect to the total pool of shared variance accounted for by a factor. Factor loadings range from 0.0 indicating the absence of any relationship, to 1.0 showing "a perfect correlation". Only features with values above a pre-determined cut-off point are considered when interpreting a factor. In the 1988 model of variation, features with loadings below 0.35 were not considered as salient and important (Contrad and Biber, 2001: 21). By comparison, in the new MD analysis reported in the next chapter, only features with loadings larger than 0.30 are used in the computation of dimension scores. Dimension scores (or "factor scores") are computed by summing the frequencies of the features with salient (above the designated cut-off point) loadings on a particular dimension and then subtracting the frequencies of features with negative loadings. In MD studies, frequencies are standardized to a mean of 0.0 and a standard deviation of 1.0 before computing the dimension sores (Conrad and Biber, 2001; Biber, 2006). This procedure ensures that all features identified for a given factor have equivalent weights in the computation of dimension scores. There are seven factors extracted for the 1988 study of register variation but only the first five are considered as most readily interpretable and relevant to the present analysis. These are as follows:

1. Involved versus Informational Production
2. Narrative versus Non-narrative Concerns
3. Situation-Dependent versus Elaborated Reference
4. Overt Expression of Persuasion
5. Non-Impersonal versus Impersonal/Abstract Style

These are interpretive labels proposed after qualitative analysis of the dimensions' underlying functions. The 1988 analysis was based on a broad range of 23 major register categories including academic prose, press reportage, fiction, letters, conversations, interviews, official documents, etc. (a full list can be found in Biber, 1988: 209) and it includes a relatively large set of linguistic features. Detailed results of tests and other statistical procedures carried out using the framework of the 1988 MD analysis can be found in Appendix B. Consequently, the present study is based on the assumption that the dimensions remain valid for the description of variation in the more specialized domain of law. It is felt that only by applying both the 1988 MD model and by conducting a new multi-dimensional analysis is it possible to provide a comprehensive description and analysis of legal genres. The former type of analysis makes it possible to understand the specialized legal genres relative to a number of spoken and written genres or registers in English. This can be achieved only by means of the broad-based 1988 dimensions. Genres within the legal register can be thus analyzed in a much wider context. On the other hand, carrying out a new MD analysis of the legal genres enables one to establish the dimensions of variation valid for this domain of language use and it provides more effective ways to capture the niceties of variation among such genres.

2.9. Overview of linguistic analyses

This book aims to provide a relatively comprehensive linguistic description of legal genres. In order to accomplish this, the descriptions are based on a wide range of linguistic characteristics carrying functional associations and indicating important differences among legal genres. The selection of linguistic features was motivated in part by previous corpus-based studies of non-specialised varieties of English. Insights from previous studies of legal discourse were useful in adding relevant domain-specific characteristics. The analyses vary from the corpus-driven, such as the KeyWord Analysis and the analysis of lexical bundles to the corpus-based as in the case of the Multi-Dimensional Analysis. At their core lies the belief in the centrality of syntagmatic patterns and the use of text corpora as the principal source of data for language analysis. As the following chapters demonstrate, new lines of argument begin to emerge based on the perception of stretches of text as repeated events, and the use of frequency-based statistical measures. The latter part of the book shows how legal genres use different patterns of co-occurring linguistic features to achieve their particular communicative goals.

CHAPTER III: VOCABULARY USE ACROSS DIFFERENT LEGAL GENRES

3.1. Introduction

This chapter takes an innovative approach to the study of vocabulary in legal texts by focusing on lexical distributions and patterns of vocabulary use in legal genres. Unlike most previous studies of legal discourse, this approach does not prioritize terminology but rather it deals with the totality of vocabulary explicitly incorporating the genre perspective. There are many important research questions concerning word use in legal genres. Do different legal genres use the same words? Are there any lexical categories unique to a particular legal genre? Is there any overlap across the genres? Can we talk about "core" legal vocabulary? Do some legal genres use a greater range of different words? Are some genres more repetitive, formulaic, specialized?

Traditionally, legal lexicon has been usually discussed as just one of many factors useful in explaining the nature of legal language. In one of the earliest comprehensive studies on written legal discourse and taxonomic in presentation, Mellinkoff (1963) sets out to describe general syntactic and morphological characteristics of legal language in the hope of isolating what people find difficult about it. The same approach to the presentation of the legal lexicon can be found in Danet (1985). The so-called technical terms are listed first followed by a category of 'common terms with uncommon meaning'. This somewhat lengthy label refers to the polysemy of certain words which can have one general meaning and then an additional specialized meaning. The term *assignment* is a case in point. Apart from its meaning of "something assigned, a task or duty", it also means "the transference of a right, interest or title" (Black, 1990). Other categories proposed by Danet include archaic expressions, mostly archaic deictics such as *hereinafter, hereto, herein, thereof,* etc, and doublets (*cease and desist, will and bequeath, aid and abet, etc.*). Tiersma (1999) devotes one chapter to the legal lexicon. He focuses on vocabulary items which contribute to the perception of legal language as different from ordinary speech and writing. His interest seems to lie with the degree to which such items are semantically transparent and which help to ensure effective communication. Set against such background, it is hardly surprising that the category of "legal archaisms" is discussed first and at considerable length. This category includes vocabulary which, as we will see below, is relatively rare and/or confined to a specific text genre. For example, the verb form *witnesseth* appears only 22 times in the ALC and, somewhat predictably, it is only found in contracts. Another example from the same category are adverbs of the type *here-, there-* and *where-* (such as *herein, thereby,* and *wherewith*), which have a relatively large frequency but their distribution is also restricted to one category, i.e. contractual instruments. Clearly, Tiersma (1999) intends to account for the peculiar use of the legal lexicon by the legal profession in light of the highly conservative nature of legal vocabulary and in the wider context of formal and ritualistic language (Tiersma, 1999: 100). In terms of the traditional classifications of specialized lexicon, the focus is on technical terms, the so-called terms of art and jargon. While extremely useful and informative, such presentation of the legal lexicon tends to perpetuate certain conventional and stereotypical views of the legal lexicon, namely that of centrality of terms and the perception of legal language as a language variety marked by frequent occurrence of archaic and opaque words.

More recently, in a book addressed to legal translators, *Legal Translation Explained,* Alcaraz and Hughes (2002) start by classifying legal vocabulary into symbolic or representational items and functional items (2002: 16). The first category consists of technical terms or phrases (e.g. *court, tort, misrepresentation*), the other covers words or phrases without direct reference to concrete objects or legal concepts. Examples include deictics, modals, auxiliaries, and more complex units like *unless otherwise stated* or *as in section 2 above*. Just as Tiersma (1999), Alcaraz and Hughes do not attempt to provide an exhaustive account of the legal lexicon. Instead, they want to introduce aspiring legal translators to the problem of unfamiliar legal vocabulary in the context of legal translation. Accordingly, in their classification, they propose three subgroups for the category of symbolic or representational vocabulary. The first one is called 'purely technical terms' and it groups terms which "are found exclusively in the legal sphere and have no application outside it"(Alcaraz and Hughes, 2002: 16). Terms or terminological phrases such as *mortgage*, *estoppels, usury, terms and conditions,* or *refuse leave to appeal* etc., are monosemic, semantically stable and have become standardized and institutionalized terms, i.e. they are listed in authoritative terminological resources. The second group, referred to as 'semi-technical' or 'mixed terms' includes words or phrases from the general lexicon which underwent the process of specialization, i.e. they acquired a more precise specification or an altogether different additional meaning. While this process seems to be characteristic of specialized discourse in general (see Gotti, 2003 54-56), many legal terms tend to be highly polysemic. For example, a word such as *consideration* has, apart from the common meaning of "careful thought before making a decision or judgment", the technical legal meaning of "the inducement to a contract. The cause, motive, price, or impelling influence which induces a contracting party to enter into a contract. The reason or material cause of a contract" (Black 1990). Finally, Varo and Hughes propose a third group which consists of words frequently found in legal texts but which "unlike the previous group, have neither lost their everyday meanings nor acquired others by contact with the specialist medium" (2002: 18). For this category, referred to rather generally as 'everyday vocabulary found in legal texts', examples include *subject matter, paragraph, section, subsection* or *summarize* as in "the judge *summarized* the facts of the case". Defined in this way, the category strikes one as extremely broad and imprecise. Indeed, as the authors assert "any non-technical term" could be included in this class of the legal lexicon. While the expression "non-technical term" seems to be a contradiction in terms, it is worth noting that words such as *section* or *paragraph* are used in the specialized sense of a part of a legal document. Such generalizations about legal vocabulary are motivated by pedagogic concerns. They conveniently introduce LSP users to the intricacies of legal texts by giving them some idea of potential translation problems linked to what is perceived in legal vocabulary as unique or deviant from the standard LGP usage.

Gibbons (2003) can be viewed as yet another recent attempt at explaining and justifying the need for the specialist language of law. Legal vocabulary is discussed in the context of pursuing precision and the need for technicality. Just as any other specialist field, law has developed numerous unique processes and institutions which require a specialist language to refer to them. In a chapter entitled "The Pursuit of Precision" (which seems to echo one of Tiersma's (1999) chapters "The Quest for Precision"), Gibbons (2003:40-50) provides a more refined taxonomy of legal vocabulary in that he adds certain categories which have not been mentioned before. Apart from specialist terms, archaic deictics, terms derived from Latin and Norman French, doublets and triplets, complex function expressions (such as *in pursuance of, during the time that,* etc.) and ordinary words used with specialist meanings, Gibbons points to the frequent use of short forms, i.e. abbreviated forms of longer technical terms and expressions conveyed, for instance by way of acronyms. For example, *TRO* stands for *Temporary Restraining Order, UCC – Uniform Commercial Code* (2003: 45). This is typical of efficient professional communication and the knowledge of such forms may mark membership to the specialist group of legal professionals.

Proper names are another important lexical class listed in Gibbons (2003). The use of the name of a person can refer to a particular legal concept associated with that person. For example, *Miranda Warning* refers to a warning given by the police to criminal suspects held in police custody before they are asked questions related to the commission of a crime. The name *Miranda* refers to the name of an appellant in a landmark US Supreme Court decision *Miranda v. Arizona* in 1966. The Court held that any incriminating statements made in response to interrogation by a defendant in police custody will be admissible at trial only if the prosecution can show that the defendant was informed of the right to consult with an attorney before and during questioning and of the right against self-incrimination prior to questioning by police, and that the defendant not only understood these rights, but voluntarily waived them (cf. also terms such as *Miranda hearing* or *Miranda Rule* as explained in *Black's Law Dictionary*). Thus, in our view, no classification of the legal lexicon can claim to be comprehensive and exhaustive without including proper names.

Worth mentioning is also what Gibbons refers to as slang (2003: 46) and Tiersma classifies as legal jargon[14]. Tiersma provides several useful examples of words which would be classified as jargon rather than terms of art. *Arguendo, conclusory, grandfather clause, judge-shopping or predecease* are just some examples from a fairly broad category (1999: 107). Indeed, the distinction between jargon and a term or term of art might not always be clear. Terms are usually regarded as more precise. Their use involves some degree of institutionalization and standardization.

3.2. Terms and words

Certain difficulties inherent in distinguishing between legal jargon and legal terms are related to problems encountered by terminologists when determining the distinction between terms and words and between different types of terms (Pearson 1998). The domain of law is no exception. The dilemmas faced by terminologists are relevant to this discussion in the context of studying real text situations. The classifications of the legal lexicon provided above reflect, to some extent, certain pragmatic approaches to the distinction between various categories of terms which seem to favour a tripartite system of classifying terms. For instance, according to Trimble and Trimble (1978) terms can be divided into "highly technical terms", "technical terms" and "sub-technical terms". "Highly technical terms", also referred to as "subject specific terms" (Hoffmann, 1985) are monosemous terms used in one domain and considered to be unique to one specific domain. The restriction to one domain appears to be an important criterion in distinguishing between terms as can be seen in another category of "technical terms". Technical terms are referred to by Trimble and Trimble (1978: 92) as "a bank of technical terms from which all disciplines can draw". In other words, technical terms are understood as words which have a special reference in more than one domain. Hoffmann (1985) refers to them as "non-subject-specific specialized vocabulary". Finally, the category of "sub-technical terms" is used in reference to "common words that have taken on special meanings in certain scientific and technical fields" (Trimble and Trimble, 1978: 93).

It is not entirely clear how the distinctions provided above could be applied to legal terminology. The label "highly technical terms" could be used to refer those terms which function only in the domain of law, such as, for instance, *estoppel, possessory lien, punitive damages,* etc. Technical terms might refer to those terms that appear in law and other domains, for instance, accounting, such

14 Mellinkoff (1963) uses the term "argot" in a slightly pejorative sense to refer to certain type of in-group specialised communications probably intended to exclude the layperson. Importantly, he distinguishes between the rather abstruse argot and the more precise technical terminology.

as *retained earnings, surplus* or *undistributed profits*. However, the question worth asking is whether it would make sense to propose further distinctions based on different subfields within legal discipline. "Highly technical legal term" could then be used with reference to terms used solely in one subfield, for example, civil law or criminal law. There might be valid pedagogic reasons for doing so. Still, it remains to be seen whether it is feasible to establish specific cut-off points for such terms. "Technical terms" could refer to those legal terms that are found commonly across different legal fields. To date, there does not seem to be any empirical research to confirm that there exists core legal vocabulary in English[15]. In legal terminology, this problem is compounded by the broad nature of law, its many different disciplines, the absence of clear-cut distinctions between legal terminology and the terminology of and other disciplines, for instance, finance or banking. The category of "sub-technical terms" is amply represented in legal discourse. It corresponds to what Danet (1985, see above) calls "common terms with uncommon meaning". However, the label "sub-technical terms" strikes one as oddly inappropriate since it seems to suggest reduced technicality of such terms. In that respect, it is similar to the category of "semi-scientific" or "semi-technical" terms (Herbert, 1965). Both designations, "sub-technical terms" and "semi-technical" terms, stress the dual nature of general language words which may have different meanings when used in special subject domains. However, it should also be stressed that the meanings ascribed to such words in particular domains are strictly technical. For example, a legal term *direct attack* consists of word forms which are relatively frequent in general English (this phrase is found 100 times in the *Corpus of Contemporary American English*). In legal English, *direct attack* on a judicial proceeding is an attempt to void or correct it in some manner provided by law (after Black, 1990). In addition, general language words may find their way into legal English via the language of legislation, which as a rule, attempts to make use of ordinary words. Hence, even seemingly familiar words such as *child, driver, husband,* or *household* are also part of the legal lexicon with corresponding specific definitions. As can be seen, the traditional ways of distinguishing terms and words and different types of terms do not seem suitable for dealing with legal vocabulary. Essentially, it seems there are no objective and reliable methods of distinguishing between terms and words. Moreover, the subject-specific/non-subject-specific criterion appears to be of little practical use. The tripartite system of classifying terms is a good example of a pragmatic approach motivated by the need to design an LSP curriculum. However, after Pearson (1998: 40), we could wonder whether it really matters if a term has special reference in one domain or in more than one domain. For a

15 Pieńkos (1999) postulates the existence of a great number of 'ordinary' legal vocabulary which he refers to as basic, key words fundamental to a legal lexicon in any language , such as words derived from the Roman law.

terminologist, it is by far more important to determine when words are used as terms and then to retrieve them. Pearson's seminal book *Terms in Context* demonstrates the advantages of integrating terminology and corpus linguistics in order to develop a methodology for retrieving information about terms from corpora.

As can be seen, previous studies of the legal lexicon outlined above tend to reflect traditional theory and practice of terminology. Consequently, they concentrate on proposing overly broad classifications of legal terminology motivated by pedagogic concerns or issues related to (in)comprehensibility of legal discourse. This approach suffers from two major drawbacks. First, it is preoccupied with terms at the expense of other important vocabulary found in legal texts. Second, it is not concerned with usage, i.e., the way terms or other vocabulary items are actually used in texts.

The present study differs from the previous ones in that it is not confined solely to the analysis of terms Indeed, this chapter intends to provide a more comprehensive and systematic description of how vocabulary is actually used in authentic legal texts on the basis of extensive language evidence. Crucially, such investigation should shed more light on lexical variation among legal genres. First, we will look at the overall patterns of vocabulary use by examining the breakdown of words by frequency level for each genre. The findings should enable one to gain insights into the diversity of lexical choice across legal genres.

3.3 Vocabulary use across legal genres

This analysis starts by examining the proportion of overall number of words (tokens) and types (different words). Since the comparison involves textual categories of differing size, Table 3.1. provided below, lists not only the total number of tokens but also the number of all types normalized per million words[16].

16 Since word type distributions have a non-linear relationship, the following formula was adopted to compute an approximate estimate of the number of words in a one-million word corpus: *normed number of words = (number of word types/Square root of corpus size) x 1,000* (cf. Biber 2006: Appendix B).

Table 3.1. *Use of different words across legal genres*

	Number of tokens (running words)	**Number of word types per million words**
academic journals	583,901	26,088
legislation	1,369,344	12,011
briefs	769,154	20,372
contracts	1,182,616	10,402
professional articles	202,668	23,050
opinions	1,264,564	20,661
textbooks	520,078	19,048

Despite the fact that all the genres are written and therefore carefully planned, revised and edited, radical differences can be noticed across the genres in terms of a number of different word types they use. Legislation and contracts use a markedly smaller number of distinct words (12,011 and 10,402 respectively) than the other text genres. This corroborates the perception of these two operative genres as highly repetitive and relying on a relatively small set of word types. On the other hand, academic articles and professional articles tend to employ the largest set of different words. Legal academic journals are related to a wide range of topics and they deal with issues originating from different legal subfields. The same applies to the category of professional articles. The diversity of topics is reflected in the wide range of word types. Finally, briefs, opinions and textbooks have roughly the same number of different word types. Textbook samples have been taken from books related to commercial law and thus they represent a fairly uniform vocabulary set. The picture emerging from Table 3.1. can be further refined in terms of different frequency levels illustrated in Figure 3.1.

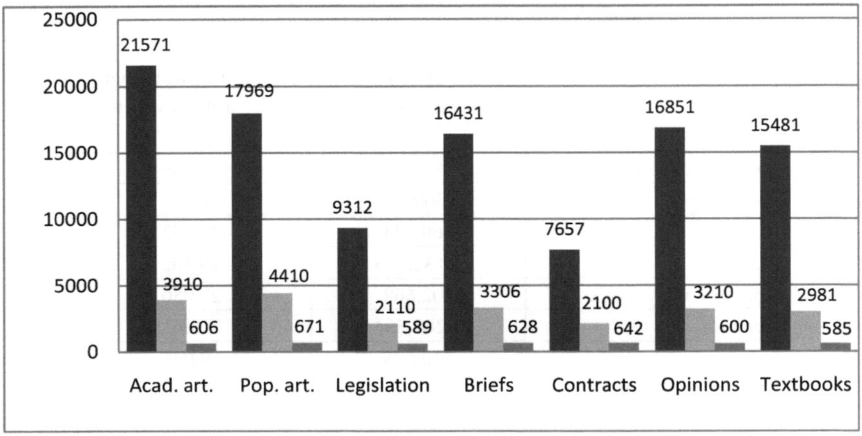

Figure 3.1. *Number of word types at three frequency levels (rates per million words)*

On closer examination, it appears that the diversity in word choice is attributable to the use of specialized vocabulary. Figure 3.1 plots the breakdown of word types by frequency level. Thus, there are very common words (occurring more than 200 times per million words) represented for each genre by the left-hand columns, moderately common words (between 21 and 200 times per million words), illustrated by the middle columns, and rare words (occurring fewer than 20 times per million words) shown in the right-hand columns. All the genres use a similar number of high-frequency word types. This might suggest that there is indeed a relatively small set of words shared by most legal genres. However, some genres differ radically in the use of low-frequency words. Both legislation and contracts tend to rely on the smallest number of rare words while academic journals and professional articles use a wide range of rare word types. Academic journals use a much larger set of such specialized words than, for instance, contracts or legislation. At the same time, professional articles, briefs, opinions and textbooks are fairly uniform in using a largely similar number of low-frequency word types. Substantial differences can also be noticed in respect of the use of moderately common words. Both academic journals and professional articles use nearly twice as many such words as legislation and contracts. The difference in the use of medium word types between legislation and contracts on the one hand and briefs, opinions and textbooks on the other is not so marked but also considerable. In a recent study (2006), Biber documents vocabulary use for classroom teaching and textbooks. Textbooks from different disciplines employ circa 27,000 while classroom teaching around 15,000 different word types. Thus, overall, legal genres would appear to be marked by a more restricted lexical diversity. Figure 3.2, below, plots the approximate number of word types in textbooks (normalized per 1 million words) across a range of disciplines (based on Figure 3.5 in Biber 2006: 42) with the legal discipline added.

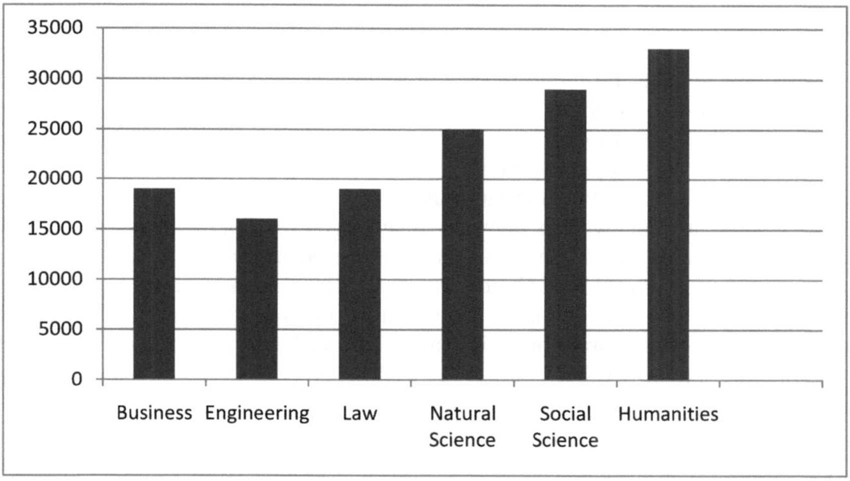

Figure 3.2. *Number of word types in textbooks across academic disciplines*

Legal textbooks appear to be similar to business and engineering in terms of the number of different word types used.

It seems then that the functions associated with different legal genres may have a strong influence on word choice. The two operative (creating and modifying legal relations) genres of legislation and contracts differ dramatically from the other genres. They tend to use a similar number of high-frequency word types but the scarcity in word choice is mostly due to the limited use of rare and moderately common words. So far, legislation and contracts appear to be far more restricted than the other genres, especially academic journals and professional articles.

3.3.1. High-frequency verbs

We now turn to a more detailed presentation of vocabulary use across the seven genres that will show which words are actually used at a particular frequency level. The following discussion will be confined to verbs which appear very frequently, i.e. at least 200 times per million words. As can be seen in Table 3.2, there is a certain degree of lexical overlap across the genres. Words marked in bold (*apply, base, determine, file, find give, hold, include, make, provide, require, see, use*) have been found in six or seven text genres grouped in the ALC. This is a small set of words which represent 'core' vocabulary used to express essential meanings and functions in legal discourse. These verbs are found in predictable lexico-grammatical and collocational patterns across all the genres. For example, the verb *give* tends to be found as part of a phrase co-occurring with a restricted set of nouns: *give rise to {a claim, lawsuit, obligation, right}, give priority to {activities, applicant, projects}, give effect to {language, evidence}* or *give (such, written) notice {e.g. of a meeting}, give preference to {applications, eligible entities, proposals}*, etc. In a similar vein, certain high-frequency verbs signal that there is some lexical overlap between related genres. For instance, briefs and opinions are related in that the two genres are used in proceedings between the Supreme Court of the United States. All the high-frequency verbs appearing in briefs are also found in opinions. Briefs and opinions both share a number of communication verbs (underlined in Table 3.2) such as *allege, conclude, deny, explain, state,* etc. (cf. Biber et al, 1999: 362). However, opinions make use of a larger set of such verbs (e.g. *argue, assert, describe, suggest,* etc.).

Certain genres tend to use specific vocabulary not found in the other categories (at least not with the same frequency). High-frequency verbs in contracts contain many highly specialized words (marked in italics in Table 3.2) such as *accrue, construe, deem, demise* or *incur*. This strikes one as surprising because high-frequency words are usually common words (cf. Biber, 2006: 37) and one would expect to find rare and difficult terms among low-frequency words. Table 3.2 shows that many of these verbs are in fact extremely frequent, appearing even more than 500 or 1000 times per million words. These are not only words usually not found in general English but words which are not found in other legal genres. Findings obtained in this analysis suggest that contracts use the greatest number of high-frequency specialized words but further analysis is needed to confirm this. One explanation could be that contracts are terminologically denser than the other genres.

Table 3.2. *High-frequency (>200 per 1 million words) verbs (lemmatized) broken down by legal genre; word appears *over 500 per one million words **over 1000 per million words*

ACADEMIC JOURNALS
base, consider, expect, **find**, follow, **give**, **hold**, **include***, **make****, note, offer, **provide***, receive, represent, **require**, **see****, set, take, **use***
PROFESSIONAL ARTICLES
base, **determine**, **file**, **find**, **hold**, **include**, limit, **make***, pay, propose, **provide**, **require**, **see***, purchase, **use**

LEGISLATION
add*, advance, allow, amend**, apply**, appropriate, approve, base*, carry*, concern, conform, consider, cover, define**, describe*, designate, determine**, distribute, ensure, enter, entitle, establish*, exceed, exist, file, follow, give, impose, include**, insert**, institute, involve, issue, limit, locate, make**, meet, pay, propose, provide**, prescribe, publish, read, receive, redesignate, refer, register, relate**, require*, specify*, strike**, submit, substitute, take*, treat, use*
BRIEFS
add, <u>allege</u>, apply, base*, challenge, <u>conclude</u>, consider, <u>deny</u>, determine, enact, entitle, establish, <u>explain,</u> file, find*, follow, give, grant, hold*, include, intend, involve, issue, limit, make**, <u>note</u>, omit, present, prevent, protect, provide*, <u>quote</u>, recognize, <u>reject</u>, relate*, require*, see**, <u>state</u>, use,
CONTRACTS
accrue, affect, agree*, amend*, apply, arise, assign, attach, authorize, become, bind, borrow, cause*, consolidate, constitute, construe, contain, contemplate*, continue, contribute, date, deem*, define*, deliver, demise, describe, designate, determine, enter, execute, exceed, exercise*, exist, file, give, grant, hold, include**, incur, indemnify, issue, lease, limit*, maintain, make**, mean*, obtain, offer, own, pay**, perform, permit, prefer, propose, provide*, purchase**, qualify, receive, refer, register, relate*, release, remain, request*, require**, restrict, result*, retain, say, secure, sell, set**, sign, specify, take, terminate, transfer*, use**, vote
OPINIONS
add, <u>address</u>, adopt, <u>affirm</u>, allow*, agree, <u>allege</u>, amend, appear, apply*, <u>argue</u>, <u>assert</u>, authorize, avoid, base*, believe, bring, call, challenge, charge, cite, conclude, concur*, consider, control, create, decide, define, deliver, <u>deny</u>, <u>describe</u>, determine, dissent*, enact, entitle, establish, <u>explain,</u> fail, file*, find*, follow, give*, grant, hold, impose, include, intend, involve, issue, join, justify, leave, limit, make**, note, omit, order, pay, permit, present, prevent, proceed, propose, protect, provide**, quote, raise, reach, read, recognize, reject, relate, require**, reverse, <u>say</u>*, see**, seek, sentence, set, show, <u>state</u>, <u>suggest</u>, support, take*, think, turn, use**, violate,
TEXTBOOKS
accept*, agree, apply, arise, base, bind, claim*, consider, discharge, do, enforce, entitle, enter, find, fix, give*, grant, hold*, imply, intend, make*, pay, perform*, prevent, provide, recover, receive, require, say*, see, seem*, sell, set, state*, sue, take, use, write

Many high-frequency words occur with heavily restricted occurrence. Primarily, this restriction concerns terms employed to deal with some aspect of the legal procedure. For example, it is only in opinions that we find two verbs *concur* and *dissent* used in highly predictable and fixed patterns to signal a judge's agreement or disagreement, as shown in the example below:

(1) Justice Breyer, with whom Justice Scalia and Justice Ginsburg join, **concurring**.(emphasis added)

Similarly, only legislations use *insert* and *strike* in the more technical meaning:

(2) The Act entitled "An Act concerning tonnage duties on vessels entering otherwise than by sea", approved March 8, 1910 (36 Stat 234; 46 U.S.C. App. 132), is amended by **striking** "through 2002," and **inserting** "through 2006".

However, unlike in the case of certain terms in contracts (see above), *strike* and *insert* are not words unfamiliar for the lay reader. Legislative language is expected to use vocabulary from the general stock of the English language, a requirement not binding for private law documents such as contracts. Genre-specific verbs are more likely to appear in more restricted genres. As already noted, restricted, domain-specific varieties employ relatively fixed, formulaic expressions to convey highly specialized meanings. In our study, Table 3.2 shows that legislation, contracts and opinions rely on a relatively large set of very frequent verbs. Judicial opinions represent an interesting case of a genre which is essentially expository (Tiersma, 1999: 139) but also one which contains persuasive elements, even if couched in very formal objective form of expression. However, the significant number of very frequent verbs in opinions can be ascribed to the fact that opinions contain a judgment or order which constitutes the disposition of the case. The disposition part of an opinion is more "operative" with a well-defined set of vocabulary and ready-made formulaic expressions. In our view, the somewhat heterogeneous characteristics of judicial opinions are reflected in their lexical make-up. The same observation applies to briefs. Briefs, as we recall from Chapter 2, are written legal arguments constructed by appellate attorneys in an attempt to persuade appellate courts to rule for their clients (Brostoff and Sinsheimer, 2003: 147). Briefs are very formal documents which require particular formatting prescribed by the Rules of Appellate Procedure for each jurisdiction. Apart from the persuasive elements provided by attorneys advocating a certain legal position, briefs also contain more "operative" language. On the other hand, two more open-ended genres (academic journals and professional articles) tend to rely on a small set of very frequent common verbs which, to a large extent, are shared by the other genres.

3.4. A keyword approach to studying variation across legal genres

In this section a different methodological approach is adopted to examine in greater detail variation in terms of vocabulary choice across different types of legal texts. The concepts of keyword and keyword analysis as well as the corresponding methodology were introduced in Section 2.6 of Chapter 2. As a result, 700 keywords (100 hundred for each genre) listed in Appendix A were identified. The keywords were then carefully examined in their immediate co-texts as well as in the larger macrostructure of a particular genre. In what follows, tentative classifications of keywords are provided for each genre. It should be stressed that the proposed categories of keywords are neither watertight nor absolutely clear-cut. The labels introduced for each category represent so-called *ad hoc labels,* which aim to show the typical characteristics of the category. Table 3.3 shows the overall organization of the keyword sections.

Table 3.3. *Functional classification of keywords across legal genres*

Academic Journals	**Examples**
Citation keywords	*citation, see, supra*
Self-mention keyword 'we'	
Legal terms as keywords	*discovery, harm, penalty, sentencing*
Keywords used to illustrate and support legal reasoning	*beliefs, estimates, model, probability*
General language keywords	*care, patient, school, social, child, death*
Legislation	
Keywords marking internal organization of a legislative text	*section, paragraph, title, chapter*
Keywords denoting legal instruments	*act, code, document, plan*
Keywords marking time/place/text-deixis	*beginning, date, end, following*
Keywords used to change or modify legislative provisions	*inserting, striking, amending*
Institutional keywords	*agency, commission, entity*
General language keywords	*conservation, education, health*
Briefs	
Communication keywords	*concluded, explained, testified*
Institutional keywords	*circuit, court, federal, government*
Legal terms as keywords	*acquittal, defendant, probation, seizure*
Keywords denoting legal instruments	*amendment, decision, statute*
Academic keywords	*ibid., id., see,*
Keywords related to crime and incarceration	*criminal, inmates, offenses, offenders*
Keywords expressing evaluation	*compelling, constitutional, harmful*
Keywords referring to public interest	*access, advocacy, race, sex*
Contracts	
Keywords marking temporal relations	*date, day, prior, time*
Keywords marking text deixis	*herein, hereto, thereto*
Keywords marking participation	*agent, buyer, holder, stockholders*
Legal terms as keywords	*default, indemnification, liabilities*
The keyword	*deem*
Professional articles	

Legal terms as keywords	*appeal, certification, defense, litigation*
"Advisory" keywords	*must, should, you*
Opinions	
Keywords marking judicial stance	*concurring, dissenting, joined*
Personal pronouns as keywords	*he, his, we, our*
Legal terms as keywords	*claim, evidence, rule, remand*
Keywords used to identify and interpret legal issues	*argument, interpretation, issue, text*
Textbooks	
Legal terms as keywords	*acceptance, assignee, breach*
"Function" keywords	*may, should, would, he, his*

Table 3.3 shows salient functional categories of keywords identified in the legal genres. Two fundamental lexical characteristics appear to be emerging. First, the only category shared by all the genres is that of legal terms. Sometimes, a given category can be shared by only some of the genres, indicating some similarity between them. For example, only legislation and contracts have keywords marking time/place/text deixis. Second, the functional categories range from narrow, highly specialist ones (e.g. keywords used to change or modify legislative provisions in legislation, judicial stance keywords in opinions) to general language keywords (as in academic journals or legislation). It seems therefore that the Keyword Analysis provides a useful means of identifying further areas of overlap and specificity among legal genres. In what follows, each keyword section is discussed in detail.

3.4.1. Keywords in academic journals

Citation keywords

Predictably, academic journals are marked by the presence of keywords that contribute towards the construction of academic discourse. They are all related to the academic register in that they identify and refer readers to relevant sources on which propositions made in the articles are based. Indeed, as Hyland (forthcoming) notes: "One of the most striking differences in disciplinary uses of language is in citation practices". Legal texts appear to have their own format for constructing legal citations. Understanding them is extremely important because they help locate the original documents. For example, in *See 43 U.S.C. 1603,* the interested reader is referred to Section 1603 of Vol. 43 of the United States Code. Any citation referring to a case will contain the name of the parties involved in the litigation, i.e. its heading (cf. Lee *et al.* 1999), as in another corpus example: *See Rice v. Rehner, 463 U.S. 713, 726 (1983).*

Citation keywords form a relatively small but salient category. There are as many as five such keywords found among the top ten keywords (*Id., supra, note* (in fact these two word forms are very often used as one expression *supra note,* and *see*). The other keywords include *citation, journal,* and *literature.* The word *supra* or the expression *supra note* are clearly unique to academic and legal citation practice. *Supra* is a Latin term for 'above'. It signals a situation where a writer wants the reader to look up a previously-cited source. Thus, *supra* is used to indicate that the current citation is from the same source as the previous one. This word is often used in legal research to denote that matter under current consideration has already appeared somewhere before in the text or document in which the reference is made. For instance, if a writer wants to mention a source in his or her fifth footnote, then s/he would denote it in this manner: *see supra note 5* or *see supra text after note.*

Id. is the most common abbreviated form which stands for the Latin *Idem*, meaning 'the same' and it is used to indicate a reference made earlier in the text, as in the following corpus example (emphasis added):

(3) An exception to the Santa Clara Pueblo rule has emerged in the Tenth Circuit, in Dry Creek Lodge, Inc. v. Arapahoe and Shoshone Tribes, 623 F.2d 682 (10th Cir. 1980). There the court permitted federal judicial relief against a tribe when a non-Native lacked a tribal forum in which to litigate his claim. *See id.* at 684-85.

The extremely frequent occurrence of the directive *see* illustrates how legal academic articles are replete with references to statutes and cases. The frequent use of *see* is not confined to academic genres. It is also a key directive in briefs and opinions (ranking as 8th and 7th keyword, respectively). Interestingly, *see* is not found as a keyword in legal textbooks. However, it appears that it is the preferred form of directing readers to other parts of a text or other texts in much of what we could refer to as the expository-persuasive mode of legal writing. Clearly, it is also a fairly common device in other disciplinary discourses (cf. Hyland, 2009).

Words derived from Latin seems to suggest specificity in terms of language resources appropriated for citation in legal academic genres. Citation keywords tend to cluster in the top ten keywords (except for *article*). Legal academic articles display the general tendency of legal writing to cite the authorities from which a legal principle has been drawn. Legal writers may draw the legal principle from one controlling authorities or from several (Brostoff / Sinsheimer, 2003: 88). As Bhatia notes, this tendency is one of the reasons for "an extremely high degree of intertextuality and interdiscursivity in legal discourse, whether it is the case of textbooks, cases, judgments or legislation" (2004: 35).

The self-mention keyword *"we"*

Self mention is another important feature which varies both *across* and *within* disciplines. It concerns how far writers want to intrude into their texts through the use of *I* or *we*, or by using impersonal forms. Hyland (forth.) argues that presenting a discoursal self is central to the writing process, and we cannot avoid projecting an impression of ourselves and how we stand in relation to our arguments, discipline, and readers. To some extent, this is determined by seniority, experience, confidence, personality, and so on, but the presence or absence of explicit author reference is a conscious choice whereby writers adopt a particular community-situated authorial identity. In our corpus, academic journals make frequent use of *we,* which ranks as 62nd in the keyword list:

(4) In the next issue of the Journal of Employment Discrimination Law, *we* will consider how an organization moves from a compliance culture based on rules of conduct to a values culture that is based on shared norms of behavior and relationships. (emphasis added)

In the example above, the personal pronoun fulfils a text-organizing function by specifying how the author intends to arrange the content of the article and what aims are envisaged by him or her. As can be seen in the following example, the first-person pronoun is used to express authorial stance quite unequivocally:

(5) *We* do not agree that the corporation's property interests settle the question. The State urges in effect that the corporation's right to control the inhabitants of Chickasaw is coextensive with the right of a homeowner to regulate the conduct of his guests. *We* cannot accept that contention. (emphasis added)

Indeed, stance structures with a 1st person subject are frequently used, which is evidenced by the co-occurrence between *we* and mental verbs (Biber et al 1999: 364) such as *assume, consider, find, know, see* and *think*:

(6) However, *we* <u>think</u> it more realistic to analyze the case in which there is a distribution of views and the government punishes only the extremist speech. (emphasis added)

We is typically used even if an article is single-authored. An additional examination of its most frequent collocates reveals that there is also a strong co-occurrence between *we* and modal verbs such as *can, may, must, should* and the verb *need*:

(7) It is then that *we may*, in good conscience, begin the process of rationing our health care technologies. My position is that *we must* begin to set out our criteria for making these decisions now. (emphasis added)

Excerpt (7) illustrates how *we* is employed as a useful device to engage the reader by signalling mutual obligation and commitment to shared ideas or values. Worth noting is the presence of an overt expression of author stance: *my position is that...*

Legal terms as keywords

Compared to other legal genres, legal academic articles are clearly marked by their reliance on a relatively limited number of keywords denoting legal concepts. In our analysis, these include: *discovery, governor, harm, Miranda, penalty, prosecutors, sentencing, sovereignty, treaty.* These keywords are typical of criminal and constitutional law and obviously do not reflect the fact that terms from many other branches of law are widely discussed in academic journals, e.g. business law or family law. What the keyword output shows is a more general trend showing the overall proportion of legal terms in the one hundred keywords across the range of legal genres.

Strictly speaking, this category also includes the so-called 'semi-technical' or 'mixed' terms, i.e. words from the general language which "have acquired additional meanings by a process of analogy in the specialist context of legal activity" (Alcaraz / Hughes 2002:17). If we look at the list of keywords provided above, *discovery* and *harm* are a fine example of this type of terms, which also includes words whose meaning does not differ substantially from their everyday meaning. For instance, the keyword *child* is defined by *Black's Law Dictionary* (1990) as "progeny; offspring of parentage. Unborn or recently born human being [...] At common law one who had not attained the age of fourteen years". Thus, the legal definition may be more accurate in the way it specifies the age of a young person, his or her rights, etc.

What this analysis seems to suggest is that legal journals contain relatively few purely technical terms. At the same time, there is a fairly large category of words from the common stock such as *child, parents, higher, school, students, university,* etc. which seem to signal a broad range of issues embedded in the highly social context of much legal research.

Keywords used to illustrate and support legal reasoning

There is growing evidence to suggest that each disciplinary discourse may have its own knowledge-system structure, which in turn affects the preferred modes of communication (see, for instance Berkenkotter / Huckin, 1995). To address this aspect I looked at keywords that are associated with the process of advancing argument in scholarly writing: *beliefs, estimates, model, probability, problems, results, responsibility, theory*. The two examples (italicised) below corroborate the presence of empirical and social research trends in legal research with a clear focus on the evaluation of its outcome:

(8) Empirical evidence generally supports this idea with respect to the relative propensity of stock insurers to exist when future cash flows are more uncertain or business income is generally more risky (Lamm-Tennant and Starks 1993). Through observation of the behaviour of insurance companies involved directly in litigation, the *results* of this study are consistent with this idea as well.

(9) This paper *estimates* the effect of judicial characteristics (political affiliation, race, and sex) on federal criminal sentencing using variation in judicial characteristics at the district level. The *results* suggest that judges' race and sex have little influence on prison sentences in general but do affect racial and sex disparities.

The keyword *model* is also strongly indicative of how legal research is constructed and carried out. It signals the presence of logical tools employed to model legal argument:

(10) Robert Pollack has built a *model* in which the donor's utility depends on the recipient's consumption of certain goods, as opposed to the recipient's utility. In this "paternalistic" *model*, the donor's utility rises if, but only if, the recipient consumes more of those goods that the donor wants the recipient to consume. Yet, in this *model*, as in Becker's, the donor might derive more utility from transferring a dollar to the recipient than by increasing his own consumption.

The keyword *beliefs* is noteworthy for its co-occurrence in rather atypical co-texts. In our corpus data, *beliefs* are discussed in the context of their *distribution* among the parties to a dispute as a result of a discovery procedure:

(11) In the wake of the papers by Shavell and Sobel, several authors have modeled the discovery process. Cooter and Rubinfeld (1994) develop a model of discovery in which plaintiffs and defendants have subjective

beliefs about the outcome at trial. Settlement occurs if a contract zone exists, while a trial occurs when the contract zone fails to exist. The effect of discovery depends on how it changes the *distribution of beliefs* of the two parties to the dispute. In this context, discovery can either raise or lower the probability of trial depending on whether it makes the litigants more or less optimistic about the outcome.

Of course, this does not mean that *beliefs* do not co-occur with more predictable collocates. There is in fact evidence that these include *common, cultural, personal, philosophical, prior, religious, subjective,* etc., which indicate a very broad range of use for this keyword.

General language keywords

By far, the largest category of keywords indicates a broad range of topics raised in the articles. These can be generalized, as health care (*care, patient, recipients*), education (*higher, school, students, university*), welfare (*poor, social, welfare*), family (*child, children, families, parents*), crime (*crimes, death, penalty, victim*), and ethics (*ethical, moral, morally, values*).

Inevitably, there is considerable overlap between these categories when, for example, family matters are discussed in the context of social welfare or crime and capital punishment are viewed from the perspective of ethics. These keywords are, in my view, indicative of how the law, as a set of rules, may be examined at several different levels. At one level, it divides social behaviour into actions that society regards as either obligatory and permissible or forbidden. It specifies when and how people are held responsible for shirking obligations, or for engaging in forbidden behaviour. At another level, it organizes private processes of dispute settlement. At yet another level, it allocates *welfare* (understood here as things such as wealth, status, and social power).

The occurrence of *responsibility* as a keyword is perfectly understandable if we bear in mind that law is a process determining responsibility for socially consequential behaviour (Lempert / Sanders, 1989). Furthermore, allocating responsibility is a central legal task. Applying the law often involves deciding what people did or did not do, determining what they could (not) have done and distinguishing the intended from the unintended consequences of behaviour. There is a consensus among legal theorists that the term *responsibility* is particularly hard to define (Lempert / Sanders, 1989: 5):

> One of the difficulties with discussions of responsibility is that the term *responsibility* has different meanings. We sometimes fail to distinguish these

meanings and, consequently, the various ways, in which individuals may be held responsible.

Collocational analysis shows that *responsibility* tends to be qualified by such adjectives as *moral, personal* and *professional*:

(12) Taking responsibility for one's actions means taking responsibility for any foreseeable consequences of those actions. A doctor cannot shirk *moral* or *legal responsibility* for such consequences by saying that bringing them about was not the primary intention of his actions. It is inconsistent, therefore, for a doctor practicing active euthanasia to be seen as morally inferior to a colleague who is doing exactly the same thing while merely claiming he has different intentions.

Interestingly, the keyword *responsibility* also collocates with other keywords identified as belonging to the category of illustrating and supporting legal reasoning. In the following example, we can note how discussion in a legal journal revolves around different theoretical perspectives on the concept of responsibility:

(13) One recent critic, Jean Roberts, equating his *theory* of voluntary action with his *theory* of *moral responsibility*, goes on to argue that Aristotle holds a *theory of moral responsibility* that is alien to our modern conception of *responsibility*.

Responsibility appears to provide a glimpse into a complex and interrelated network of legal concepts characteristic of a great deal of legal thinking.

3.4.2. Keywords in legislation

Keywords marking internal organization of a legislative text

Legislation is the only legal genre with such a proliferation of keywords denoting different textual units. They divide the text into macrostructural units and help to ensure unity and cohesion of individual legal provisions. They are the product of legislative drafting standards known as *paragraphing* (Thornton, 1987: 64), *sculpturing* or *paragraph sculpture* (Dick, 1985: 117). There are as many as fourteen keywords belonging to this category found in the top one hundred keywords (see Appendix A for a complete list of one hundred keywords identified for legislation). In fact, there are as many as six such keywords in the top ten keywords. These include: *section, subsection, paragraph, subparagraph, title, subtitle, subclause, chapter* etc.). They are uniformly used to mark endophoric reference in order to locate the textual source of a particular legislative provision as is evidenced in the following examples:

(14) The protection provided for a mask work under this chapter shall commence on the date on which the mask work is registered under section 908, or the date on which the mask work is first commercially exploited anywhere in the world, whichever occurs first.

(15) GENERAL REQUIREMENTS- A security program established under paragraph (1) shall provide a security program and capability at that seaport that is adequate to ensure the safety of the public from threats of crime and terrorism. (emphasis added)

More importantly, such expressions are not used merely to mark textual deictics but in fact they indicate *legal basis* for the preceding provision. This category of keywords is marked by both uniformity of their discourse function as well as by recurrent patterns of use. For instance, out of the total of 2745 occurrences of the keyword *section,* 1114 instances of its use are found in the form of a three-word sequence *under this section,* 530 instances were identified as a four-word formulaic sequence *as defined in section,* yet another 382 instances are phrased as *described in section,* etc. In other words, keywords from this category tend to be found in longer fixed and formulaic expressions which will be discussed in more detail in the next chapter. Such lexical items are regarded as everyday vocabulary frequently found in legal texts (cf. Alcaraz and Hughes, 2002: 18) chiefly due to their semantic transparency. In fact, they are specialized and genre-specific.

Keywords denoting *legal instruments*

A separate but related category has been distinguished for keywords denoting various legal instruments or other documents referred to or relied upon in the texts of different legislative acts. These are several keywords which can be grouped in this category such as, *act, amendments, code, plan, document, program, report, study, project,* and *works.*

For example, the keyword *Act* is found as part of the title of a legislative act. It is then usually located at the beginning of an act immediately after the enacting clause as in the following example:

(16) Be it enacted by the Senate and House of Representatives of the United States of America in Congress assembled,
SECTION 1. SHORT TITLE, ETC.

a) SHORT TITLE- This **Act** may be cited as the `Retirement Opportunity Expansion **Act** of 2001'.
(b) AMENDMENT OF 1986 CODE- Except as otherwise expressly provided, whenever in this **Act** an amendment or repeal is expressed in terms of an amendment to, or repeal of, a section or other provision, the reference shall be considered to be made to a section or other provision of the Internal Revenue Code of 1986. (emphasis in bold added)

It is found in legislative definitions where a reference is made to a given act as a source of legal authority:

(17) Clearing bank. - The term "clearing bank" means an uninsured State member bank, or a corporation organized under section 25A of the Federal Reserve **Act**, which operates, or operates as, a multilateral clearing organization pursuant to section 409 of the Federal Deposit Insurance Corporation Improvement **Act** of 1991.(emphasis in bold added)

The four-word expression *for the purposes of* specifies the scope of application of a definition:

(18) For purposes of this subsection, in the case of an individual who is absent from work on leave required to be given to such individual under the Family and Medical Leave **Act** of 1993, the **plan** shall treat as hours of service--

In other words, the keyword *act* is characterized by specific *textual positions* in which it is found in legislative texts. On closer examination, other keywords from this category are similar to the keywords from the previous category in that they also signal a source of authority for a specified activity or action as the examples below illustrate:

(19) The number of individuals provided assistance <u>under</u> the **program** as of the date of the **report.**
(20) The average dollar amount (monthly and annually) of the premium assistance provided <u>under</u> the **program**. (emphasis added)

The keyword *document* serves as a generic term for different types of instruments and it is thus usually postmodified as in the following example:

(21) EASTERN PLANNING AREA- The term "Eastern Planning Area" means the Eastern Gulf of Mexico Planning Area of the outer Continental Shelf, as designated in the **document** entitled "Draft Proposed Program Outer

Continental Shelf Oil and Gas Leasing Program 2007-2012", dated February 2006.

Consequently, this keyword is used extensively in statutory definitions (emphasis added):

(22) (3)(A) For purposes of this subsection, the term "satisfactory documentary evidence of citizenship or nationality" means--
`(i) any **document** described in subparagraph (B); or
`(ii) a **document** described in subparagraph (C) and a document described in subparagraph (D).
`(B) The following are **documents** described in this subparagraph:
`(i) A United States passport.
`(ii) Form N-550 or N-570 (Certificate of Naturalization).
`(iii) Form N-560 or N-561 (Certificate of United States Citizenship).

Keywords marking *time/place/text-deixis*

A few keywords are invariably employed to mark deictic relations in legislative texts. The most frequent are *end, beginning, following*, and *this*. As we will see in the next chapter, the keyword *end* is found in highly frequent lexical bundles *at the end of* and *the end of the* to mark text and place deixis respectively. It is also found in highly productive phrase-frames. The cluster analysis shows that a three-word cluster *at the end* is often preceded by words used to modify or change the text of a legislative provision (see next section for detailed discussion of this category of keywords).

(23) (a) Requirements- Part 3 of title V of the National Energy Conservation Policy Act (42 U.S.C. 8251 et seq.), as amended by section 101, is amended by *adding* at the **end** the following:
(24) SALES OF TIRES- Section 6416(b)(4)(B) is amended by *striking* "or" at the end of clause (i), by striking the period at the **end** of clause (ii) and inserting ", or", and by adding after clause (ii) the following: (emphasis added)

Worth noting in the above examples is the presence of another keyword from this category – *following* – to mark cataphoric reference. Interestingly, *end* is frequently employed to mark explicitly the end of a bill and it is then used on its own:

(25) (b) Effective Date- The amendments made by subsection (a) shall take effect as if included in Public Law 107-159 (116 Stat. 122).
Speaker of the House of Representatives.
Vice President of the United States and
President of the Senate.
END (emphasis added)

The keyword *beginning* is similar to *end* in that it is part of numerous lexical bundles (e.g. *beginning on the date, beginning after December 31*) but it differs in terms of the type of reference, which is temporal rather than spatial. The presence of a keyword *this* in our analysis corroborates findings obtained in earlier studies of deixis (see Kurzon, 1985). *This* was found to serve exclusively as a deictic in nominal expressions or (rarely) as a demonstrative pronoun. The present analysis documents the use of *this* in nominal phrases where *this* tends to modify keywords denoting legal instruments or their parts (e.g. *section, act, subsection, paragraph*, etc.). Its use is further constrained by the co-occurrence with the preposition *under* (3415 instances, as in *under this section*[17]) and the modal *shall* (1579 occurrences) which seems to suggest that, in many instances of its use, *this* is often part of a larger, more general pattern which imposes mandatory legal force by referring to the source of its authority enshrined in a particular macrostructure of a legislative text.

Finally, there are two frequent **referential keywords** which are used to ensure unity and cohesion within the legislative texts: *relating* and *reference*.

(26) (c) Certain Transfers Included. - Any **reference** in this section to transfers of liabilities includes a ratable transfer of liabilities within a priority class.
(27) `(3) any **reference** to the education of children with disabilities or the education of all children with disabilities shall be considered to be a **reference** to the provision of appropriate early intervention services to infants and toddlers with disabilities.

As the two examples illustrate, *reference* can be found in a fairly fixed pattern which serves as a signpost to the reader by helping them to interpret the scope of a particular provision. In the first example, the more general expression *transfers of liabilities* is interpreted as inclusive of a more specific one (*ratable transfer of liabilities within a priority* class). As will be seen in the discussion below, legislative and contractual genres share a great deal of similarity in that they have many keywords marking temporal and spatial orientations in texts.

Keywords such as *after, date, effective, period, year, years* testify to the presence of a yet another subcategory of **referential keywords marking time**

17 This appears the total of 11309 times in legislation.

relations. Since they are all found in fixed multi-word expressions, they will be discussed in detail the next chapter. Let us note however, as in the case of the categories proposed above, that there are certain constructional tendencies which account for a great deal of co-occurrence among these keywords[18]. For instance, *effective* appears 2192 times in the legislative genre and it precedes another keyword *date* 1660 times. *Date* (in total 5593 occurrences) is found 1135 times in the bundles *after the date of* or *after the date on.* The co-occurrence between *after* and *effective* is confirmed by 147 instances where *effective* is found within the span of five words of *after* either to its left or right:

(28) A) **Effective** 18 months **after** the date of the enactment of this chapter, no person shall manufacture, import, offer to the public, provide or otherwise traffic in any (…)

In fact, there are as many as 56 instances of the bundle *after the effective date of.*

Keywords used to *change* or *modify legislative provisions*

Another distinct category is made up by extremely frequent verb forms such as: *apply, inserting, striking, amended, adding, carry, redesignating* which are usually combined to produce formulaic sequences of the type provided below:

(29) EXTENSION OF DUTIES- **Section** 36 of the Act of August 5, 1909 (36 Stat. 111; 46 U.S.C. App. 121), is **amended** by **striking** "through 2002," each place it appears and **inserting** `through 2006,'.

(30) CONFORMING AMENDMENT- The table of sections for subchapter I of chapter 13 of title 11, United States Code, is **amended** by **adding** at the end the following: (emphasis added)

These keywords are clearly patterned in that they appear in highly predictable lexico-grammatical patterns. For example, by scrutinizing the concordance lines for *amended,* two patterns emerge:

- It is predominantly used in the Passive Voice;
- Whenever *amend* is found in a *to*-infinitive clause (51 instances), it appears at the beginning of an act followed immediately by an enactment clause to express the purpose of the act:

18 The term "constructional tendency" is used to mean the ratio of a word overall frequency and its frequency in a recurrent string. See also Renouf and Sinclair, 1991; Kjellmer, 1990; and more recently Stubbs, 2009.

(31) A BILL **To amend** the Food Security Act of 1985 to establish the conservation security program. Be it enacted by the Senate and House of Representatives of the United States of America in Congress assembled.

The Past Participle form *amended* is used 3391 times and it is preceded by IS in 2716 cases (in only 25 cases, it is preceded by ARE). It has a fixed lexical core in the form of two lexical bundles *is amended by* (1668 occurrences) and *is amended to* (220 occurrences). *Is amended to* is in fact part of a longer lexical bundle *is amended to read as follows.* Its pragmatic function is to introduce a change or modification into a legislative provision. The word form *amended* is also found in a different variant: *as amended by* (353 instances of use):

(32) Subsec. (c)(3)(C). Pub. L. 103-369, Sec. 2(4)(C)(iii), as amended by Pub. L. 105-80, Sec. 1(2), inserted before period at end "or July 1, 1997, whichever is later".

The two bundles *as amended by* and *is amended by* differ in respect of the slots that follow them. While the former is invariably followed by a reference to a specific part of the legislative act (see example above), the latter tends to co-occur with a limited range of verbs such as *adding, inserting, redesignating, striking* which specify the exact nature of the effected change. Thus, our findings demonstrate how the five keywords tend to co-occur in a largely fixed lexical pattern and within a single semantic set. It also emerges that it is useful to distinguish between 'lemmas' or 'lexemes' and 'word-forms'. For example, the lemma ADD is found almost exclusively in legislative texts as the word-form *adding,* the lemma STRIKE as *striking* rather than *strike*, etc. In other words, the keyword analysis output suggests that the absence of lemmatization can be an advantage because phraseological patterns appear to be attached to a particular word form rather than lemma.

Finally, the keyword *carry* (in fact a phrasal verb *carry out*) which collocates with keywords related to the internal organization of a legislative act as in the following example:

(33) IN GENERAL- Not later than 18 months after the date of enactment of this Act, the Commission, after consultation with States and other stakeholders, shall issue final regulations establishing such requirements as the Commission determines to be necessary to carry out this section and the amendments made by this section.

On closer examination, it emerges that it tends to co-occur with expressions connected with money and the way money is meant to be spent by an appropriate authority:

(34) Extended Authorization- There are authorized to be appropriated to the Secretary to carry out section 912 $50,000,000 for each of fiscal years 2010 through 2013.

(35) There is authorized to be appropriated to carry out this subtitle $200,000,000 for each of fiscal years 2007 through 2011, to remain available until expended. (emphasis added)

Thus, the keyword *carry* is found in a fairly fixed lexical structure which can be generalized as follows:

> THERE + BE + AUTHORIZED TO BE APPROPRIATED TO CARRY OUT + section/subtitle {reference to part of a legislative act}+ {specified sum of money}+ {some extension, usually a time reference} (e.g. *fiscal years 2010 through 2013*).

The capitalized words represent the full canonical form of this phrase with optional elements in brackets. In terms of the pragmatic function, this is a conventional way of earmarking specific funds in accordance with a specific legislative provision.

Institutional keywords

There are several keywords which can be grouped in a category referring to various institutional bodies or positions of authority: *administrator, agency, commission, entity, organization, secretary.* They are extremely frequent keywords in legislation because they represent general designations for various government or other administrative departments. For instance, *secretary* is a name given to various heads of executive department in the government of the United States, such as for instance, the *Secretary of State, Secretary of Commerce, Secretary of the Treasury,* etc. Such keywords denoting positions of authority tend to be followed by the keyword *shall* to signal obligations or duties which such posts entail or prerogatives vested in this position (e.g. the keyword *secretary* co-occurs with *shall* in 38% of the total number of its occurrences and in 13% with *may*):

(36) b) Development of Verification Procedure. – The **Secretary** of Commerce shall establish a procedure to verify, upon the petition of an interested party, that a system meets the standards set forth in subsection (a)(2).

In terms of institutional names, *agency* is used with reference to a range of local (for instance educational), state, federal or government entities. *Organization* is another general designation often used in defining various bodies as is evidenced by the extremely frequent clusters *organization described in,* or *organization as defined in.* Finally, *entity* is a designation referring to an organization or being that possesses separate existence for tax purposes. Examples are corporations, partnerships, estates and trusts (cf. *Black's Law Dictionary*). It can therefore refer to a very wide range of objects such as different types of corporations, even person or government units. An example from our data illustrates the frequent use of this keyword in legislative provisions which aim to determine an addressee of a legal norm in the most accurate manner:

(37) An **entity** other than an **entity** of the kind specified in paragraph (1) of this subsection is not an underwriter under section 2(11) of the Securities Act of 1933 (!1) with respect to any securities offered or sold to such **entity** in the manner specified in subsection (a)(1) of this section. (emphasis added)

This use of *entity* is corroborated by the analysis of its collocates. It is found the total of 1010 times in the legislation. It is preceded, among others, by *an* (117 times), *any* (43), *such* (52), other (30) and followed by *means* (26), *shall* (48), *described* (26), etc.

Other relatively small categories include keywords related to **measurements** (*amount, percent*), **definition** (*term, means*) and **requirements** (*appropriate, eligible, requirements, qualified, individual*).

General language keywords

A considerable proportion of keywords identified as significant for legislation belongs to the category which has been dubbed *general language keywords.* They cover a variety of topics (even if not as varied as in the case of academic journals) which can be subsumed under the following headings:

Finance: *commodity, fiscal, funding, futures, security, taxable*

Education: *demonstration, education, educational, research*

Technology: *facility, transmission,*

Welfare/public policy: *assistance, conservation, coverage, disabilities, health, housing, service, services, security*

The presence of such keywords is indicative of major legislative policies adopted by the US Congress over the last few years.

So far, keywords in legislation have been grouped into relatively stable, if not entirely clear-cut, categories, according to their meaning and/or function. However, keywords can be also grouped in a separate category collectively labelled as "function keywords", where individual items represent "closed class" words. Scott cites such example as *because, shall* and *already* (2008: 143). Culpeper (2009) points to the fact that some such keywords may be borderline open class words. For example, adverbs are considered as a varied and thus problematic category, which is deemed as open class by some linguists and closed by others. Examples of such keywords in the present analysis include: *by, for, under, of, and, such, shall* and *or.* Some of the keywords have already been mentioned, such as *shall* which has been shown to co-occur with the other "function" keywords, for example, *under.* The presence of certain function keywords seems to be motivated by general features of the legislative genre, e.g. the preposition *of* is key because of the highly nominal style found in legislative provisions, *or* is largely due to the presence of word lists and noun strings favoured in legal definitions. We will return to this point in Chapters 5 and 6 devoted to the Multi-Dimensional Analysis.

3.4.3. Keywords in legal briefs

Communication keywords

Briefs are marked for the presence of several keywords which can be classified as related to "communication verbs" in terms of general language grammar (cf. Biber *et al.,* 1999). This distinctive category includes verbs such as: *concluded, denied, explained, found, testified, presented, rejected.* Just as in the case of keywords in legislation used to change or modify legislative provisions, these verbs appear consistently as a specific word-form, i.e. the Past Simple Tense form. The use of some of them reflects the legal procedure that is necessary before a case is heard by the Supreme Court.

This clearly applies to the keyword *denied.* Cases or controversies normally reach the Supreme Court for the purpose of review in one of the three principal ways (Abraham, 1998): (1) on a writ of appeal, as a matter of right (usually simply called right); (2) on a *writ of certiorari,* as a matter of Court discretion (usually simply called certiorari or cert); and *by certification,* i.e. the consideration by the Supreme Court of "errors of law", allegedly committed by a court of lower instance. In the instance of a writ of appeal, the aggrieved party (known as the *appellant*; the answering party is the *appellee* or *respondent*) has an absolute and statutorily granted right to carry a case to the U.S. Supreme Court, which in theory must review it. However, this right was seriously curtailed by Congress in 1988. In any case, since 1928, the Supreme Court has had the discretionary power to reject an appeal if the federal issue is 'insubstantial'. For example, in *Kohrigh v. Illinois,* the Court rejected the appellant's appeal, based on an alleged violation of her privacy on account of Illinois's mandatory seatbelt law, as lacking a substantial federal question. Moreover, the federal question must have been validly raised early in the state court, when the matter begins as a state issue. Even then, the Supreme Court might not take the case if the state court's judgment can be sustained on an independent ground of state law. The requirements mentioned above mean that, in practice, many appeals and petitions are dismissed (Abraham 1998: 190) provides that over 90 per cent of them never reached the Court in the 1986-87 term. In all other cases involving a "federal question of substance", the disappointed litigant has no *right* to appeal to the Supreme Court the adverse decision he sustained; but he or she does have the *privilege* of petitioning the highest bench in the land to grant writ of certiorari (a Latin term meaning "made more certain", or "better informed". Generally, each such petition, a copy of which goes to every Justice with a record of the proceedings below, comprises the two sides' arguments both for and against its grant. The party bringing the action is known as the *plaintiff* or *petitioner*, the other as the *respondent.* More than ninety percent of the cases decided by the Supreme Court reach it by that method. Needless to say, the Court is wary of granting its writs of certiorari unless it considers a given case is of substantial significance or controversy. In many cases, the writs are rejected with a terse "certiorari denied". This negative trend is confirmed in this study by the presence of both *denied* and *rejected. Denied* is found the total of 435 times and in 249 instances it is preceded by *cert.* or *certiorari.* In briefs, this expression is found in footnotes when a reference is made to a particular holding contained in a judicial decision as in the following expression:

(38) In re Long Term Admin. Segregation, 174 F.3d 464, 472 (4th Cir.) (isolation associated with administrative segregation or maximum custody does not deprive prisoners of any basic human need), **cert. denied**, 528 U.S. 874 (1999); cf. Hewitt, 459 U.S. at 466-467 ("austere and restrictive administrative segregation quarters" do not violate the Fourteenth Amendment).

Worth noting is that *denied* can also be found in an equally succinct sentence expressed in the active voice as in the following two examples:

(39) […] The district court **denied** the motion.
(40) […] The California Supreme Court **denied** Petitioner's review.

We should recall now that briefs are formal legal documents that are drafted in accordance with a specific format required by the Rules of Appellate Procedure for each jurisdiction. The purpose of a brief is to present the important legal issues of the appeal to the court. Most briefs consist of several different sections such as "cover page", "table of contents", "table of authorities", "statement of authorities", "statement of jurisdiction", "question presented for review", "statement of the case", "summary of the argument", "argument" and "conclusions", also known as "prayer for relief"(See also Brostoff and

Sinsheimer, 2003: 147-153). Keywords in this category are located in "statement of the case". They are used to narrate the procedural and substantive facts of the case, and especially the procedural history of the case. In collocational terms, this is corroborated by the statistical fact that keywords in that category show a strong co-occurrence with *court* and *judge*. For example, the keywords *explained* and *rejected* co-occur with *court* and *judge* in over 60% of all the instances when they are used in briefs. In other words, these keywords are typically employed in briefs to report on previous relevant court activities. In addition, *explained* is used to show legal reasoning applied by a court of lower instance:

(41) As the district court **explained** in upholding the rational basis of this legislation, "the Iowa Legislature could have concluded that river boats should receive a beneficial tax rate because it is a needed or useful industry." Pet. App. 34.

Finally, worth noting is the presence of the keyword *found,* which (also used in the better known but less frequently used expression *found guilty*) is used predominantly to mark what a court has determined in the course of a discovery process:

(42) The court ultimately **found** that Laidlaw had violated the permit's mercury limitation 489 times, including nine times after petitioners filed their complaint.

Institutional **keywords**

Predictably, many keywords in briefs refer to types of courts, government bodies, the legislature or other entities (*appeals, circuit, Congress, court, district, federal, government, officials, states*). This category corresponds to what was distinguished as "institutional keywords" in legislation. The reason for their frequent use in briefs is, to a large extent, self-evident in as much as the court names are concerned. In the case of the Congress and the government, these are often referred to as sources of authority in the "Argument" sections of a brief:

(43) Significantly, in this case, not only has **Congress** explicitly <u>authorized</u> (and the **President** <u>approved</u>) the filing of a Clean Water Act citizen suit, but this suit involves a claim against a private firm, not another branch of government. (emphasis added)

Legal terms as keywords

Briefs are further noted for the presence of many subject/domain-specific keywords related to the **appeal system** in the US jurisdiction. This is a broad category that could be further subdivided into keywords denoting **participants in appeal proceedings:**

amicus [curiae], assistant, counsel, defendant, petitioner, plaintiffs, prosecution, respondent, solicitor [general]

and **procedure keywords:**

*acquittal, [en] banc, cert. (certiorari), challenge***,** *count, evidence, hearing, plea, probation, rehearing, seizure, search***,** *testimony, trial,* etc.

Some keywords in the above category are also found in professional articles and opinions. These include common terms such as *petitioner, respondent* or *defendant.* However, there might be certain differences in the patterns in which they are found due to genre-specific formulations. For instance, *petitioners* tend to be frequently found with the keyword *amicus* and the verb *supporting* or the prepositional phrase *in support of* which immediately signals a subcategory of *amicus curiae briefs.* Amicus Curiae (Lat. "friend of the court") refers to a person "with strong interest in or views on the subject matter of an action, but not a party to an action, who may petition the court for permission to file a brief, ostensibly on behalf of a party but actually to suggest a rationale consistent with its own views" (cf. Black, 1990). Such amicus curiae briefs are filed in appeals concerning matters of a broad public interest, e.g. civil rights cases. They may be filed by private persons or the government. In language terms, this type of briefs is signalled by certain formulaic expressions placed routinely at the beginning of briefs, where amicus curiae appear:

(44) Amicus curiae in support of petitioners
(45) Brief for the united states as amicus curiae supporting petitioners in part and respondents in part

Also, note the frequent co-occurrence of *petitioners* with *rejected* and *denied* which can only be explained on the grounds of the specific legal procedure:

(46) The district court <u>rejected</u> **petitioners'** argument that the state court lacked subject matter jurisdiction to determine the plan's lien rights. Pet. App. C5-C7 (emphasis added)

A specific perspective on *defendant* is signalled by a set of collocations, e.g. *advise, assistance, aware, conflict, counsel, error, plea, represented,* etc. The emphasis appears to be put on ensuring that a defendant is not denied his or her rights to a fair trial (e.g. *the ability of a medicated defendant to receive a fair trial and due representation, the creation of possible trial prejudice to the defendant was unjustified,* etc.). As we will see below, such perspective differs considerably from that adopted in judicial opinions.

Finally, two keywords, *seizure* and *search* do merit some attention as their use in briefs seems to be genre-specific. For one, these two keywords collocate as in:

(47) The court held that the Tribe's sovereignty did not preclude the **search** and **seizure** of the Casino's personnel records.(emphasis added)

They are not reversible, i.e. *seizure* does not normally precede *search*. Such fixedness in the order of these nouns results from the wording of the Fourth Amendment to the US Constitution where we read:

> The right of the people to be secure in their persons, houses, papers, and effects, against unreasonable searches and seizures shall not be violated (…).

A closer examination shows that *seizure* collocates with *Government's*. This is not surprising because the Fourth Amendment had been intended to protect US citizens again the abuse of Governmental powers. *Seizure* also co-occurs with prefixes such as "pre" and "post" and other time expressions (*before, initial*). In other words, it appears that argumentation in briefs very often centres upon the temporal aspect of an act of seizure. It is of utmost importance when seizure is made and what results it brings at a given point in time. This is well illustrated in the example below:

(48) Furthermore, the only evidence in the record of any **pre-seizure** involvement on the part of Jimenez Recio and Lopez-Meza consisted of a handful of phone calls, for which there was uncontroverted evidence that some of the calls made on the phone card possessed by Lopez-Meza could not possibly have been made by him. The conclusion is therefore inescapable that the defendants would almost certainly not have been involved in the transaction were it not for the government's intervention.

The Fourth Amendment with its two key elements, i.e. search and seizure, has provoked a great deal of controversy concerning the way in which such elements should be properly interpreted. Solan notes that "over the past twenty-five years or so, the Supreme Court has ruled on many occasions whether a particular police activity constitutes an unreasonable search. (…) These rulings have produced a body of law so dependent on the unique facts of each case that it takes enormous effort to sort it out" (1993: 163). It is therefore little wonder that such fundamental issues related to human rights and citizens' rights have found their way to briefs.

Keywords denoting *legal instruments*

There are two categories which are related to what we can find in other genres. Just as in legislation, there are several keywords in briefs which can be classified as relating to documents relied on or invoked in the texts of the briefs. These are *amendment, cong., decision, pet. record, statute*. For example, *statute* is often found in the terminological phrase *the statute of limitations,* which is a statute that sets forth the maximum period of time, after certain events, that legal proceedings based on those events may be initiated. It is thus a crucial statute for legal proceedings. Interestingly, statute is found also in the cluster (13 occurrences) *the language of the statute,* in arguments aimed at interpreting a contested meaning of a legislative provision:

(49) We are not convinced. First, *the language of the* ***statute*** does not indicate or imply that the district court is deprived of jurisdiction to review the Commissioner's assignments unless the assigned premiums have first been paid.

Academic keywords

The other category shared by other genres is that of certain **academic** keywords. We have used the word "academic" because keywords found in this category are frequently employed in legal academic texts (for instance, in academic journals discussed above). These are *ibid. , id., see,* used to refer to relevant legislation or previous cases of precedential value.

Keywords related to *crime* and *incarceration*

A few keywords in briefs can be classified as covering the issue of crime and incarceration: *criminal, inmates, offenses, prison, offenders*. In 60% of the cases, the keyword *offenders* was used with the preceding adjective 'sex' or "sexual". Wider patterns of use feature this keyword in clusters such as *information about sex offenders* or *protecting the public from sex offenders*. In other words, offenders are mentioned in briefs in a very specific and negative context in the argumentative parts of briefs. On the other hand, *inmates,* in a manner similar to the way *defendants* were treated above (see Section 2.4.4.3), appear in contexts related to *(constitutional) rights, visiting privileges, their illiteracy, assistance, adequate food, clothing,* etc.

Keywords expressing *evaluation*

There are several keywords which express evaluation through value-laden word choice (*compelling, constitutional, error, harmful, unconstitutional, guilty, plain, political, punitive, racial*). In the example below, *constitutional* is used to evaluate the decision reached by a court of lower instance

(50) The district court's order that petitioner be involuntarily medicated to restore his competence is **constitutional.** (emphasis added)

The keyword *unconstitutional* is strongly patterned in briefs. A large proportion of all occurrences is preceded by BE/IS/ARE/WAS (33%). There is a strong co-occurrence with *held* (60%) to signal judicial decision and a reason clause, typically signalled by *because* (44%):

(51) The court of appeals, however, **held** that the ban on visits for prisoners found guilty of two, in-prison, major substance abuse infractions **is** unconstitutional under Turner **because** prison officials had "produced only anecdotal evidence to show that the permanent ban on visitors has deterred drug abuse in the prison population." Pet. App. 20a. (emphasis added)

Further, a three-word cluster *as applied to* frequently (in 33% of all cases) follows the statement of unconstitutionality in order to limit the scope of such statement to a particular addressee, e.g. a corporation:

(51) As discussed above, the Supreme Court held this statute unconstitutional **as applied to** Massachusetts Citizens for Life, a non-profit, ideological corporation similar to NCRL.

Note also the co-occurrence with value-laden adverbs: *facially, plainly, presumptively* in 12% of all cases.

Another evaluation keyword, *compelling* is used in two senses. Its more everyday sense of "convincing" is relatively rare in briefs. There are only four attested instances of this use reflected in the expression *compelling evidence.* More technical meaning prevails as evidenced by the expression *compelling interests* or *interest* to denote an interest which the state or government "is forced or obliged to protect" (cf. Black 1990). This term is used to uphold state action in the face of an attack on Equal Protection or First Amendment rights. It is also employed to justify state action under police power of state. Statistically, *compelling interest* or *interests* is found in over 50% of all cases when *compelling* appears in briefs. However, the co-occurrence patterns could involve some distance between the two items as in the following example, where the court may have to assess whether "compelling interest" really occurs:

(52) Part V-C made explicit that five Justices believed Davis should not be prohibited from any consideration of race in making admissions decisions. It did not however, purport to describe what **interests** would be sufficiently **compelling** to justify preferences in a "properly devised admissions program." (emphasis added)

The presence of this category of evaluative keywords is hardly surprising given its highly persuasive function. Briefs are meant to advocate a certain legal position. In an appeal, the appealing party seeks to overturn a decision of a lower court by alleging an error of law (hence the presence of the keyword *error*).

Keywords referring to public interest

It was already noted, when discussing the amicus curiae briefs, that this class of legal texts usually concerns matters of broad public interest. This is confirmed by the presence of several keywords such as: *access, advocacy, conspiracy, jeopardy, motive, race, sex, suspicion*, which signal themes vital to the general public interest. For example, *access* is most often used in the contexts of *counsel, courts, information, Internet, legal services, records, federal office-holders* etc. *Advocacy* is used in the prevalent contexts of *non-profit advocacy groups* or *corporations*. In 38% of all cases, *advocacy* is found in the expression *express advocacy*. The express advocacy standard was first articulated by the Supreme Court as a way to distinguish independent issue ads that could be paid for with soft money from candidate advocacy, which could be regulated under federal law. Another keyword *sex* is used almost exclusively in conjunction with words carrying negative connotations: *conviction, discrimination, offender(s), offense.* The last two words co-occur with *sex* in almost 90% of all instances.

Finally, worth noting is a category of functional words which include: *also, at, because, indeed, moreover, that, did, those, was.* The presence of *did* and *was* suggests that Past Simple forms may play an important role in narrating the procedural history of a given case. This text genre appears to be much more restricted in terms of lexis than legislation.

3.4.4. Keywords in contracts

Keywords marking temporal relations

Legislation and contracts are similar in having a number of keywords which mark temporal relations. In contracts, these are, for example, *closing, date, day, prior, termination , time.* Just as in legislation, these time keywords are also found in extremely frequent lexical bundles. For instance, the keyword *date* is found in as many as eighteen different bundles (see next chapter for more details). Interestingly, *date* is also a keyword in legislation where it functions as a time expression in (the same as in contracts) highly productive bundles such as, for example, *after the date of* or *after the effective date.* Equally, the keywords *time* and *day* are also found in both legislation and contracts. However, only in contracts, *termination* and *closing* are key. The presence of the former is motivated by the need to mark the end of a contractual relation. The latter is found as an adjective and then it usually precedes another keyword *date* (e.g. *dated as of the Closing Date*). *Closing* can also be a noun to denote the end of an accounting period):

(53) After the Closing, no agreements relating to the voting of HMI Common Stock, irrevocable proxies or restrictions on the transfer of HMI Common Stock exist except as provided under (…).

Keywords marking text deixis

Contracts are clearly marked for the strong presence of numerous keywords marking textual deictics. The present analysis has identified the following keywords as belonging to this category: *foregoing, herein, hereof, hereto, hereunder, thereof, thereto.* Much has already been written on the origin and the function of archaic deictics (see, for instance, more recent treatments in Tiersma, 1999: 93-95; Gibbons, 2003: 41; Jopek-Bosiacka, 2006). They are usually discussed in the context of extreme conservatism and archaism of legal language. The use of such constructions is criticized for leading to difficulties in the interpretation of legal texts. Our findings confirm that these expressions are still very much in use despite extensive efforts to discourage their use in contemporary legal texts[19]. At the same time, their distribution is highly restricted and largely genre-specific. This lexical category is not key in any other genre but in contracts.

19 Such efforts are usually attributed to the Plain English Campaign and more generally to the Plain Language Campaign (see, for example, Garner, 2001).

The available corpus data shows that the distribution of this lexical set is restricted to legal operative documents, especially, to various contractual instruments.

Keywords marking participation

Contracts appear to be unique in relying on a relatively large group of keywords denoting parties to a contract (legal or natural persons) or other entities. There are in fact as many as twenty such keywords found in the one hundred keywords. Below is a list of some: *affiliates, agent, borrower, buyer, company, corporation, directors, employee, group, holder, lender, parent, partner, partnership, party, seller, stockholders, subsidiaries.* There is a certain symmetry reflected in such pairs as *borrower, lender* or *buyer* and *seller,* which indicates the essentially reciprocal nature of contractual relations. Both natural and legal persons are conferred rights and obligations by means of contractual provisions. In terms of surface linguistic features, this is most frequently realized by means of colligations with *shall* and *may.* For example, *lender* is followed by *shall* 12% of the time and it is the most frequent collocate appearing to its right. There is also strong co-occurrence with *such* (30%), *any* (14,5%) and *each* (13,5%) as illustrated in the following example:

(54) Each ***Lender*** shall remit its Commitment Percentage of each requested Committed Borrowing to Administrative Agent's principal office in Dallas, Texas. (emphasis added)

Another example illustrates the observation that keywords from this category tend to colligate with verbs in the Present Simple Tense:

(55) Each ***Borrower*** agrees that any ***Lender*** so purchasing a participation or subparticipation from another ***Lender*** pursuant to this Section 2.15 may, to the fullest extent permitted by law, exercise all its rights of payment (including the right of set-off) with respect to such participation as fully as if such Lender were the direct creditor of such Borrower in the amount of such participation or subparticipation.

The use of *any* and *each* is meant to ensure all-inclusiveness of a given contractual provision. Note also the atypical way in which *such* tends to co-occur with nominal forms as a deictic (see also Tiersma, 1999: 91).

Corporations and other legal entities display much the same pattern as natural persons. *Company* which is the fourth keyword in contracts has very distinct colligational patterns. In 70% of the occurrences *company* is preceded by *the* as it is used to refer to a clearly designated entity. In 22% of the time, it is found as a head noun in an *of*-phrase (e.g. *general assets of the Company*). In 20% of all the cases, it is followed by either *or* or *and* to appear in longer coordinated phrases (e.g. *as a result of the actions of Company or any of its subsidiaries or any affiliate of Company*). It co-occurs with *shall* and *may* in 16% of all instances.

Legal terms as keywords

Several keywords in contracts are highly technical terms referring to various types of obligation, entitlement or failure to do something required by law: *default, indemnification, indemnified, liabilities, obligations, payable , rights*. These keywords represent fundamental terms in contract law. For example, *default* is central to the concept of obligation. A highly patterned word, it co-occurs with *event* in 34% of all its occurrences in the form of a nominal phrase *event of default*. This expression co-occurs with *constitute* and *mean* and it is typically found in the definition part of a contract:

(56) **Default** <u>means</u> any **Event of Default** or any event that would <u>constitute</u> an **Event of Default** but for the requirement that notice be given or time elapse or both. (emphasis added)

Event of default is found in *if*-clauses (80 instances), where the main clause specifies the rights assigned to a particular party to a contract which was harmed by the failure to fulfil an obligation by the other party:

(57) If an **Event of Default** occurs, BandT will have all rights and remedies available to it under applicable law or in equity.

The assignment of rights to a harmed party is expressed through *will, shall* or *may,* hence the co-occurrence of *default* with these modal verbs. In fact, the tendency for *default* to co-occur with *if* –clauses is not restricted to its collocation with *event* because it tends to appear in the so-called qualificational insertions (Bhatia 2004) This keyword is primed to appear in contexts where negation is expressed by certain explicit markers (e.g. *no, not*). This both includes cases where *default* is directly preceded by *no* (40 occurrences) as well as when *no* is found within the span of 25 words either left or right of *default* (103 occurrences). The following example is illustrative of how *default* tends to be used:

(58) ii) **No** distributions on Series A Preferred Units shall be authorized or paid or set apart for payment at such time as the terms and provisions of any agreement of the Partnership, including any agreement relating to its indebtedness, prohibits such authorization, payment or setting apart for

> payment or provides that such authorization, payment or setting apart for payment would constitute a breach thereof, **or** a **default** thereunder, **or if** such authorization or payment shall be restricted or prohibited by law.

Worth noting is that negation does not need to appear in the immediate co-text. Obviously, *default* itself implies negation because it means an omission to do something, usually required by law (cf. Black, 1990). The collocational analysis further reveals that *default* is directly followed by *or* (104 occurrences) and this coordinator is found even more frequently (310 times) within the span of five words. This is by no means an exhaustive account of the phraseological behaviour of *default*. However, it should shed more light on why certain words are key and why this keyness can be linked to a specific genre.

There are more subject-specific keywords, i.e. legal terms which can be grouped in a thematic category related to **financial matters**: *amount, assets, cash, expenses, merger, securities, shares, stock, borrowing, payment, purchase, taxes.*

The keyword *deem*

There are several keywords which elude clear-cut categorization but which, nonetheless appear central to the contractual expression. The keyword *deem* is a good example. It is listed in the *Black's Law Dictionary* and explained as synonymous with *to hold; consider; adjudge; believe; condemn; determine; treat as if; construe.* Gibbons (2003: 47-48) refers to it when discussing the practice of deeming and legal fictions. *Deem* is very often used in legal definitions to define or redefine a word in accordance with the goal of a statute or contract. It is worth pointing out that the meaning assigned under a statutory definition may differ (and indeed it often does) from the normal, everyday sense of this word. Tiersma (1999: 116) cites a definition of a person, which for the purpose of the Consumer Legal Remedies Act in California, defines a person as "an individual, partnership, corporation, limited liability company, association, or other group, however organized." Unlike lexicographical definitions, the legal ones are prescriptive and have a mandatory force. The meaning thus defined is usually valid only within a strictly defined context. This is reflected in the frequent use of such lexical bundles as *for the purpose of* or *for purposes of this,* which are then followed by a reference to a specific legal instrument (see next chapter for a more detailed treatment of lexical bundles used in definitions). The presence of the keyword *deemed* is evident of the ubiquity of such declaratory definitions in contractual instruments. From the phraseological perspective, *deemed* is found in highly restricted patterns of use. There are 858 (out of 1015) instances of its use in the Past Participle form. This keyword tends to appear in the Passive Voice. It is found in the colligational combination with *be* in 84% of the time. In 61% of all the instances, *deem* co-occurs with *shall* and in 58%, it is followed by the *to*-infinitive. This pattern of NOUN + *shall be deemed to* VERB is frequently used in declaratory definitions as illustrated below:

(59) The term "Base Tax" **shall be deemed to** mean the Taxes for the Tax Year commencing July 1, 1998.

However, *deemed* is also found in other parts of contractual instruments in slightly different patterns. It can be preceded by the negative particle *not* and followed by a noun or noun phrase (an adjective is also possible in that position). The following example comes from a dispute resolution clause. The use of *deemed* is more interpretative than descriptive, as shown in the previous example. Admittedly, such interpretation is imposed and it is highly prescriptive:

(60) The requirements of this Article 7 shall **not** be **deemed** a *waiver* of any right of termination under this Agreement.

Shall is commonly (and somehow routinely) viewed as the most characteristic modal verb in legal language used to express a command or obligation. Indeed, it is probably one of the best described modal verb in legal discourse and it has been approached from a number of different perspectives. Importantly, as Tiersma asserts (1999: 105), *shall* is not restricted to giving commands nor is it only used in legislation. Tiersma aptly summarized its use by explaining:

> Generally, however, *shall* indicates that the verb and phrase that follow are part of what is being enacted, promised, and so forth. Consequently, legal documents have at least one performative, express or implied, that indicates the overall force of the document: enacting (a statute), promising (a contract), and so forth. That which is being enacted or promised is indicated by *shall*.

As Table 3.3 shows, there is a stark contrast between the frequency of *shall* in contracts and legislation and the other genres. Quantitatively, *shall* can be regarded as one of many distinctive features that set the operative genres apart from other legal genres.

Table 3.3. *The distribution of "shall" across different genres*

Genre	***shall* frequency per million words**
academic journals	183
legislation	**10,248**
briefs	728

contracts	**13,700**
professional articles	263
opinions	616
textbooks	470

By way of comparison, it should be noted that *shall* is the least frequent modal (around 250 words per million words in the LSWE Corpus) in general English. Interestingly, the most frequent modal noted there is *will* with frequency slightly above 3500 hits per million words (Biber, 1999: 486). It seems that it is too early to announce the demise of this verb in American normative texts (cf. Williams 2005). However, what should be stressed is that its frequency varies dramatically across the different genres. Legal academic journals have on average fewer *shall* forms than the general English. *Shall* should not be associated with legal language in general but only with its operative genres. Its frequency is unusually high even for legal texts.

Shall is found in very frequent lexical bundles performing different functions such as expressing obligation/promise, prohibition and creating legal fictions (deeming). The use of s*hall* will be further discussed in the next chapter devoted to multi-word patterns.

Several keywords in contracts have been identified because of their occurrence in extremely frequent clusters or bundles.[20] Keywords such as *event, connection, respect* or *accordance* are almost exclusively found in longer phrases, such as *in the event, with respect to/in respect of,* or *in accordance with.*

3.4.5 Keywords in professional articles

Legal terms as keywords

Professional articles represent a new emerging informative and instructive genre offering limited legal advice over the Internet. The texts examined in this section were culled from the popular American website www.findlaw.com (see also section 2.2 in Chapter 2) The keyword output shows a clear focus on highly specialist communication as evidenced by the fact that over 50% of the top one hundred keywords are terms. Most terms are linked to various aspects of **litigation procedure** (*action, appeal, appellant, appellate, certification, claims, class, conflicts, counsel, court, decision, defence, defendants, evidence, exercise, filed, joint, judgment, lawsuit, litigation, motion, objections, plaintiff, represent, representation, rule, settlement, summary (judgment), Supreme (Court) trial, lawyer).*

20 The definition of "lexical bundle" is provided in the next chapter.

Another group of specialist keywords is related to the area of **finance** (*bank, companies, compensation, corporate, financial, firm, ease, estate, loan, loans, market, merger, mortgage, option, options, purchase, risk, stock, value*).

The presence of keywords such as *represent* and *representation* along with frequent references to members of the legal profession *lawyer, counsel, attorney* and *client* suggests a strong interest in lawyer – client relationships and the issue of **legal representation** in court.

"Advisory" keywords

The advisory nature of this type of text is reflected in two modal verbs *must* and *should* and their co-occurrence with the keyword *you.*:

(61) First, **you should** examine whether there was adequate consideration for the restrictive covenant. If the underlying agreement would not have been enforceable by the company that was acquired, it will not be enforceable by the successor corporation.

(62) After a tenant files Bankruptcy **you must** get an order for "relief from automatic stay" from the U. S. Bankruptcy Court.

You and *your* rank as second and third keywords, respectively. There appears to be a strong co-occurrence between the modal forms, the personal pronoun and *if* (also a keyword), suggesting a highly instructive and interactive type of discourse[21]:

(63) **Should you** also suggest that the Assistant Controller retain his own attorney? Comment [7]to Rule 1.13(d) recommends this additional step, but there are practical considerations suggesting that **you** may want to postpone this warning. **If you** begin the interview by telling the Assistant Controller that he should consider retaining his own counsel, he may want to postpone the interview while he looks for an attorney.

Such instructive, advisory and authoritative mode of discourse can be further detected in the widespread use of such keywords as *sure, important, actually* and *fact*. For example, *sure* is used in direct references to the interested reader:

(64) When you do get the refund, **make sure** your premium or taxes weren't paid by both lenders.

21 This point will be further discussed in Chapter 6.

(65) **Be sure** you feel comfortable with the attorney before making a decision. **Make sure** you hire an attorney who has the time and interest to pursue your interests and advise you of the pertinent aspects of your case.

Fact appears to be the preferred choice for expressing stance. In 30% of the cases, it is found in the lexical bundle *the fact that the* (example 66) and in 20% in the collocation *material fact* (67):

(66) Approximately 90% of this amount is paid by banks, which reflects **the fact that the** banking sector has been the primary focus of the FCAC's activities.
(67) On appeal, appellant contended that the trial court erred in granting a no evidence summary judgment in favor of appellee because he presented evidence that raised genuine issues of material fact about the reason for his termination.

As can be seen, keywords in professional articles represent a fairly homogenous lexical set, which is largely due to the considerable terminological density documented in this genre. The other most readily recognizable categories suggest that this text genre is characterized by a degree of interactivity not found in the other genres and it provides a focus on communicating specialist content to semi- or non-experts.

3.4.6. Keywords in opinions

Keywords marking judicial stance

This genre is marked by the presence of several keywords related directly to the expression of judicial stance (*dissent, dissenting, concurring, joined, opinion, plurality*). They fall into a distinctive, genre-specific class of lexical items employed in highly formulaic patterns and marked by a clear textual positioning. Before we continue, a brief overview of a US opinion and its corresponding terminology seems desirable. Just as in the case of briefs, opinions follow a clear organizational format. The term *opinion* is used in two senses. More generally, opinion may refer to the official decision of a court of justice and it is thus interchangeable with the term *judgment,* which is defined as "the official and authentic decision of a court of justice upon the respective rights and claims of the parties to an action or suit therein litigated and submitted to its determination. The final decision of the court resolving the dispute and determining the rights and obligations of the parties" (Black 1990). The term *opinion* is also used to denote the reason which the court gives for its decision. It then refers to the statement made by a judge or court of the decision reached in connection with a case heard before them. Such a statement explains the law as applied to the case and provides the reason on the basis of which the judgment is made. In this study, the term *opinion* is used primarily in the first sense as a convenient label for the entire genre. Opinions are characterized by a fixed generic structuring. Indeed, there are several models employed by different scholars to describe their discourse structure. For example, Bhatia (1993) has analyzed legal cases from the perspective of their communicative purpose and structural interpretation. He has proposed a typical four-move structure:

a) Identifying the case
b) Establishing facts of the case
c) Arguing the case
    i. Stating the history of the case
    ii. Presenting arguments
    iii. Deriving ratio decidendi
d) Pronouncing judgment

The structure of legal judgments varies depending on the court and its function (trial court of first instance or appellate court). Opinions delivered by the Supreme Court of the United States generally have the following structure (cf. Brostoff and Sinsheimer, 2003; Lee et al., 1999):

Headnote – this section includes the names of the parties, identification of parties (petitioner, respondent, an identification of the court in which the recorded case was heard, and the date of the opinion.

Procedural History – This is a brief description of how the lower-instance courts have dealt with the case. This section usually includes the basis for review.

Holding- Invariably signalled by the use of the word *held,* this section provides the decision (ruling) reached by the Supreme Court in a particular case ended with a disposition of the case (e.g. *affirmed, vacated and remanded, etc*).

Opinion – This part of a judgment includes the names of the judges who heard the case and it specifies what type of opinion a given judge expressed. The example provided below well illustrates the way in which some of the keywords are used:

(68) Kennedy, J., delivered the opinion of the Court, in which Rehnquist, C. J., and Stevens, O'Connor, and Breyer, JJ., ***joined***, and in which Scalia and Thomas, JJ., ***joined*** as to Parts I, II, III, and IV. Stevens, J., filed a concurring opinion. Thomas, J., filed an opinion ***concurring*** in part and ***dissenting*** in part, in which Scalia, J., ***joined***. Ginsburg, J., filed a ***dissenting*** opinion, in which Souter, J., ***joined***.

Thus, there may be (as evidenced by the keywords provided at the beginning of this section) a *plurality opinion* which occurs when the final outcome is agreed by majority but for differing reasons. For example, in a 6:3 decision (there nine members of the US Supreme Court), two judges (or justices as they are usually referred to in legal documents) could write one concurring opinion, three judges could write another concurring opinion, one judge could write his or her own opinion and three judges could dissent. *Concurring* opinions are those which agree with the majority decision for different reasons, while *dissenting* opinions are given by judges who do not agree with the majority. The excerpt taken from an opinion and provided above well illustrates the strong presence of keywords signalling judicial stance in relation to a given case. The opinion of the court is obviously provided first followed by concurring opinions and finally there are the dissenting ones. The disposition given immediately after the procedural history section is provided again and elaborated at the end of the opinion of the court:

(69) We granted certiorari. 540 U. S. ___ (2003). We now vacate the judgment of the Court of Appeals and remand the case for further proceedings to reconsider the Government's mandamus petition.

Goźdź-Roszkowski (2009) demonstrates the highly formulaic nature of the language used in disposition parts of judicial opinions by studying three common terms and keywords (albeit not found in the top one hundred keywords) *reverse, overrule* and *overturn.*

This class of keywords has clear collocational, colligational and textual patterns. By way of example and a small case study, consider briefly the term *reverse* (for a full discussion, see Goźdź-Roszkowski, 2009). The term *reversed* was found to be a high-frequency verb (cf. Biber, 2006) with a rounded frequency of 318 tokens per million words and a relatively broad distribution in 88 different opinions. It is usually found in its past participle form (68% of the time) and it appears to be highly formulaic. In terms of textual positioning, *reverse* is usually placed in the disposition of the case after the recitation of the procedural history or facts and at the end of the opinion. The textual position of this term can be illustrated by the following excerpt:

(70) FMCSA has no ability to countermand the President's decision to lift the moratorium or to act categorically to prevent Mexican carriers from registering and Mexican trucks from entering the country; and once the regulations are promulgated, FMCSA will not be able to regulate any aspect of vehicle exhaust from those trucks. Pp. 17-19. 316 F. 3d 1002, **reversed and remanded**
Thomas, J., delivered the opinion for a unanimous Court.

In addition, the sentence final position of *reverse* is not accidental. In fact, *reverse* is placed there in 32% of all instances. Syntactically, *reverse* appears to be found frequently in coordinated phrases:

AND L1: 20; R1: 80 (27%)

The above notation shows that in approximately one third of all instances when *reverse* is found, it is either immediately preceded (in twenty instances) or followed (in eight instances) by *and*. This tendency can be illustrated by the following sentence examples:

(71) *We* ***granted*** *certiorari* <u>*and*</u> ***reversed***
(72) *Relying on cases such as Hawaii Housing Authority v. Midkiff, 467 U. S. 229, and Berman v. Parker, 348 U. S. 26, the Connecticut Supreme Court* ***affirmed in part*** <u>*and*</u> ***reversed in part****, upholding all of the proposed takings.*

Reverse has also been found frequently in passive constructions (in 20% of all instances):

(73) <u>*Held*</u>*: The judgment* ***is reversed****, and the case* ***is remanded****.*
(74) *The judgment of the Fifth Circuit* ***is reversed****.* <u>*It is so ordered.*</u>

Examples in (73) and (74) show that *reverse* tends to co-occur with words that signal judicial disposition such as: *held, it is so ordered.* The highly formulaic nature of *reverse* is then further evidenced by the unusually frequent co-occurrence (14%) with the pronoun "we" as in:

(75) *(Accordingly/consequently) We (therefore) now reverse.*

Bracketed words in (75) signal possible variants in this formulaic expression. *Reverse* can be used as both transitive and intransitive verb (although the latter significantly less frequently in only 13%). Note, however, example (76):

(76) *We reverse the Court of Appeals' judgment.*

Personal pronouns as keywords

The co-occurrence pattern between *reverse* and *we* helps to account for the presence of keywords which are personal pronouns (*we, our, it, us, his, he*). The first person plural pronouns are used to refer to the court *en block* when giving a majority or plurality opinion. The use of the third person singular is largely confined to procedural history to describe a person's wrongdoing:

(77) On May 13, 1994, respondent Mathew Musladin shot and killed Tom Studer outside the home of Musladin's estranged wife, Pamela. At trial, Musladin

admitted that **he** killed Studer but argued that **he** did so in self-defense. (emphasis added)

Legal terms as keywords

Keywords marking judicial stance could be subsumed under a more general category of specialist terms employed in the course of legal proceedings held in appeal cases (arranged below in an alphabetical order):

> (*appeals, circuit, claim, court, district, evidence, jury, ninth, rule, judge, respondent, petitioner, plurality, process, remand, sentencing, suit, trial*)

As can be seen, some keywords indicate parties to a case and their role in the proceedings (*respondent, petitioner*), other keywords denote courts and their designations (*court, district, ninth*), the proceedings themselves (*process, suit, trial*), yet other are related to certain mechanisms of reaching judicial opinions (*remand, sentencing*).

Keyword analysis proves to be useful in identifying terminology but more importantly, terms specific to a given genre emerge. Similar to legislation and briefs, opinions contain keywords which can be categorized as referring to legal instruments and other documents, as the following list exemplifies: *brief, certiorari, Constitution, habeas, judgment, statute, writ.* What differs opinions from the other genres are the actual keywords. The presence of most of these keywords is self-explanatory because they refer to specific legal proceedings. For example, this applies to *certiorari* and *writ.* As noted above, cases reach the Supreme Court *on writ of certiorari.* A *writ of certiorari* is thus a document issued by a superior court requiring that an inferior court produce a certified record of a particular case tried before it (cf. Black, 1990). However, the keyword *certiorari* can be used on its own, as in *We granted certiorari and reversed.* On the other hand, *writ* is found with *habeas* to denote a legal instrument of a *writ of habeas corpus.*

Keywords used to identify and interpret legal issues

Another distinct category in judgments groups several keywords which are used to identify and interpret legal issues. These are *argument, interpretation, issue, question, reading,* and *text.*

Consider the keyword *text.* In 40% of the time, it appears in the cluster *the text of* to signal text-based interpretive analysis of a legal (usually statutory) provision. The examination of the keyword's collocates indicates the existence of a semantic set with other keywords present. The collocates include *statutory, history, statute, amendment, structure, legislative, reading*:

(78) The **text** of the statute does not, however, so limit its reach, and the legislative history of the provision shows its placement in Title 18 was not meant to render the statute more restricted than its terms. (emphasis added)

Interestingly, when interpreting, judges tend to mark their stance by using value-laden words such as *clear* or *plain*:

(79) Although the statute is **clear**, and hence there is no need to delve into the legislative history, this history merely confirms that the **plain** reading of the text is correct.

The presence of these keywords reflects the enormous role of the judiciary, especially, of the Supreme Court of the United States in interpreting legislation. The Anglo-American framework in effect now, consists of a mixture of common law and statutory law. A great deal of contemporary law is statutory, i.e. it is coded. Still, common law has remained an important basis of legislative motivations and actions, and often an enacted statute simply spells out certain aspects of the common law. Moreover, no legislative body, and sometimes not even the executive, is capable of pinpointing in writing all the aspects and ramifications of a statute or order. Probably, this would not be even desirable even if it were possible. The result is interpretation, usually first by administrative units, then often by the courts. This interpretation becomes part of the statutes and orders, thus giving them meaning in the spirit and application of the common law.

If we recall the typical structuring of a judgment provided above, it is clear that any such document consists of different rhetorical segments with differing discoursal functions. From the phraseological perspective, some segments are likely to contain a great deal of highly formulaic language (for example, *headnote* and, to some extent, the *procedural history* and *background*) while some other will contain less constrained, more idiosyncratic language (employed in the opinions, particularly in concurring and dissenting opinions). Legal analysis found in legal opinions is carried out by relying on tried and tested academic devices of invoking sources of authority. Keywords such as *footnote, footnotes, see, ibid., quoting, supra* have been already identified in journal articles and briefs. In addition, opinions also use Latin abbreviations (*ante, v. J.*). But these are not uncommon in other types of legal expository writing. Lexically, opinions stand out by using *could* and *would* much more often than other genres. Apart from the rather obvious use of these two keywords in reported speech (in the more narrative part of the procedural history) and to mark the hypotheticality of an analyzed case, *would* tends to be used in the opinion of the court to voice the court's opinion or after a concurring or dissenting opinion to express a single judge's decision, as shown in (80) and (81).

(80) **We would** not defer to a legislature's determination of the various circumstances that establish, for example, when a search of a home would be reasonable, see, e.g., Payton v. New York, 445 U. S. 573, 589-590 (1980)
(81) **I would** therefore vacate the judgment of the Court of Appeals and remand for proceedings consistent with this view.

Finally, several keywords (*commerce, government, jurisdiction, justice, police, religion, immunity, sovereign, war*) indicate certain abstract and fundamental areas on which the Supreme Court tends to concentrate in its adjudicative practice, e.g. protecting an individual from excessive governmental power, the role of religion in public life (neutrality), discrimination, etc.

3.4.7. Keywords in textbooks

Legal terms as keywords

It turns out that there are very few distinctive categories of keywords in this type of legal texts. Just as in the case of professional articles, textbooks are marked by considerable terminological density. Almost half of the top hundred keywords represent highly specialist, domain-specific terms. In terms of a law area, these terms belong to the domain of business law[22]:

acceptance, arbitration, assignee, assignment, bound, breach, clauses, consideration, contract, contracting, contracts, contractual, creditor, damages, debt, debtor, discharge, equitable, executor, frustration, goods, implied, innocent, intention, land, liable, liability, loss, misrepresentation, mistake, obligation, party, parties, perform, performance, plaintiff, promise, promisee, recover, reliance, repudiation, specific, sue, terms, vendor, void

These keywords represent basic and fundamental concepts indispensable for any business law student. This high density of specialist terms results from textbooks' genre-specific role of disseminating discipline-based knowledge and the somewhat narrow focus on business law. The examples of keywords provided above demonstrate that technical legal content is often expressed by means of

22 Under the Anglo-American legal system, business law usually comprises the law of contract, the law of torts, commercial law, company law and partnerships and employment law. See, for instance Abbott and Pendlebury, 1996.

commonly found words (e.g. *acceptance, frustration, implied, innocent, party*, etc.), which is a lexical phenomenon already discussed in Section 3.1. At the same time, law uses specialized terms found exclusively in this discipline and such words do not have a counterpart in everyday usage (e.g. *assignee, breach, equitable, promise, etc.*). In our analysis, contracts and textbooks share a similar terminological focus in that these two genres are related to contract and company law. Despite this shared domain, they differ in terms of terminological usage. Textbooks contain terms found exclusively in this genre. For example, *frustration* is a case in point. Not a single instance of this word was found in the operative genre of contracts simply because this term belongs to the realm of legal doctrine. Moreover, even if a term is found in both genres, its usage may differ depending on the type of texts in which it is found. In contracts, terms are used in more restricted lexico-grammatical patterns. For example, *intention,* (which is actually not a keyword in contracts even though it appears there 96 times), is found in the following pattern:

It is the intention of X (e.g. the agreement, company, parties) + *that*-clause or *to*-infinitive, as the example below illustrates:

(82) **It is the *intention* of** the parties to this Agreement **that** payments made pursuant to this Agreement be treated as relating back to the pre-Distribution transactions. (emphasis added)

This construction has a pragmatic and legal function of communicating specifically what the two parties intend to be done with respect to the subject matter of their mutually binding contract. By contrast, in textbooks, *intention* is more freely distributed in terms of its lexico-grammatical environment. It appears to be a widely used term due to its significance in the theory of contract. As such, it tends to be discussed in terms of intention to create legal relations[23].

"Function" keywords

It seems that "content" keywords represent a fairly uniform and homogenous set and thus 'functional' keywords play a greater role in characterizing this genre than in the other genres discussed so far. Textbooks are marked by the presence of a wide range of modal and auxiliary verbs: *can, cannot, could, may, must, should, will, would* and the frequent of use of third person singular (nominative and accusative) and its possessive and reflexive forms (*he, him, his, himself*), *it* and

23 See also Goźdź-Roszkowski (2007a) for a detailed study of the term *consideration* and its collocational behaviour in four different legal genres.

the third person plural pronoun *they*. Legal textbooks appear to be highly conservative in using masculine pronouns to refer to nouns of dual gender:

(83) If any mortgage, other than a mortgage accompanied by transfer of the title-deeds, is unregistered, it is void as against a subsequent mortgagee, whether **he** registers **his** mortgage or not.

The use of coordinated pronoun forms is very rare (with only 7 attested corpus examples):

(84) If such a spouse is not in occupation, **he or she** may enter and occupy the home with leave of the court.

There is no corpus evidence that the third person plural form *they* is used as a plural co-referent pronoun.

Another example of a functional keyword is ***where.*** In a manner common for academic prose (Biber et al., 1999:626), *where* is used to mark logical rather than physical locations:

(85) The law of nullity covers not only cases **where** the purported marriage was void, but also those **where** the marriage, though initially valid, is voidable, and thus may be set aside.

For instance, there are 105 corpus examples of the cluster *in cases where.* In the next two examples, *where* is used as a preferred subordinator to express habitual condition, a legal principle:

(86) **Where** the contract price is equal to the value which the good would have had if it had been as warranted there is no difference between these two measures of damages.

(87) Under the Administration of justice Act 1982, **where** a will contains a devise or bequest to a child or remoter descendant of the testator, and the intended beneficiary dies before the testator, leaving issue who are living at the time of the testator's death, then, unless a contrary intention appears in the will, the devise or bequest passes to the issue living at the testator's death.

The use of *where* in sentence-initial or clause-initial positions is both a style marker and an indication of extensive intertextuality because the use of *where* in this position is typical for legislative provisions. Put differently, textbooks rely on the almost verbatim wording of a legislative provision by incorporating it into its own texts, albeit without the original layout:

(1)Where—
(a)a will contains a devise or bequest to a child or remoter descendant of the testator; and
(b)the intended beneficiary dies before the testator, leaving issue; and
(c)issue of the intended beneficiary are living at the testator's death,

then, unless a contrary intention appears by the will, the devise or bequest shall take effect as a devise or bequest to the issue living at the testator's death. [*Administration of Justice Act 1982* extracted from the UK Statute Law Database (SLD)]

Finally, there are few keywords which represent non-specialist lexis and which are found in very frequent and productive clusters: *circumstances* (*in certain/these circumstances*) *favour* (*in favour of*) *words* (e.g. *in other words, in the words of*).

3.5. Conclusions

This chapter adopted a different approach to vocabulary study than most previous studies of legal discourse. First, it focused on the diversity of vocabulary and the frequency distribution of common and rare words across different legal genres. This perspective revealed important differences between operative genres and expository or persuasive genres. Overall, operative genres (contracts and legislation) were found to use a relatively small set of different word types, which are employed with extremely high frequencies. In contrast, other genres, especially academic articles and professional articles were found to use a substantially larger set of different word types. The comparison of vocabulary patterns across different genres highlighted the important relationship between word use, genre and discipline. Legislation and contracts were found to have less diversity in word choice. The subsequent analysis of high-frequency verbs showed that contracts tend to use more terms not normally found outside the domain of contract or business law, while legislation uses words adapted from general language use but with specific technical meanings. At the same time, both the operative genres use extremely frequent formulaic expressions related to the fulfilment of specific legal and procedural functions. In contrast, academic and professional articles show more diversity in vocabulary, reflecting a wide range of issues expressed through more rarely- occurring terms. Further, professional articles in particular address matters that are more often part of our everyday experience. Genres such as opinions and briefs are found between the two opposites described above. Such 'intermediary' position may be attributed to containing both operative technical elements (e.g. in the disposition part) and persuasive, more idiosyncratic language found in the opinions of individual judges or attorneys.

Finally, the analysis of high-frequency verbs revealed the occurrence of a small set of words shared by all the genres. More work would be needed to determine the full extent of such 'core' legal vocabulary.

The subsequent keyword analysis identified for each genre one hundred most common words appearing with uniquely high frequencies after cross-tabulations. The scrutiny of the keyword lists led to the emergence of several distinct categories. They neither offer an exhaustive account of the legal lexicon nor classify the keywords into clear-cut categories. The classification proposed above should be regarded as tentative and necessarily arbitrary. For example, the keywords placed in the category of marking judicial stance (e.g. *dissenting, concurring*, etc.) could be equally subsumed under the more general category of legal terms because they are part of judicial practice and procedure. Still, it was felt that creating a separate category helps to highlight more readily and effectively what distinguishes opinions from the other legal genres. Some keywords have remained elusive and could not be assigned to any of the categories. Certain 'function' keywords were also not included in the analysis because they were not found in discernible patterns unique to a given genre. This omission is to a large extent remedied by way of Multi-Dimensional Analysis presented in Chapters 5 and 6, which deal with a large pool of linguistic features.

The categories proposed in this chapter effectively reflect major trends in the overall lexical composition of each genre. The genres under examination differ with respect to the number and types of different categories. Some, like legislation and briefs contain several classes of keywords marked by a clear functional focus. Others, like professional articles and textbooks, appear to be marked by terminological density, which is reflected in the prevalence of single, roughly homogenous groups of terms. Some functional groupings are genre-specific. For example, in legislation, there is a class of keywords marking internal organization of a legislative text. Contracts are characterized by several keywords marking temporal relations and participation in legal acts. Academic journals contain keywords used to illustrate and support legal reasoning. At the same time, certain functional categories are found in more than one genre albeit with different members. For example, both legislation and contracts contain keywords marking text and time deixis. Both legislation and briefs have keywords referring to various bodies, entities and institutions. The statistical dimension of keyword analysis was extended by further qualitative explorations of selected keywords. It appears that many keywords are found in fixed lexico-grammatical patterns. Such patterns of use may well be constrained by different generic conventions. Co-occurrence patterns can be observed not only at collocational and colligational levels but also at the textual one. A large corpus offers endless possibilities to investigate patterns and provide quantitative information. It is then easy to forget that the patterns originate from the accumulation of individual texts, with each text having a specific purpose and textual structure. Some legal genres, such as legislation, briefs, contracts and judgments contain a fixed textual structure which consists of clearly defined units. Certain lexical items appear to have strictly designated textual positions. A case point is the verb *reverse,* discussed above, which is invariably placed at the end of a judicial opinion in the disposition part of a judgment.

The keyword perspective helps to notice that the legal lexicon should not be perceived as consisting primarily of terms in the sense defined by the traditional theory of terminology (e.g. Wüster, 1979; Sager, 1990). Many words identified as key in legal texts are not endowed with a special reference only within the legal discipline (cf. Sager, 1990: 19) but nevertheless they fulfil very important local functions. This observation applied to several categories of keywords distinguished in this analysis, as, for example to keywords used to mark text and time deixis in legislation and contracts, communication keywords in briefs, or keywords expressing evaluation. Such words do have special reference and, in some cases, may also form part of the lexicon of another subject field. In other cases, many keywords may function both in general reference and in special reference within the legal discipline (e.g. *access, responsibility, sex*). At the same time, in the process of term extraction, keyword analysis could be to some extent used to generate candidate terms.

No matter how useful the keyword analysis has turned out to be, it is not without some limitations. Many keywords have unusually high frequencies because they are found in extremely frequent multi-word expressions. Accordingly, the next chapter will explore variation between legal genres as reflected in multi-word patterns.

CHAPTER IV: MULTI-WORD PATTERNS IN LEGAL GENRES

4.1. Introduction

Although the previous chapter has focused on words and keywords, the importance of recurrent lexical patterns in which a particular word is found has become already apparent. For example, in legislation some keywords were found in extremely frequent and productive phrases, such as *under this section, as defined in section* or *for the purposes of.* It was also noted that some keywords can co-occur to produce formulaic sequences which serve definite legal functions as in the following example from Section 3.4.2 in the previous chapter:

> Section 36 of the Act of August 5, 1909 (36 Stat. 111; 46 U.S.C. App. 121), is amended by striking "through 2002,"each place it appears and inserting "through 2006"

This chapter adopts a different approach to the study of variation in legal English by considering the distribution and functions of multi-word expressions across the different legal genres. It starts from the premise that the analysis of how multi-word expressions are used in contexts provides a reliable indicator of variation between different text types, genres and registers. The central principle that collocations differ in different text type can be traced back to the seminal text of the "OSTI Report" (Sinclair et al;. 1970/2004). In fact, as early as in 1966 Sinclair stressed the relationship between collocation and register. He gave the examples of *vigorous depressions* and *dull highlights* as expressions which could be perceived as odd when taken out of context. However, if encountered in the textual domains of meteorology and photography, they are perfectly normal and acceptable.

The importance of word combinations in legal language was noticed and discussed in Kjaer (1990). In her analysis of word combinations in German legal language, Kjaer claims that failure to employ prefabricated word combinations which are directly prescribed by law "will result in the invalidation of the whole text of which they form a part"(1990: 28). In other cases, legal force or the security of the law could be affected. However, there are very few studies that deal with multi-word combinations in English legal language. This issue has been usually studied as a case of lexical doubling or binomials (Gustafsson 1984: 123) and discussed in the context of redundancy in specialised discourse (*cf.* Crystal and Davy (1969), or Gotti (2003: 50-52).

This chapter intends to fill a gap in phraseological research devoted to legal texts by documenting the patterns of distribution and usage of lexical bundles. Section 2.7 in Chapter 2 provide an overview of various methodological perspectives on multi-word expressions and introduce the concept of lexical bundle adopted in the present study. Section 4.2 below further elaborates on the methodological considerations and research questions pursued in this chapter.

4.2. Methodology employed in the present analysis

The decision to adopt a similar methodology as in previous studies of lexical bundles, especially those in academic language, was largely motivated by two factors. First, the highly formulaic and repetitive nature of many legal genres (especially, the operative genres, such as legislation) makes such texts particularly amenable to a methodology which focuses on very frequent uninterrupted sequences of word forms. Second, this study intends to obtain findings that could be potentially comparable with those reported in studies of other disciplinary genres or discourses.

In this analysis, the frequency cut-off point was set at 40 times per million words with an additional criterion that a multi-word sequence must appear in at least five different texts to qualify as a lexical bundle. As already noted above, these parameters are arbitrary. In this case, these numbers represent a trade-off between the quantity of lexical bundles that would be manageable for the analyst and the quality of actual analysis. In addition, many of the bundles identified according to these criteria occur much more frequently, as shown in Table 4.1. In fact, there are bundles which are extremely common and are found in the corpus more than 200 times per million words. To further narrow down the scope of the analysis, only four-word sequences are considered. Four-word sequences appear to have a more readily recognizable range of structures and functions than three-word bundles. Finally, the parameters in this analysis correspond to those in other studies (e.g. Biber, 2006; Cortes, 2004; Hyland, 2008[24]), which could potentially facilitate comparative and descriptive work between different registers, genres or disciplinary discourses. It should be stressed that the analysis presented below does not aim to focus on individual lexical bundles. Instead, the main goal is to examine the patterns of use of such expressions as a means to study variation among legal genres. In other words, the analysis seeks to demonstrate the overall degree to which lexical bundles are used and the major structural and functional associations of bundles in each genre. In what follows, we will consider the following questions:

- Are there chunks of language – sequences of words – that are used repeatedly in legal genres?
- What are their functions?

---

24 Hyland also focuses on four-word sequences but he sets a minimum frequency at 20 times per million words

- Are there any genre-specific bundles?
- To what extent, if at all, the genres overlap?
- How do different genres compare in their use of lexical bundles?

4.3. Overall distribution of lexical bundles in legal genres

915 different bundles were identified in the entire corpus and they were categorized structurally in terms of grammatical types and functionally with respect to their meanings in the texts. This section compares the lexical bundles across the full range of legal genres. First, the overall number of lexical bundles in each genre is discussed.

Table 4.1. *Bundle frequency information*

Genre	Different bundles	Total cases	% of total words in bundles
Legislation	216	27879	9.4
Contracts	309	29939	10.1
Opinions	41	3676	1.2
Briefs	79	4408	2.3
Textbooks	157	5471	4.2
Academic journals	28	1445	1.0
Professional articles	86	1235	2.4

Table 4.1 shows the overall number (raw counts) of different lexical bundles across the full range of legal genres. The figures provided there should be interpreted with caution because they are expressed in absolute frequencies in relation to corpus components of varying size. It appears that it is not methodologically appropriate to normalize raw counts of different lexical bundles because their distribution is not linear. As a result, direct comparisons can only be safely made between genres with approximately the same word counts. Table 4.1 shows basic bundle information in a way that reflects the size of individual corpus components, i.e. legislation, contracts and opinions are sized almost identically. Both legislation and contracts show a similar pattern by containing the greatest range of different bundles, the largest number of all bundles and the highest proportion of texts comprised of words in bundles. In our view, this is further evidence of an extremely high degree of formulaicity and repetitiveness in these two genres. Legislation and contracts use a relatively wide range of very frequent bundles. In contrast, opinions rely on a relatively small (albeit frequent) number of different bundles. Table 4.2 provides the number of high-frequency bundles

(occurring one hundred times and more) as well as the proportion of such bundles with regard to the overall number of bundles in each genre. From this perspective, opinions rely on the greatest proportion of very frequent bundles. As already noted, opinions represent a legal genre which is largely expository but also operative in that it communicates judicial decisions in a highly formulaic and conventional manner. For example, opinions employ procedure-related bundles such as *it is so ordered, the case is remanded,* etc. On the other hand, the expository part, which consists of a legal analysis provided by the judges, by far prevails in quantitative terms. Cheng Le and King Kui Sin (2007) report that in American judgments this part accounts for 68% of an entire judgment. This seems to suggest that legal reasoning is expressed in a highly idiosyncratic manner, which results in avoiding repetitive sequences of words. Such 'mixed' nature of this type of texts could account for the dramatically different way in which opinions rely on bundles in comparison with identically-sized legislation and contracts.

Interestingly, textbooks employ a relatively wide range of different lexical bundles, especially in comparison with academic journals (in terms of word count, textbooks and academic journals are of almost the same size - 519,116 and 552,487 respectively). Biber (2006:136) reports that textbooks and academic prose are noted for using relatively few different lexical bundles, but this observation seems to apply to academic journals only. Both textbooks and academic articles contain relatively few high frequency bundles (22% and 19% respectively). However, textbooks contain a much higher proportion of texts consisting of words in bundles than the academic journals.

Table 4.2. *High-frequency (over 100 per million words) lexical bundles*

Genre	No.	%
Legislation	117	54
Briefs	29	37
Contract	121	39
Opinions	26	63
Academic journals	5	19
Professional articles	15	18
textbooks	34	22

Our preliminary explanation for this pattern is that both textbooks and academic journals belong to expository type of academic legal writing but they address very different audiences. Legal academic journals are much more specialised and they are intended for experts in the field, while textbooks are meant to provide state-of-the-art knowledge to semi-specialists in a possibly most accessible way (see discussion in Pearson 1998 on different levels of specialised communication). Textbooks sampled for our corpus are homogenous in content because they almost exclusively deal with one domain of law (business law). As we will see in the next sections, this results in a large number of domain-specific terminological phrases which tend to be repeated over and over again.

Briefs are similar to opinions in that they also consist of language elements which are marginally operative and those expository that are prevalent (see the previous chapter for more details on briefs' macrostructure). As a result, briefs employ a limited range of different lexical bundles and relatively few high-frequency sequences. Briefs use twice as many different bundles as opinions while the total number of bundles is similar for both genres. Still, if we consider the percentage of total words in bundles, bundles appear to play a slightly more important role in briefs than in opinions (2.3% and 1.2% respectively).

Finally, professional articles contain a relatively wide range of different, low-frequency patterns. They show the smallest proportion of high-frequency bundles (18%) and the smallest number of total cases. However, in terms of the percentage of words in bundles, professional articles tend to rely on lexical bundles more extensively than academic journals, opinions and briefs. This pattern of use could be partly explained by a great diversity of legal issues addressed in this genre.

4.4. The structural characteristics of lexical bundles

We first turn to consider the structural characteristics of lexical bundles found in different legal genres. To that end, a taxonomy based on Biber et al (1999: 1002-1023) was adopted. This framework turned out to be sufficient to capture the structural complexities of lexical bundles in legal texts. A preliminary analysis (Goźdź-Roszkowski, 2006) carried out on a 500,000 word corpus of judgments delivered by the Law Lords in the House of Lords demonstrated the presence of ten structural categories: noun phrase with *of*-phrase fragment, noun phrase with other post-modifier fragment, prepositional phrase with embedded *of*-phrase fragment, other prepositional phrase fragment, anticipatory *it* + adjective phrase, passive verb + prepositional phrase fragment, (verb phrase +) *that* clause fragment, pronoun/noun phrase + be, (verb/adjective+) *to*-clause fragment, personal pronoun+ verb phrase (+complement clause fragment). However, no frequency information was available at that time. In what follows I provide a list of structural types identified in the entire American Law Corpus. This list overlaps with that found in Goźdź-Roszkowski (2006). Thus, the bundles in legal texts have been found to contain the following structural types:

- **noun phrase with *of*-phrase fragment:**

e.g. *the amount of the, any portion of the, the nature of the*
- **noun phrase with other post-modifier fragment:**
  e.g. *the extent to which, date on which the, summary judgment on the*
- **prepositional phrase expressions:**
  e.g. *at the request of, to the benefit of, on the part of, of the parties hereto*
- **verb phrase with passive verb**
  e.g. *shall be entitled to, is amended by striking, shall not be treated as, the case is remanded, this Act may be cited as,*
- **verb phrase with active verb**
  e.g. *shall be in writing, does not apply to,*
- **anticipatory it + verb phrase (usually passive)**
  e.g. *it is so ordered, it was held that,*
- **adverbial clause fragments**
  e.g. *as defined in section, as provided in section, if the contract is,*
- **(verb/adjective+) *to*-clause fragment**
  e.g. *to meet the requirements, to carry out the,*
- **(verb phrase +) *that*-clause fragments**
  e.g. *that it is not, that there was no, that there is no, the court noted that, the court found that,*

It should be stressed that this list is not exhaustive. These are categories frequently found in most genres. This means that there are even smaller categories confined to only one genre. For instance, the so-called "quantifier expressions", i.e. bundles beginning with *all* (*all or any of, all or any part, all or any portion,* have been found only in contracts where they account for 6% of all the bundles. Table 4.3 gives the percentages of the main structures in each genre. As can be seen, lexical bundles in legal texts are primarily phrasal. Noun phrase expressions and prepositional phrases account for over 70% of all the bundles. In fact, in most legal genres these categories account for over 80% of all bundles. At the same time, bundles containing verb phrase and dependent clause bundles tend to be extremely infrequent.

Table 4.3. *Proportional breakdown of lexical bundles across major structural categories*

	legislation	contracts	opinions	briefs	academic journals	textbooks	prof. articles
noun phrase with *of* phrase fragment	34	31	24	17	20	33	38
noun phrase with other postmodifier	21	15	12	30	11	10	11
prepositional	18	29	39	35	54	32	35

phrase expressions							
verb phrase with passive verb	8	6	3	x	x	2	x
verb phrase with active verb	5	3	5	3	4	6	10
anticipatory *it* with verb phrase (pass.)	x	x	2	x	x	6	x
adverbial clause fragment	5	3	2	x	x	x	x
To-clause fragment	3	1	1	1	x	2	2
That – clause fragment	3	1	5	13	7	3	1
Other	3	5	7	1	4	6	3

In that respect, bundles in legal texts are remarkably similar to those in academic prose. Biber reports that almost 70% of bundles in that register are NP/PP-based (Biber, 2004, 2006). These percentages tend to be substantially higher than what Hyland 2008 documents for biology (54%) and electrical engineering (52.2%) and similar to applied linguistics (76.8%) and business studies (76.6%). Certain legal genres tend to be even more phrasal (briefs – 82%, academic articles – 85% and professional articles – 84%). In legal texts, prepositional phrase expressions are the most common structure overall, comprising, on average, one-third of all lexical bundles. In some genres, the proportion is even higher. For instance, in academic articles, over half of all forms include this structure. On the other hand, only 18% of prepositional phrase expressions have been found in legislation. Just as in other disciplinary genres (Hyland, 2008: 10), this structure is used typically to mark logical relations between propositional elements:

(1) Traditionally, the appropriate bank regulator, e.g., the Federal Reserve Board, would notify DOJ of a pending transaction, and DOJ would then conduct its assessment largely *on the basis of* the bank regulatory application. [professional article]

(2) *In the case of* a probationer or parolee, prior approval for the visit is obtained from the warden of the institution and the supervising field agent [brief]

(3) *In light of the* force crime requirement, the prosecutor's initial charging decision is critical [academic journal]

Further, prepositional phrase expressions serve other functions, In most genres, especially in legislation and contracts, this structural type tends to mark time, place and text deixis:

(4) This Agreement shall become effective *on the date of* its signature by the parties hereto [contract].

(5) Joint Authorship. - Under section 304, a grant of renewal rights executed by joint authors during the first term of copyright would be effective only as to those who were living *at the time of* renewal; [legislation]

(6) With these general principles in mind, let's return to the three scenarios described *at the beginning of* the article. [professional article]

Other more disciplinary-specific uses include indicating parties in a legal process and expressing stance, in the sense of marking the source or perspective of knowledge:

(7) A court having jurisdiction over actions under this chapter may grant injunctions *in accordance with the* principles of equity to prevent infringement of a design under this chapter, including, in its discretion, prompt relief by temporary restraining orders and preliminary injunctions. [legislation]

(8) The defendants anticipated that the eventual contract would be made on their standard terms which included a provision for unlimited liability *on the part of* the plaintiffs in the event of consequential loss due to late delivery.[opinion]

The noun phrase with *of* phrase fragments accounts for over a quarter of all the bundles. It covers a range of meanings in legal genres and in particular it is widely used to refer to various legal and other entities (e.g. *court of competent jurisdiction, directors of the company*), legal concepts (e.g. *a breach of contract, the doctrine of privity*), legal instruments or their parts (e.g. *the provisions of the, the judgment of the*), quantity (e.g. *the amount of the, the total number of*), other attributes (e.g. *the nature of the, the name of the*).

Bundles containing adverbial clause fragments have been found in three major legal genres: legislation, contracts and judgments. These bundles are introduced by the subordinator *as* and they function as a text deictic:

(9) For purposes of this Plan, a “Change in Control” shall occur automatically if and when an "Acceleration Date" occurs *as defined in the* Company's 1998 Incentive Stock Plan. [contract];

(10) To accept or reject rate adjustment petitions as provide in section 804 and petitions to participate *as provided in section* 803(b) (1) and (2). [legislation]

In terms of structural types, there appears to be relatively little variability across the legal genres. By and large, they all make dense use of noun phrase and prepositional phrase bundles. Such distribution of structural types contributes to the perception of legal genres as linguistically highly nominal. Similarly, all the text genres are marked by the presence of a small proportion of bundles incorporating verb phrases. We now turn to look at lexical bundles and the functions they perform in their relevant co-texts.

4.5. Lexical bundles and their functions in legal genres

One has a much better understanding of the distribution and significance of lexical bundles, if their discourse functions are also analysed. An inductive approach to function identification was adopted. First, lexical bundles were grouped depending on whether they shared similar functions. This was only possible by studying concordance lines of each bundle and examining its co-texts in order to determine typical meanings and uses. After assigning the bundles to different groups, the groups were then labelled according to their predominant functions. Some bundles can be problematic because they serve different functions depending on the context in which they are found. For example, a bundle like *at the end of* can function as a time reference, place reference , or text deictic reference. However, most bundles tend to have one prevalent function. If a bundle was found to be multi-functional, it was classified according to its most common use. A framework for functional analysis of lexical bundles in legal texts was designed in such a way as to reflect the specificity and somewhat unique nature of legal data. In doing so, we relied on insights from earlier classifications proposed in Biber et al., 2004; Biber, 2006, and Hyland, 2008. Similar to these earlier classifications, lexical bundles in legal genres are classified into three broad categories of lexical bundles marking legal reference, stance and text-oriented lexical bundles. Bundles grouped in the first category make direct reference to abstract or physical objects in the world of law: its institutions, instruments, concepts, processes, etc. Stance bundles serve to express different attitudes or assessments while text-oriented bundles are used to signal relationships between different textual segments. Table 4.4 provides the percentages of the three major functional categories for each genre. Referential bundles form the largest group overall, with legislation, contracts and professional articles containing the largest proportion of such expressions. At the same time, academic journals and opinions contain a markedly lower proportion of referential bundles but the largest percentage of text-oriented and stance bundles. Stance bundles are the smallest category in all genres however, their distribution varies more substantially than in the case of referential bundles. Proportionally, both legislation and contracts contain less than half of the stance bundles in comparison with the other genres. This difference is even more conspicuous if we compare the percentages for legislation and contracts with those in briefs, textbooks and academic journals. A similar trend can be noticed in respect of text-oriented bundles. In academic journals and opinions, a third of all bundles are used to signal textual organization, while the percentages for legislation, contracts and professional articles are considerably lower.

Table 4.4. *Proportional breakdown of lexical bundles across major functional categories*

	Legal reference	**Stance**	**Text-oriented**
legislation	77	6	17
opinions	59	12	29
contracts	78	5	17
briefs	65	15	20
textbooks	65	15	20
academic journals	54	14	32
professional articles	75	11	14

Thus, in all legal text genres, the largest proportion of bundles is used to mark legal reference. In some genres (briefs, textbooks and professional articles) the percentages between stance and text-oriented bundles is relatively small. However, there are important differences in terms of the three major functional categories, there is a clear difference in the way bundles are used across the genres. Legislation, contracts and professional articles are clearly focused on legal reference, with relatively few bundles expressing stance and a moderate number of text-oriented bundles. This pattern of use is in stark contrast to opinions and academic journals which contain considerably fewer referential bundles but significantly larger proportions of stance and text-oriented bundles. Briefs and textbooks represent intermediary genres and are marked by a relatively even distribution of stance and text-oriented bundles.

4.5.1. Legal reference

Bundles collected under this broad category are used to refer to legal concepts, institutions, instruments, processes, etc. As a result, seven subcategories have been distinguished: *temporal bundles* referring to particular points in time, *location bundles* the function of which is to mark places or locations; *attributive bundles* which describe legal entities, concepts, instruments and processes by specifying their attributes, *participative bundles* signalling the role performed by various participants or parties in a legal process; *institutional bundles* referring to legal instruments and entities (such as, for instance, courts, government agencies, corporations, constitutional amendments, etc.); *domain-specific terminological bundles* denoting nominal term phraseology (e.g. *a breach of contract, right of first refusal*) and finally *procedure-related bundles* indicating verbal expressions used to effect a particular legal act.

Table 4.5. *Proportional breakdown of lexical bundles with legal reference*

	Temporal reference	Location	Attributive	Participative	Institutional	Terminological	Procedure-related
Legislation	23 (18)	5 (4)	10 (7)	4 (3)	25 (19)	2 (1.9)	31 (24)
Judgments	4 (2)	17 (10)	17 (10)	4 (2)	39 (22)	9 (5)	9 (5)
Contracts	19 (15)	.4(.3)	21 (9)	10 (7)	17 (14)	9 (4)	24 (19)
Briefs	2 (1)	10 (6)	12.5 (8)	2 (1)	64.5 (39)	2 (1)	7 (5)
Textbooks	5 (3)	3 (2)	21 (13)	19 (11)	29 (18)	23 (14)	-
Academic Article	13 (7)	40 (21)	13 (7)	7 (4)	20 (11)	7 (4)	-
Professional Article	16 (11)	11 (8)	29 (20)	3 (2)	19 (14)	17 (13)	5 (4)

Table 4.5 provides the percentages of each subcategory across the legal genres. The figures in brackets show the proportion of bundles from a given category against the total number of bundles, while the other figure shows the proportion within the category of legal reference bundles. For example, with regard to legislation, bundles with temporal reference account for 23% of all bundles with legal reference. At the same time, they make up for 18% of all bundles indentified for this genre.

4.5.1.1. Temporal bundles

As can be seen in Table 4.5, legal genres exploit this type of bundles to a varying degree. It has a strong presence in all legal genres but contracts and legislation appear to make the most extensive use of time expressions. On average one-fifth of all bundles with legal reference in these two genres are used as time expressions. Structurally, these expressions are typically realised as prepositional phrases:

(11) Discovery in such proceedings shall be permitted **for a period of** 60 days, except for discovery ordered by the Copyright Royalty Judges in connection with the resolution of motions, orders, and disputes pending **at the end of** such period. [legislation]
(12) **At the time of** the hearing, he requested a continuance which was denied. [professional article]

As documented in Goźdź-Roszkowski (2006), time bundles are particularly important in contracts where marking temporal deixis is clearly crucial. Goźdź-Roszkowski (2006) documents further distinctions of contractual temporal bundles according to the key element appearing in a given sequence. Thus, temporal lexical bundles are grouped depending on the occurrence of such words as *time, day* or *date*:

(13) Assignee agrees to pay all rent due after **the effective date of** this assignment, and to assume and perform all duties and obligations required by the terms of this lease. [contract]

More specifically, temporal bundles in contracts are often used to mark *duration* or *process*:

(14) Should employee die **during the term of** employment, the Company shall pay to Employee's estate any compensation due through the end of the month in which death occurred. [contract]

Worth noting is the extremely frequent occurrence of *from time to time*. It is found 495 times per million words in contracts. In fact, it is the most frequent bundle in this type of legal writing[25]. Its high frequency in contractual instruments, where precision of expression should be in principle prioritized, suggests that this

25 By comparison, the *Corpus of Contemporary American English* shows that this bundle is most frequent in fiction (15.77 words per million) and in spoken language (7.98 w.p.m.)

expression is employed in a unique, genre-specific sense divorced from its everyday imprecise meaning:

(15) In addition, there shall be payable to the employee such additional salary by way of bonus as the Board of Directors of the company shall **from time to time** agree.

(16) Company may furnish the Sales Representative **from time to time** with a reasonable supply of such brochures, price lists and other materials concerning the Products as may be available to Company.

In English legal language, the lexical bundle *from time to time* implies that an activity is not a one-off but it can occur over and over again[26]. One can wonder to what extent such use is strategic and is meant to ensure flexibility and discretion for one party to a contractual relationship. For example, in excerpt (15), the Board of Directors exercise some discretion with regard to the amount and frequency of the payment of an additional salary to the employee. Interestingly, in ten cases, the word *discretion* is found within the span of five words to the left of this lexical bundle. In a similar vein, in excerpt (16), there is no precise indication of how often the Sales Representative should be supplied with brochures, price lists, etc. In fact, unlike in the previous example, there is no obligation on the part of the Company to provide the Sales Representative with the materials. The act of furnishing the Sales Representative is dependent on the availability of the materials. Finally, note also the presence of the notoriously imprecise word *reasonable* (cf. Gotti, 2003:49) on imprecision in specialised discourse).

On the other hand, very few temporal bundles have been found in opinions, briefs and textbooks. As a result, there is a clear difference in the extent to which formulaic expressions are employed in the two operative genres of legislation and contracts and the expository genres of legal writing.

4.5.1.2. Location bundles

Location bundles in legal genres are used to refer to institutions, such as courts or corporations, or types of lawsuits. These bundles provide vital information which helps to identify the type of case and elaborate on the wider institutional background:

(17) Petitioners filed refund suits **in the district court** to recover wagering excise taxes paid for July 1993... [brief]

26 See Berezowski 2009 for more comments and examples of how the bundle *from time to time* is used in various contractual instruments.

(18) It remains an open question, however, whether a defendant **in a class action** that was filed prior to February 18.... [professional article]

Not surprisingly, location bundles are frequent in briefs and opinions where frequent references are made to courts at various levels of the US judicial structure. The significantly large proportion of location bundles in academic articles (40%) can be attributed to citation practice, where references are made to past cases:

(19) On the heels of Booker/Fanfan, the Second Circuit issued its opinion **in United States v.** Crosby,(102) and its companion decisions **in United States v.** Fleming and Green v. United States,(103) setting forth the method by which Booker/Fanfan would be implemented in that circuit.

Unlike in the previous category, contracts have almost no bundles marking location. The same applies to legislation. This pattern can signal rare reference to places outside of the documents, in the real world.

4.5.1.3. Attributive bundles

Another substantial subcategory of referential bundles, not infrequent in other disciplinary genres identifies "specific attributes of the following head noun" (Biber, 2006:145). In legal genres, a large proportion of such bundles is used to specify quantity or amounts:

(20) If **a portion of the** Collateral is or will become a fixture, it will be affixed to the real property as described above. [contract]
(21) The submission of any periodic payment offer-in-compromise shall be accompanied by the payment of **the amount of the** first proposed instalment. [bill]

In contracts, one third of attributive bundles are used to indicate quantities or amounts. In fact, Goźdź-Roszkowski (2006) lists them as a separate subcategory of *quantifying bundles*. These include *the amount of the, at the rate of, one or more of, all or any part, any part of the, part of the property*. Many of these bundles contain the quantifiers *all* and *any,* which tend to co-occur in the form of a three-word bundle *all or any*. There are as many as 214 instances of this bundle in the contract section of the ALC, and they co-occur with nouns such as *part* and *portion*:

(22) Any Stockholder, may at any time [...] by notice in writing require the Company to repay *all or any part* of each payment. [contract]

Interestingly, the search for *all or any* in legislation returns only ten hits but five of them are also followed by either *part* or *portion.* By comparison, there are only 21 instances of *all or any* in the 400-million-word *Corpus of Contemporary American English (COCA).* This extensive use of quantifying bundles in legal texts could be attributed to attempts at achieving the effect of 'all-inclusiveness' so pervasive in legislative and contractual provisions. There is no evidence of quantifying bundles, especially of the *all or any* type in the other genres. Its distribution is, to a large extent, confined to contractual instruments and could be thus regarded as a marker of genre-specificity.

Other attributive bundles are often used to contribute to the description of legal concepts by signalling the scope of the following objects, their nature, value, validity, etc in broader contexts:

(23) Flexibility in determining **the nature of the** relief that is appropriate in a given case is characteristic of suits in equity. [briefs]
(24) Here, by contrast, Congress has textually narrowed **the scope of the** term by using the modifier "valuable."5 [judgment];
(25) It seems clear that if **the validity of the** assignment is undisputed, due notice of it has been given, and the assignee is willing to complete, the other party to the contract must complete with the assignee and not the assignor. [textbook]

In addition, some legal genres use attribute-specifying bundles to describe the manner in which a particular course of action is carried out:

(26) If an Intervening Offer is undertaken, in whole or in part, **in the form of** a tender offer, at the consummation of such tender offer, (...) [contract]
(27) Except for the price, the other option terms, such as vesting, generally stay the same, although many companies extract some consideration from the optionees, usually **in the form of** a delayed exercisability of the new option or by extending the vesting term or by reducing the number of option shares. [professional article]

There is a relatively even distribution of attributive bundles in legal discourse. Still, professional articles tend to have the largest proportion of such bundles (29% of all legal reference bundles), while legislation has only 10%. There are 21% of attributive bundles in contracts and textbooks and 13% and 12.5% in academic journals and briefs, respectively.

4.5.1.4. Participative bundles

There are a number of bundles which signal the presence and participation of various legal or natural persons in a particular legal process or transaction. They help identify individuals or corporations that may benefit or, more generally, be affected by legal provisions or transactions or other actions. They are found to a varying extent in all genres but they have their largest proportions in textbooks (19%) and contracts (10%):

(28) However, covenants **on the part of** the landlord are implied in the cases of houses let at a low rent or for a short term. [textbook]
(29) This Insurance may be cancelled at any time **at the request of** Assured in writing to the Broker who effected the Insurance (…) [contract]
(30) Such time limitation shall be tolled for minors for any period during which a parent or guardian and a health care provider or health care organization have committed fraud or collusion in the failure to bring an action **on behalf of the** injured minor. [legislation]
(31) There does not appear (at least as a general rule) to be any similar possibility where the promise claims damages for breach of a contract **for the benefit of** a third party. [textbook]

The use of participative bundles seems to be linked to the domain of business law in general rather than to a particular genre. Contractual relations between individuals and corporations are based on the principle of reciprocity and they hinge upon the participation of various, sometimes more than two parties. The importance of this category of lexical bundles is self-evident, especially in contractual documents as parties' respective duties, obligations and benefits need to be defined clearly and unequivocally. This is further corroborated by an extensive use of such bundles in textbooks, which suggests a more content-oriented specificity.

4.5.1.5. Institutional bundles

The term *institutional bundles* is here understood in the sense of expressions which refer to legal entities (such as courts, government agencies, corporations, etc.) and legal instruments (e.g. statutes, codes, constitutional amendments, agreements or contracts, individual clauses). Bundles in this category are usually proper names, inextricably linked to the US legal system and culture:

(32) **The Due Process Clause** prohibits the criminal prosecution of a defendant who is not competent to stand trial. [briefs]

(33) Whenever **the Internal Revenue Code** of 1986 provides that the amount excluded from gross income in respect of the discharge of indebtedness in a case under this title shall be applied to reduce the tax attributes of the debtor or the estate, a similar reduction shall be made under any State or local law imposing a tax on or measured by income to the extent such State or local law recognizes such attributes. [legislation]

(34) On appeal to the **Court of Appeals for** the Sixth Circuit, Lewis prevailed. Id., at 67. [judgment]

(35) Any event, action or condition with respect to an employee benefit plan of the Company subject to Title IV of ERISA results in any penalty or action pursuant to ERISA that has a material adverse effect on the business or financial condition of the **Company and its Subsidiaries**, taken as a whole. [contract]

Unlike in the previous excerpts (31-33), example (34) contains a bundle that is less culture-bound and more generic. As Table 4.5 shows, institutional bundles are one of the most numerous categories overall, with briefs, opinions and textbooks having the largest percentages not only across the full range of the genres but also in their own respective categories. In briefs, institutional bundles account for as much as 64% of the referential bundles and 40% of all the bundles in this category. As we recall, appellate briefs are written for an extremely demanding audience since appellate courts (especially the Supreme Court) are concerned with developing new legal doctrines, applying existing law, and remedying errors of law. A good brief has to contain numerous institutional references to explain the legal issues in the case and to educate the court of the precedential authority. On the other hand, more operative genres, such as contracts contain markedly lower proportion of culture-bound, institutional references because they are much less constrained institutionally.

4.5.1.6. Terminological bundles

Terminological bundles represent highly technical and specialised vocabulary the occurrence of which is confined to the legal discipline. In other words, they are, what lawyers refer to, as "terms of art" as illustrated by the following examples:

(36) The question whether the sum stipulated for is a penalty or liquidated damages can only arise when the event upon which it becomes payable is **a breach of contract**. [textbook]

(37) The Shereleigh court, however, declined to give lead plaintiff's counsel the **right of first refusal**, reasoning that a **right of first refusal** would "

unnecessarily abrogate the court's duty to carefully weigh the interests of the class", (...). [professional article]

The statistical data in Table 4.5 show that textbooks contain by far the largest proportion of terminological bundles (over one fifth of all referential bundles). This terminological density is certainly linked to the textbooks primary function of disseminating state-of-the-art disciplinary knowledge. It should be also borne in mind that the disciplinary knowledge is fairly homogenous in that the textbooks deal almost exclusively with the sub-discipline of business law. The more homogenous and domain-specific the data, the greater probability that a number of fixed and specialised expressions will be used over and over again. That is indeed the case with textbooks in this study.

Professional articles also contain a large proportion of such expressions. Their function is somewhat similar to that of textbooks in that they also focus on providing specialist knowledge albeit with a view to dispensing free legal advice. Interestingly, legislation and briefs have relatively few terminological bundles which could be explained by the immense diversity of issues dealt with in individual documents. As a result, it is less likely that a particular combination becomes recurrent. Further, legislative texts eschew highly specialist expressions because they are intended for a more general public.

Interestingly, there is relatively little overlap between terminological bundles in textbooks and contracts despite the shared subject matter. This discrepancy could be attributed to different communicative and professional goals associated with these two legal genres. For example, textbooks tend to contain terminological bundles related to legal theory (e.g. *the doctrine of frustration, the doctrine of privity, total failure of consideration*), while bundles in contracts reflect the realities of business practice (e.g. *assets of the company, shares of common stock, consummation of the transactions*).

Finally, lexical bundles of this type could provide initial input for manual term extraction. Obviously, labelling such expressions as terms might raise questions concerning terminological validation criteria. However, some of them, such as terminographic documentation and usage frequency can indeed be overcome by using the lexical bundle methodology.

4.5.1.7. Procedure-related bundles

This last category of referential bundles groups verb-based expressions which are used to serve various specialist functions related to legal procedure and practice. Predictably, they are most frequently found in two operative genres of legislation and contracts:

(38) CONFORMING AMENDMENT- The Act entitled "An Act concerning tonnage duties on vessels entering otherwise than by sea", approved March 8, 1910 (36 Stat 234; 46 U.S.C. App. 132), **is amended by striking** "through 2002," and inserting "through 2006". [legislation]

(39) **Be it enacted by** the Senate and House of Representatives of the United States of America in Congress assembled (…) [legislation]

Excerpt (38) illustrates the use of an extremely frequent bundle *is amended by striking* which introduces changes made to the wording of a particular legislative provision. In the next example (39) we can see the bundle being part of a larger enacting formula routinely employed at the start of each US statute. Such bundles can be viewed as "performatives", i.e. marking a special class of speech acts. In many procedure-related bundles, a speech act is explicitly marked by the presence of *shall*. It is usually associated with carrying the illocutionary directive force of expressing command, imposing obligation or conferring legal rights (see, for instance, a recent discussion in Witczak-Plisiecka, 2007). The traditional, somewhat stereotypical legal understanding of *shall* can be summarised by the following quote from Robinson (1973: 39):

> "the use of '*shall*' indicates that the legal subject is under obligation to act in accordance with the terms of the provision (...) it does not indicate something in relation to the future"

Admittedly, expressing obligation is very frequently expressed by means of lexical bundles containing *shall*, as illustrated in (40):

(40) Report- Not later than July 1, 2009, the Secretary **shall submit to Congress** a report describing the effectiveness of the program under this section.[legislation]

Equally frequent is the use of *shall* to confer rights. The following bundle *shall be entitled to* has 258 occurrences per million words):

(41) The Bank **shall be entitled to** rely upon any written or telephone request from persons it reasonably believes to be authorized by the Borrower to make such requests without making independent inquiry.[contract]

Contracts provide many examples of overusing *shall.* In the example below (42), there is one lexical bundle containing *shall* which expresses an obligation as to how a process of valuation must be carried out:

(42) The valuation **shall be made by** two valuers, one selected by each partner or his representatives and in case the two valuers shall be unable to agree they **shall** appoint a third valuer whose valuation **shall** be final.

At the same time, the use of *shall* (underlined) placed in the conditional clause following *in case,* is not motivated by deontic modality and it is clearly redundant. The other uses of *shall* signal the obligatory nature of the provision. It should be borne in mind that apart from expressing obligation or command, such bundles indicate that a given proposition is legally binding (as in example 40) and that a particular course of action or procedure is in place. A similar legally binding procedure is indicated in (43) and (44), below:

(43) This Protocol shall be signed and **shall be subject to** ratification or acceptance, or may be acceded to, as if the provisions of article VIII of the Convention applied hereto. [legislation]

(44) The decision and award of the arbitrators **shall be in writing**, shall be final and conclusive on the parties, and counterpart copies thereof shall be delivered to each of the parties. [contracts]

Bundles with deontic *shall* often contain negation to express absence of obligation (45) or prohibition (46). Both bundles are very frequent. The expression *shall not be required* appears 64 times per million words, while *this agreement shall not* was found 71 times per million words.

(45) The Committee **shall not be required** to see to the application of any payment so made, and payment to the person determined by the Committee shall fully discharge the Plan and the Participating Employer from any further accountability or responsibility with respect to the amount so paid.[contract]

(46) **This Agreement shall not** be modified or amended except by an agreement in writing signed by the parties hereto.[contract]

However, as already noted in the previous chapter, the use of *shall* goes beyond merely indicating obligation or command. Tiersma (1999:105) notes that *shall* is also used to make declarations as in the example he cites: *This Act shall be known as the Penal Code of California*. The use of *shall* here does not fulfil any of the functions mentioned above. It is not a command or an obligation. Still, it communicates that the provision is intended to be legally binding. As a result, such uses of *shall* have also been subsumed under the category of procedure-related bundles.

Further, Tiersma aptly points out that the function of *shall* depends on "the type of document in which it occurs" (1999:106). This analysis corroborates his suggestion that *shall* is typically found in legislation and contracts. Biber et al (1999) report that *shall* is the least frequent modal with roughly 250 occurrences per million words in the LSWE Corpus. In the sub-corpus of contracts used in this study, *shall* appears 13,700 times and there are 10,248 instances of *shall* in legislation (see Table 3.3 in Chapter 3). Both the sub-corpora are slightly above 1,000,000 words, so no statistical tests are not necessary to demonstrate the unusually high frequency of this modal in normative legal genres. Any analysis of *shall* should then be carried out in light of their respective generic conventions, especially that there are no bundles with *shall* found in the other genres.

Not surprisingly, procedure-related bundles account for 31% of legal reference bundles in legislation and 24% in contracts, while in academic articles and textbooks no bundles of this type were identified. Thus, the use of *shall* should be regarded as a marker of intra-disciplinary variation in legal discourse.

4.5.2. Text-oriented bundles

In this section, we turn to explore the second major type of lexical bundles which have been found to serve several different functions summarized in Table 4.6. The broad category of text-oriented bundle consists of several more specific categories: bundles expressing *conditions,* bundles related to *topic elaboration* or *clarification, focus* bundles which provide overt signals to the reader that a new issue is being introduced, bundles which *frame* arguments by specifying limiting conditions for making assertions, claims or arguments, bundles highlighting the *results* of an analysis, *structuring* bundles which are used to organize the text and finally, *transition* bundles marking links between preceding and subsequent textual segments. It becomes immediately clear that distributional patterns vary widely across the different categories. Some are strongly represented (framing, clarification and focus bundles) while some are infrequent and found in only certain genres (e.g. structuring bundles).

Table 4.6. *Proportional breakdown of text-oriented bundles across different subcategories*

	condition	clarification	focus	framing	resultative	structuring	transition
legislation	3	3	19	35	9	28	3
opinions	x	13	7	80	x	x	x
contracts	12	4	4	35	18	25	2
briefs	x	13	13	67	7	x	x
textbooks	14	10	31	34	8	x	3
academic journals	x	x	x	67	11	x	22

professional articles	18	x	x	55	18	x	9

In what follows, we will examine each subcategory and the ways in which bundles are used in their relevant contexts.

4.5.2.1. Causative/Resultative bundles

This category groups bundles which signal some logical links between arguments in a text in terms of cause and effect relationships. Expository legal genres tend to use such bundles in a way not different from what one can observe in written academic discourse:

(47) **As a result of** the Supreme Court's decision in Booker/Fanfan, the Fifth Circuit currently is considering whether Mr. Olis' case should be remanded for resentencing.[academic article]

(48) **As a result of** the 1998 amendments to Rule 23, the courts of appeals may, at their discretion, review a district court's decision to grant or deny class certification. Following this change, the federal appellate courts have developed standards for deciding which certification decisions merit interlocutory review. [professional article]

In contracts, and to a lesser extent, in legislation there are bundles which signal a causative connection between two propositions. For example, in contractual instruments, the bundles *by reason of the,* or *by reason of any* provide an explanatory basis for an entitlement to a benefit:

(49) A person becoming entitled to a share **by reason of the** death or insolvency of the holder shall be entitled to the same dividends and other advantages to which he would be entitled if he were the registered holder of the share, except that he shall not before being registered as a member in respect of the share, be entitled in respect of it to exercise any right conferred by membership in relation to meetings of the company. [contract]

In legislation, the same bundle is used to highlight a disputed incriminating link between an activity (e.g. storing copyright material) and a violation of law:

(50) For purposes of paragraph (2), no governmental body or accredited non-profit educational institution shall be liable for infringement **by reason of the** transient or temporary storage of material carried out through the

automatic technical process of a digital transmission of the performance or display of that material as authorized under paragraph (2).

Contracts are clearly marked for a dense use of multiple resultative bundles. Another excerpt illustrates the use of expressions such as *or arising out of, arising out of the* found in a highly repetitive and formulaic pattern of use in conjunction with another resultative expression *resulting from*:

(51) All Liabilities relating to, <u>resulting from</u> **or arising out of** options to purchase stock of DuPont (including, without limitation, options held by retired employees, but excluding Liabilities relating to, <u>resulting from</u> or **arising out of the** cancellation of such options upon the issuance of options to purchase stock of Conoco pursuant to Section 2.06 of the Employee Matters Agreement) other than the Employee Benefits Note.

Interestingly, opinions do not contain such lexical bundles. This does not mean that bundles such as *arising out of the* or *by reason of the* cannot be found in this type of legal texts. The analysis only reveals that such expressions do not meet frequency criteria designated for lexical bundles. It is quite likely that opinions employ a wider range of different causative/resultative expressions which were not captured by the analytical tool used in the present study.

4.5.2.2. Condition bundles

The subcategory of text-oriented bundles introduces conditions by employing prepositional combinations such as *in the event of,* and *in the event that,* which are then frequently placed in sentence-initial positions (excerpts 52 and 53). Only contracts, textbooks and professional articles tend to contain larger proportions of this type of expressions. Such constructions are characteristic of contractual provisions, where every effort is made to allow for any possible contingencies. This usually results in unwieldy sentences as illustrated in excerpt (55) which represents one sentence consisting of 154 words!

Worth noting is the use of condition bundles in textbooks to explain a legal point by providing hypothetical scenarios leading to a particular legal effect depending on a course of action taken by one of the parties (typically referred to by means of single capital letters) as in example (54) below:

(52) **In the event of** a breach or threatened breach of Tenant of any of its obligations under this Lease, Landlord shall also have the right of injunction.[contract]

(53) **In the event of** a dispute or conflict between you and the Co-defendants, there is a risk that we may be disqualified from representing all of you absent written consent from all of you at that time. [professional article]

(54) If this factual difference (i.e. the contractual duty to register) connotes a difference in principle at all, the principle would appear to be that which we have suggested: that a duty to perform a contract with A can render one liable **in the event of** non-performance to B, at least where B has relied upon one's performance and has in some way given up something in return for that reliance (albeit not directly to the defendant). [textbook]

(55) **In the event that** the Commencement Date shall be other than the first day of a Tax Year or an Operating Year or the date of the expiration or other termination of this Lease shall be a day other than the last day of a Tax Year or an Operating Year, then in such event in applying the provisions of this Article 3 with respect to any Tax Year or Operating Year in which such event shall have occurred, appropriate adjustments shall be made to reflect the occurrence of such event on a basis consistent with the principles underlying the provisions of this Article 3 taking into consideration the portion of such Tax Year or Operating Year which shall have elapsed after the term hereof commences in the case of the Commencement Date, and prior to the date of such expiration or termination in the case of the Expiration Date or other termination. [contract]

4.5.2.3. Clarification/topic elaboration bundles

This category is not different from the one identified in other studies of lexical bundles in domain-specific discourse (e.g. Biber, 2006). Bundles found here relate to the topic under consideration by further elaborating on it or clarifying it. For example, the bundles *at the same time* and *on the other hand* tend to be used in legal argumentation, to present and possibly contrast the arguments put forward (excerpts 56 -58):

(56) **At the same time**, the Government argues that in detaining Hamdi in the manner specified the President is in any event acting as Commander in Chief under the Article II of the Constitution (...). [opinion]

(57) At the least, the greater expense attached to trials and their greater complexity, taken together in the context of an overworked criminal justice system, will likely mean, other things being equal, fewer trials and a greater reliance upon plea bargaining--a system in which punishment is set not by judges or juries but by advocates acting under bargaining constraints. **At the same time**, the greater power of the prosecutor to control the punishment

through the charge would likely weaken the relation between real conduct and real punishment as well. [opinion]

(58) **On the other hand**, while the statute also requires the trial court to specify its reasons for granting or denying a motion for summary judgment, the trial courts failure to do so is usually harmless error. [professional article]

Note the use of *in the first place* in the textbook excerpt to signal a more explanatory part of the text in which justification is provided for asserting an "enormous legal significance" attached to the fact of possession:

(59) Nevertheless, possession is a fact which has an enormous legal significance, a fact to which legal rights are attached. **In the first place**, actual possession is evidence of ownership, and, except in cases where ownership is based on a system of public registration, it is hard to see how any ownership can be proved, otherwise than by going back to some prior possession. [textbook]

Table 4.6 shows that clarification bundles are more characteristic of expository type of legal writing (opinions, briefs and textbooks) with some relatively rare found in legislation and contracts:

(60) The Corporation shall require any successor (whether direct or indirect, by purchase, merger, consolidation or otherwise) to all or substantially all of the business or assets of the Corporation, expressly to assume and agree to perform this Agreement **in the same manner** and to the same extent that the Corporation would be required to perform if no such succession had taken place.[contract]

No clarification/elaboration bundles have been found in academic journals and professional articles.

4.5.2.4. Focus bundles

The presence of focus bundles in university genres has been proposed in Biber (2006: 142-143) to refer to expressions which provide overt signals that a new topic is introduced. In this study, focus bundles are used to refer to four-word bundles which indicate the purpose or purposes of a legal instrument as in the example below taken from a statute, where there is an explicit statement of the purposes of this act:

(61) Purposes. - **The purposes of this** Act [amending this section and section 902 of this title] are - "(1) to extend the period within which the Secretary of

Commerce may grant interim protective orders under section 914 of title 17, United States Code, to continue this incentive for the bilateral and multilateral protection of mask works; [legislation]

The bundle *the purposes of this* serves as an overt signal facilitating the identification of the legislative intent envisaged for a given statute.

Focus bundles are also used to increase relevance of a particular legal concept, provision or issue:

(62) That requirement, which is **at issue in this** case, is not limited to unrepresented defendants. [brief]

In quantitative terms, focus bundles are most typically found in textbooks, briefs and legislation. However, it is worth noting the presence of the bundle *any of the following* found in various contractual instruments:

(63) The occurrence of **any of the following** events shall constitute an "EVENT OF DEFAULT" under this Agreement: [contract]

What follows this sentence, is a long list of situations the occurrence of which is recognized as an event of failure, e.g. *failure to pay*, *breach of representation or warranty*, *specific defaults*, etc. Each of these points is then further described in the document. As a result we have quite an extensive and elaborate textual material, where the bundle *any of the following* helps to organize this textual space.

4.5.2.5. Framing signals

The term *framing signals* has been proposed by Hyland (2008: 14) to refer to bundles which "situate arguments by specifying limiting conditions". The examples he provides include: *in the case, with respect to, on the basis of, in the presence of, with the exception of.* Table 4.6 shows that framing bundles account for a very large proportion of text-oriented bundles in legal texts. The percentages range from 34% - 35% in the case of contracts, textbooks and legislation, through 55% in professional articles and up to 67% and 80% in academic articles, briefs and opinions, respectively. Bundles grouped in this category are used to specify limiting conditions for making assertions, claims or arguments or providing explanation or rationale:

(64) Some differences were apparent **on the basis of** the type of offense committed. [academic article]

(65) This might be explained **on the ground that** the builder is in breach of an implied term not to put it out of his power to perform or to proceed with reasonable diligence (...) [textbook]

In structural terms, these bundles tend to consist of preposition + *of* structures. They are also used to specify the conditions under which a statement can be accepted, working to elaborate, emphasize or compare aspects of an argument. While framing bundles comprise a high proportion of text-oriented bundles in all legal genres, they are found in largest proportions in opinions, briefs and academic journals:

(66) The plurality rejects any need for "specific language of detention" **on the ground that** detention of alleged combatants is a "fundamental incident of waging war." Ante, at 12. Its authorities do not support that holding **in the context of** the present case. [judgment]
(67) At common law, there was no limitation of time for prosecuting a crime. 21 Am.Jur.2d, Criminal Law, § 223, at 408. Then, as now, **in the absence of** a statutory limitation, a prosecution could be brought at any time following the commission of an offense. [brief]

A tentative conclusion is that framing bundles are particularly frequently employed in legal genres which focus on legal argumentation. Legal argumentation in opinions and briefs refers to particular cases and thus needs to be firmly contextualised and grounded in the actualities of the case. Links between the case and applicable law must also be carefully explained.

4.5.2.6. Structuring bundles

The term structuring bundles has been adapted from Hyland (2008) who uses it to refer to two text-organizing aspects[27]. The first aspect involves using structural bundles to "help organize the text by providing a frame within which new arguments can be both anchored and projected, announcing discourse goals and referring to text stages" (2008:17). The second is used to "point to other parts of the texts to make additional material salient and available to the reader in recovering the writer's intentions" (2008: 17). Such textual practice is apparently most conspicuous in the domain of electrical engineering because of the tendency to rely on graphical and numerical information which is bound to be referred to when presenting arguments. Most typical examples include *as shown in Figure* [2], or *as shown in the* [example] (Hyland 2008:17).

---

27 Hyland 2008 actually uses the term "structuring signals"

In this analysis, structuring bundles are used to signal text deixis by referring to particular legal instruments or their parts. Their function is to navigate the reader through the meanders of the frequently extremely long and complex documents by locating specific information in documents. The distribution of structuring bundles is restricted to only two genres: legislation and contracts. In contracts, these expressions are built around four verbs: *contain, define, provide* and *set forth.* Thus, the most frequent lexical bundles include *as defined in section, as defined in the, as otherwise provided in, as provided in section, as set forth in, contained in this agreement, set forth in section, set forth in the, set forth in this.*

As shown in the excerpt (68) below, in contractual instruments, structuring bundles help to direct the reader to the relevant part of the document to retrieve specific information, which in this example, is encapsulated by means of an anaphoric noun (Francis 1986) *service*:

(68) 31.02 In addition to the foregoing, either Landlord or Tenant may, from time to time, request in writing that the other party serve a copy of any notice or demand, consent, approval or disapproval, or statement, on one other person or entity designated in such request, such service to be effected **as provided in Section** 31.01 hereof.

Excerpt (69) illustrates the use of a structuring bundle, which is seemingly focused on specifying the location (*this Agreement*) but the real purpose is to stress the integrity of the document by reiterating that reference is made to representations and warranties that are included in the agreement under consideration and *not* in any other document:

(69) The representations and warranties of the Borrower **contained in this Agreement** shall be true in all material respects (...)

Interestingly, the same structuring bundles are used in legislation. Apart from the ones mentioned above, legislation typically employs bundles with the verb *describe*:

(70) (...) How to determine what property is exempt and how to value exempt property at replacement value **as described in section** 506.

(71) (...) or for the purpose of having that other person verify his or her acts of good faith encryption research **described in paragraph (2)**.

4.5.2.7. Transition bundles

This category has already been proposed in Hyland (2008), who documents how transition bundles are used to establish additive or contrastive links between elements. They usually include expressions such as *in addition to the, in contrast to the, on the other hand* (Hyland, 2008: 14). Overall, such bundles are used sparingly in legal genres except for academic journals. In this genre, transition bundles account for over one-fifth of all text-oriented:

(72) The NAFTA also contains many additional environmental provisions, namely Articles 1114(1) and 1114(2) of Chapter 11 and Article 1709 of Chapter 17.(19) Article 1114(1) permits Parties to adopt standards they believe will foster actions perceptive to environmental concerns. **On the other hand,** Article 1114(2) encourages Parties to remain steadfast in upholding their environmental regulations designed to attract or retain investment.

Interestingly, one bundle *in addition to the* is quite often (72 instances) employed in statutory provisions:

(73) Whoever, during and in relation to a crime of violence or drug trafficking crime (including a crime of violence or drug trafficking crime which provides an enhanced punishment if committed by the use of a deadly or dangerous weapon or device) for which the person may be prosecuted in a court of the United States--

`(i) discharges, uses or carries, or otherwise possesses a firearm shall, **in addition to the** penalties already provided for such crime of violence or drug trafficking crime, be sentenced to imprisonment for a term from five to ten years; [legislation]

(74) **In addition to the** remedies provided for in paragraph (1) (relating to the failure to provide contract benefits in accordance with the plan), a civil assessment, in an amount not to exceed $5,000,000, payable to the claimant may be awarded in any action under such paragraph if the claimant establishes by clear and convincing evidence that the alleged conduct carried out by the defendant demonstrated bad faith and flagrant disregard for the rights of the participant or beneficiary under the plan and was a proximate cause of the personal injury or death that is the subject of the claim. [legislation]

However, as Table 4.6 shows, except for academic journals, transition bundles form a relatively infrequent and insignificant group.

4.5.3. Stance bundles

Stance is defined as the expression of emotions, attitudes, value judgments and assessments (Biber et al., 1999). Stance bundles are understood in this analysis as expressions which provide a frame for the interpretation of the following proposition (cf Biber, 2006: 139). They convey two main types of meaning. First, *epistemic* stance bundles are used to signal writer comments on the knowledge status of the information contained in the following proposition. Such status can be expressed as certain, uncertain, probable, possible, etc. In the present analysis, epistemic stance bundles are used primarily to indicate a source of knowledge or mark the perspective from which information is given, as illustrated in excerpts (75), (76) and (77) sampled from legislation, opinions, and textbooks, respectively:

(75) The value of the Federal land and non-Federal land shall be determined by appraisals prepared **in accordance with the** Uniform Appraisal Standards for Federal Land Acquisitions and the Uniform Standards of Professional Appraisal Practice.[legislation]

(76) In line with these firm commitments, **the Court held that** the agreement and the executive order implementing it validly "suspended" litigation in United States courts against Iranian interests. See id., at 686-688.[opinion].

(77) However, section 9 (1) of the European Communities Act 1972 further confers protection on those persons dealing with a company in good faith in ignorance of **the fact that the** directors have exceeded their powers.[textbook]

In terms of structure, this type of stance bundles is primarily of two types. First, they consist of prepositional phrase expressions as in (75). Other bundles of this type include *in accordance with this, pursuant to the terms, pursuant to this agreement, pursuant to this section, under the laws of,* etc. They mark the perspective of legal authority by referring to different legal instruments. Their distribution is primarily confined to the operative genres of legislation and contracts. The second structural type consists of a verb phrase with *court* in the subject position as shown in (76). There are several other similar bundles such as *the court noted that, the court found that, the court explained that, the court concluded that*, which have a wider distribution than the previous category since they are found in all of the non-operative genres: opinions, briefs, textbooks, academic journals and professional articles. Finally, the above-mentioned genres tend to employ the epistemic stance bundle *the fact that the,* which seems to be common to many academic disciplines, and more specifically to textbooks (cf. Biber, 2006: 166).

Attitudinal stance bundles express speaker/writer's attitudes towards the actions or events described in the following proposition. Predictably, stance bundles in legal genres are predominantly impersonal, i.e. attribution of stance is not overt but it can be inferred. As it turns out, many bundles in this category are found in larger grammatical patterns: *it* v-link ADJ that (e.g. *it is clear that the problem...*) and *it* v-link ADJ to-inf (e.g. *it is important to compare...*). Goźdź-Roszkowski (2007) demonstrates how "*it* v-link ADJ that" patterns tend to be associated with the expression of validity and evaluation in judicial opinions. These findings have been now confirmed and extended to include other legal genres. Consequently, the first subcategory of attitudinal stance bundles provides writer's evaluation of the propositional content as in the following example from a textbook:

(78) In such a case, **it is clear that** the offeror cannot confront the offeree with the alternative of either refusing the offer or having contractual obligations thrust upon him by reason of his failure to reply. [textbook]

The second subcategory of attitudinal bundles is linked to the expression of "ease" or 'difficulty'. Bundles in this subcategory display the grammatical pattern of *it* v-link ADJ to-inf. Below is another sentence example from a textbook:

(79) In principle, **it is difficult to** see how this should ever be so, for there will have been no communication of the acceptance to the offeror.

In Goźdź-Roszkowski (2007: 160), it was noted that the emergence of a larger phraseological pattern can be observed in the pattern ***it is DIFFICULT/EASY to***, which in over 60% of all cases is followed by either *see* or *understand*:

(80) So **it is easy to understand** that Congress chose different meanings at different places in the ADEA, as the different settings readily show. [opinions]

The third subcategory of attitudinal stance bundles expresses obligations or directives. As in the subcategory above, bundles here follow the pattern of *it* v-link ADJ to-inf, where the adjective is usually *necessary*:

(81) Having concluded that §2a(c) applies "[u]ntil a State is redistricted in the manner provided by the law thereof after any apportionment," **it is necessary to consider** the question that the Court intentionally avoids: whether the State of Mississippi here has been "redistricted in the manner provided by the law thereof."[brief]

(82) **It is necessary to distinguish** two situations. In the first the buyer of a defective product tries to claim a reliance measure rather than a diminution in value measure.[textbook]

There are many bundles which contain *shall* and express deontic modality. In this analysis, they were grouped in the category of procedure-related bundles provided and discussed above. Table 4.7 lists many of the most common lexical bundles expressing stance broken down by genre.

Table 4.7. *Functional classification and distribution of stance bundles across legal genres*

Stance Expressions	legislation	opinion	contract	briefs	textbooks	acad. journal	pro. articles
Epistemic							
The fact that the		**		**	***	**	**
Marking the Source or Perspective							
in accordance with the	***		***		**		
as determined by the	***						
in accordance with section	***		***				
under the terms of	***						
with the requirements of	***						
the court held that		**		***		**	**
see united states v.		**					
by the terms of			**				
pursuant to the terms			**				
under the laws of			***				
pursuant to this agreement			***				
subject to the provisions			**				
subject to the terms			***				
under the securities act			***				
the court found that				**		**	**
the court concluded that				**			**

the court explained that	**			
the court noted that	**			**
court of appeal held	**	**		
the trial court granted				**
Attitudinal/evaluative				
Impersonal				
it is clear that		**		
Ease/difficulty				
Impersonal				
it is possible to		**		
it is difficult to		**		
Obligation/directive				
Impersonal				
it is necessary to		**		

Key to symbols:
'**' 44-99 per million words
'***' over 100 per million words

As can be seen, the biggest category of stance lexical bundles is used to mark the source or perspective of a proposition. Several interesting findings emerge from this comparison. First, bundles consisting of a prepositional phrase are almost exclusively found in legislation and contracts. Only *in accordance with the* is found with considerable frequency (44-99 per million words) in textbooks. The distribution of most of these bundles is restricted to contracts. Bundles such as *by the terms of, pursuant to the terms, under the laws of, pursuant to this agreement, subject to the provisions, subject to the terms* and *under the securities act* are extremely frequent in contracts and they are not found in the other genres. Briefs and professional articles share several bundles which signal the viewpoint adopted by a court. Surprisingly, most of these bundles are not found in opinions. *The court held that* is the only exception probably because of the special status of this expression. The verb *hold* signals a judicial decision and the presence of a corresponding legal principle drawn from it (the so-called *holding*). In the case of the other expressions (*the court found that* - also used in academic articles, *the court concluded that, the court explained that, the court noted that*), they are frequently used as a kind of metalanguage to analyse, clarify and comment on what judges established in their respective opinions.

Other categories of stance bundles contain relatively few expressions. *The fact that the* is a widely-occurring bundle found in all genres except for legislation and contracts to express epistemic stance. Finally, attitudinal/evaluative stance bundles are found only in textbooks. Bundles such as *it is clear that, it is possible to, it is difficult to* or *it is necessary to* are clearly not unique to legal discourse and their occurrence in legal textbooks is motivated by the conventions and constraints of academic discourse.

4.6. Conclusions

The findings reported in this study show considerable variations in the frequency of forms, structures and functions of lexical bundles across different types of legal writing. The analysis has revealed that legal genres make use of such iterative forms in varying degrees. It corroborates and explains the presence of a fundamental distinction between operative genres, such as legislation and contracts and other expository and persuasive genres. The differences are found in both quantitative and qualitative terms. Quantitatively, lexical bundles account for one-tenth of the total number of words in legislation and contracts. To date, no other genre or text type has been found to contain such a large proportion of formulaic expressions. The other legal genres, especially, opinions and academic journals use a markedly lower number of lexical bundles. It appears that the four genres are placed at two opposite ends of a cline, with legislation and contracts being most formulaic, while opinions and academic journals are the least constrained in that respect. Moreover, the operative genres display different patterns of using lexical bundles. The largest proportion of their bundles is used to refer to the universe of law, while relatively few bundles mark stance and textual relations. The figures for opinions and academic journals show a clear growth trend in bundles expressing stance and textual relations. At the same time, the proportion of referential bundles is the lowest of all the legal genres.

The analysis of the three major functional categories led to the emergence of other discernible trends. For example, in terms of bundles signalling legal reference, contracts and legislation are clearly marked by the largest proportion of procedure-related bundles and time bundles. On the other hand, they have very few location bundles. This trend is reversed in the case of expository genres, such as opinions and academic journals. In quantitative terms, text-oriented bundles are less prominent, however, structuring bundles are only found in these two genres. They reflect their shared function of organizing different textual segments.

Other interesting patterns can be observed. A widespread occurrence of participative bundles in contracts and textbooks suggests a significant role played by domain-specific subject matter. Precise delineation of parties' rights and obligations reflects the principle of reciprocity underlying contract law and company law. The same motivation seems to exist behind the strong presence of condition bundles in contracts, textbooks and professional articles.

The findings provided above suggest a considerable degree of genre specificity in terms of how bundles are distributed and used.

Table 4.8. *Percentage of bundles shared by at least two genres*

Genre	%
legislation	21
opinions	56
contracts	16.5
briefs	45.5
textbooks	20
academic journals	82
professional article	41

Table 4.8 shows the percentage of bundles shared by at least two genres revealing important differences between the genres. Over 80% of all bundles identified for academic journals can be found in at least another genre. At the opposite end, over 80% of bundles in contracts are found exclusively in this genre. The same trend is found in legislation and textbooks, where almost 80% of their bundles are specific to these respective genres. The other three genres, opinions, briefs and professional articles are "intermediate" with roughly 50% of shared bundles.

Word combinations in legal language can be also viewed in terms of the degree of influence exerted by the legal system on the writer's choice of words. Many word combinations in legal texts are prefabricated and prescribed directly or indirectly by law, others may be recommended for reasons of unambiguity. Variability within word combinations may result in affecting intended legal effects. Viewed from this perspective, the operative genres of legislation and contracts are most directly influenced by the non-linguistic world of law. Other expository and persuasive genres seem to be allowed more latitude visible in the more idiosyncratic modes of expression (e.g. in opinions written by judges or briefs prepared by legal counsel).

CHAPTER V: MULTI-DIMENSIONAL VARIATION ACROSS DIFFERENT GENRES AND DISCIPLINES

5.1. Introduction

The two preceding chapters have focused on salient word forms and multi-word expressions and their functions in legal genres. These descriptions show many differences and similarities in the way legal genres use words and extended collocations. This chapter extends the linguistic perspective developed in the previous chapters by studying the co-occurrence patterns of a large set of linguistic features across the legal genres. This analytical approach known as Multi-Dimensional analysis and described in Section 2.8 in Chapter 2 uses the multivariate power of statistical procedures to examine the quantitative distribution of linguistic features across individual texts as well as genres. The groupings of regularly co-occurring linguistic features are then studied qualitatively and interpreted in order to determine their most widely shared functions. The co-occurrence patterns are referred to as 'dimensions' along which legal genres can be compared. This is a macroscopic, exploratory approach because a wide spectrum of linguistic features is examined by means of exploratory factor analysis. The features represent many different grammatical categories and discourse functions. One of the major findings in Biber 1988 is that discourse functions are not autonomous. Rather, they form a "series of interlocking form\function sets that can only be fully understood by considering their relation to the whole range of varying linguistic features" (Biber, 2001: 216).

There are many advantages in the application of the Multi-Dimensional Analysis to study legal genres. For one, using the 1988 Model of Variation (introduced in Section 2.8, Chapter 2) enables one to adopt a much wider perspective on the overall patterns of genre variation in legal texts by comparing legal genres with other specialist and non-specialist genres in English. Second, conducting a new full MD analysis results in identifying the co-occurrence patterns that are directly relevant and specific to the discourse domain of law. Particular legal genres can then be compared with respect to new dimensions.

This chapter starts with the former type of analysis, i.e. studying variation in the specialized domain of law as set against the backdrop of previously identified dimensions and other written English genres and registers.

5.2 Variation among disciplines and genres[28]

In one of the first MD studies of variation in disciplinary texts, Conrad notes the scarcity of studies that would provide descriptions of texts within a particular discipline relative to texts from other disciplines, genres or registers (2001: 95). As a result, it is often difficult to determine whether the linguistic features found in a particular genre or register are unique or they are shared by other genres or registers. In addition, the 1988 Model of Variation computed for a wide variety of different genres in English provides a useful reference point for studying narrow and highly specialised legal genres. For example, if legal language is characterised as highly informational and abstract, then, apart from finding out whether such generalization holds true for at least most legal genres, it would be interesting to see how legal genres compare in this respect with other varieties of English. The remainder of this chapter attempts to find answers to such questions.

The analysis reported in this section is based on an explicit comparison of mean scores computed for the seven legal genres as well as for several other genres outside the domain of law. These include four specialist and disciplinary genres (textbooks and journals articles in biology and history) and five non-specialist genres (conversation, general fiction, popular non-fiction, official documents and academic prose). The mean scores and usage examples for history and biology genres were taken from Conrad (2001) and they are used for descriptions of Dimension 1 and 2. The data regarding five non-specialist genres comes from Biber (1988) and it is used throughout.

5.2.1. Dimension 1: Involved versus Informational Production

Before discussing the findings, a note on the terminology used in the MD analysis. The use of the label *informational production* results from the interpretation of particular sets of co-occurring linguistic features, which are believed to serve largely similar communicative functions. On Factor 1, the features with negative loadings are relatively few: *nouns, long words, prepositions, type/token ration, attributive adjectives*, and to a lesser extent (since they are found with larger loadings on other factors), *agentless passives, place adverbials* and *past participle postnominal clauses*). Such features have been regarded as indicative of "an informational focus and a careful integration of information in a text" (Conrad and Biber, 2001: 24). These features are found in texts which aim to convey information, primarily in a specialized context, with a carefully selected lexis in order to package the information economically to avoid

28 Some findings reported in this section (related to Dimension 1 and 2) are published as a preliminary study in Goźdź-Roszkowski 2008.

redundancy. Biber and Conrad refer to technical academic prose as one example of written expository prose characterized by its reliance on dense integration of information. Thus, the term *informational* is used in a narrow, restricted way, as a convenient label created for the purpose of a specific methodology, without the broad implications that this word could otherwise carry. In a similar vein, *involved* reflects the presence of features with positive loadings related to essentially interactive or affective purpose and on-line production circumstances. These features include 1st and 2nd person pronouns, *wh*-questions, emphatics, amplifiers, and sentence relatives. In sum, Factor 1 represents a dimension indicating affective, interactional content as opposed to high informational density and precise informational content.

Involved		
35		*Conversation*
╫		
10		
‖		
5		
‖		
0		
‖		*General fiction*
5		
‖		
10		*Popular non-fiction*
‖	**Law textbooks** (-10.7)	
‖		
15	**Opinions** (-15.4)	*Academic prose*
‖	**Professional articles** (-16.1)	
‖	**Academic journals** (-17.5)	
‖	**Briefs** (-18.0)	Ecology textbooks; *Official documents*
20	**Contracts** (-19.2)	History textbooks
‖		History Research articles
‖	**Legislation** (-23.9)	Ecology Research articles
25		
‖		
‖		
30		
Informational		

Figure 5.1. *Comparison of factor scores for Dimension 1*

Figure 5.1 plots the mean scores for the seven categories of legal texts along Dimension 1 marked in bold. There are also mean scores for four other disciplinary texts (ecology and history textbooks and ecology and history research articles), and for five genre categories (conversation, general fiction, popular non-fiction, academic prose and official documents) sampled from general English and italicised.

The scores on this dimension reveal some interesting findings. First, although all the legal genres are overall marked for a distinct presence of linguistic features associated with informational production, they should hardly be treated as a homogenous group. Their scattered scores are evident of considerable differences existing within the legal discourse. Statistically, this is demonstrated through the results of the Duncan's Test (Table 5.1) which measures whether the differences between the mean scores of individual genres are significantly different. Legislation can be found at one end with the largest negative mean score exceeding even the category of official documents, which is the most informational in the 1988 study (Biber, 1988: 128). At the other end are the textbooks with a score not dissimilar from that recorded for popular non-fiction, and clearly less informational than the academic genres and academic prose. In between, there are genres sharing similar scores (opinions and professional articles; professional articles and academic journals).

Table 5.1. *The results of the Duncan's Test for Factor 1 (different letters mean that the scores are significantly different)*

	Mean	**N**	**Genre**
A	-10.7461	101	Textbooks
B	-15.4168	114	Opinions
B	-16.1892	100	Professional Articles
C	-17.5870	71	Academic journals
C	-18.0702	63	Briefs
D	-19.2582	177	Contracts
E	-23.9590	60	Legislation

Second, there seem to be certain similarities between legal, history and biology texts. Admittedly, as Figure 5.1 shows, all the disciplinary texts along with the category of official documents have large negative scores on this dimension. This finding is scarcely surprising as virtually all of these textual categories are functionally associated, to a greater or lesser extent, with imparting information. Large negative scores simply mean that these texts have a high frequency of features usually associated with informational production (nouns, nominalization, prepositions, long words, attributive adjectives, etc.). However, the degree to which these texts are informational may vary considerably. Interestingly, there are important differences between law, ecology and history in terms of a genre category. History and ecology textbooks have much larger negative mean scores than their legal counterpart, which is reflected in the greater density of 'informational' features found there. In order to verify this claim, we now turn to examine a text sample from a legal textbook (as an example of a specialized text with the lowest negative mean score on Dimension 1), an excerpt from a popular nonfiction text, which displays roughly the same level of informational production and finally, and an excerpt from a history textbook.

Text Sample 1: Law Textbook (nouns are underlined, attributive adjectives italicized, prepositions capitalized)

> A person who signs a document which contains *contractual* terms is normally bound BY them though he has not read them, and even though he is ignorant of their *precise legal* effect. But if the document is not signed, being merely delivered TO him, then the question arises whether the terms OF the contract were adequately brought TO his notice.

This sample does not have many features associated with informational production. Although, information is conveyed, there is a relatively low density of nouns, prepositions and adjectives. The use of relative clauses contributes to the explanatory and descriptive effect of this passage. In terms of specialized lexis, there is only one terminological phrase 'contractual terms' which potentially could be difficult to grasp for the uninitiated. However, note the use of a synonymous phrase 'terms of the contract' in the next sentence, which in this context serves as a paraphrase. The following short passage from popular nonfiction seems to have a lot in common with the legal text.

Text Sample 2: Popular nonfiction (from the LOB corpus) based on Conrad 2001: 99.

> The self-teacher would seem to be a contradiction. But the contradiction is more apparent than real. It rests ON the *mistaken* notion that the teacher has something which he is passing on TO the learner. This is only superficially true. The learner is not a passive recipient.

Both excerpts have relatively few different referents and their identification is not very concise and perhaps less specific than what we will notice in other specialised texts below. For example, both passages rely on the pronoun *he* (the popular nonfiction text also has *it*). Both use relative clauses and constructions with predicative adjectives such as *ignorant, apparent* and *true,* which contribute to a lengthier description. Perhaps the major difference is the frequent use of passive constructions in the legal textbook. In that respect, the legal text is more informational than the popular nonfiction. By contrast, the following text from a history textbook is much denser in terms of informational features:

Text Sample 3: History Textbook (from Conrad, 2001: 98)

> Disappointment OVER failure to achieve a *satisfactory* peace settlement to World War I was exacerbated BY the Bolshevik Revolution OF November 1917, which had resulted IN the withdrawal OF Russia FROM the war, followed BY the confiscation OF *private* property and repudiation OF *international* debts. …

A large negative score (-20) of history textbooks is reflected in the high density of features related to an informational focus. Three such features seem particularly conspicuous: nouns, prepositions and attributive adjectives. Their function is to package information in the most economical way. In addition, as Conrad points out (2001: 98) nouns are the principal way employed by writers to refer to concepts or entities and their frequent occurrence is evident of a high density of information. Also, the use of attributive adjectives rather than clauses helps to modify nouns in a more compact manner. In terms of text type and discipline, there is a clear difference between legal textbooks and history textbooks. Even though they are both more informational in focus than most other non-specialist text types or registers in English, when compared with each other, there are significant differences between the two academic texts in terms of the density of 'informational' features. This is reflected on Dimension 1, where history textbooks have a significantly larger negative score than law textbooks.

Interestingly, Figure 5.1 shows that history textbook has its mean score at roughly the same level as contracts. Thus these two, in many ways disparate genres, contain a large proportion of linguistic features usually attributed to legalese.

Text Sample 4: Contract (Agreement of Limited Partnership)

> IN connection WITH the issuance OF Partnership Units to *certain Additional Limited* Partners, the Partnership has entered into *separate* agreements that set forth *additional* rights and obligations OF such *Additional Limited* Partners and *additional* terms and conditions of such *Additional Limited* Partner's Partnership Interests.

Linguistic features, such as excessive nominalization, avoiding pronouns, impersonal constructions, prepositional phrases etc. are linked to the abstruse and opaque quality of certain types of legal writing (cf. Tiersma 1999). What this similarity seems to suggest is that such linguistic features are not unique to legal texts. Instead, they are surface features more generally associated with increased linguistic complexity (cf. Biber, 2001: 219).

Both ecology and history texts are significantly more informational than law textbooks and journal articles. However, the difference between mean scores computed for legal journal articles and ecology research articles is considerably smaller than between law textbooks and history textbooks (see Figure 5.1 above).

Text Sample 5: (Legal Academic Article)

> The pressure ON the governor to be the "fail safe" increases when the courts limit their intervention IN capital cases THROUGH procedural barriers. Low reversal rates result IN more death penalty cases reaching the governor's desk. The Liebman et al. study indicated that Missouri death penalty cases have reversal rates OF at most 20%; a figure significantly lower than the national rates OF 40-47 %.

This sample deals with the role of a state governor in the context of death penalty. The role becomes especially important in the case when appeal courts do not tend to reverse death penalty sentences. Interestingly, this role is described by a phrase "fail safe" in inverted commas which suggests that this expression is not normally used in legal language. It is not a legal term. Overall, it seems that the vocabulary is not very technical. Even certain phrases such as "capital cases" or "reversal rates" are not totally obscure even to people ignorant of law. Even if unfamiliar at first, their meaning can be arrived at by studying the context, as is the case with "capital cases", which are somehow clarified in the text by the two references to "death penalty cases". By contrast, Text Sample 6 focuses on a specific biological phenomenon (root growth) described by means of a very technical vocabulary:

Text Sample 6: (Ecology Research Article)

> There were *marked* differences IN root growth INTO regrowth cores AMONG the three communities, both IN the distribution OF roots THROUGH the cores and IN the response TO *elevated* CO_2. IN the Scirpus community, root growth was evenly distributed THROUGHOUT the 15-cm profile, with no *significant* differences IN root biomass AMONG the 5-cm sampling intervals WITHIN a treatment.

Also, the sentences are longer than in the ecology article. In terms of the features associated with informational concerns, the highly specialist information is tightly packaged by means of numerous prepositional phrases. Irrespective of discipline, on Dimension 1, articles have larger negative scores than textbooks. Put differently, academic journals tend to be more informational than textbooks. In explaining this perceived similarity within the genre of articles, it seems useful to bear in mind its intended audiences, their background knowledge and level of expertise in the respective disciplines. The basic goal of textbooks is to provide the reader with a well-structured, carefully explained knowledge. Although this could vary, generally, textbooks are intended for readers who do not yet have specialist knowledge. So, textbooks need to facilitate the process of knowledge acquisition by addressing more general topics and providing ample exemplification. This is clearly seen above, particularly in the more descriptive, less densely packed excerpt from a law textbook (Text Sample 1). By contrast, academic journals have a different function than textbooks. They are the prime vehicles for contributing new ideas, new knowledge to the discipline. Their subject matter is usually highly specialist, technical, intended for experts in the field. As a result, journal articles use more linguistic features associated with an informational focus, which is reflected in their higher scores on this dimension.

5.2.2. Dimension 2: Narrative vs. Non-narrative Discourse

Dimension 2 was interpreted as Narrative vs. Non-narrative Discourse due to the occurrence of features (with positive weights) related to past time narration (cf. Biber 1988). These features include past tense verbs, third-person pronouns, perfect aspect verbs, public verbs, synthetic negation and present participial clauses. Since there are no negative features, this dimension represents a continuum between a strong presence of such features at one end and their absence at the other.

Narrative

6 *General fiction*
ǂ
1
‖
‖
0 *Popular non-fiction*
‖ History textbook, *Conversation*
‖ History research articles
‖
-1
‖
‖
‖ **Law Textbooks (-1.8)**
-2
‖

||	**Opinions (-2.4)**	
||	**Briefs (-2.7)**	*Academic prose*
||	**Professional articles (-2.8)**	
-3	**Academic journals (-3.1)**	
||		
||		**Ecology Research Articles**
||		**Ecology Textbooks**
-4	**Contracts (-4.2)**	
||		
||		*Official documents* **(-4.3)**
||		
-5	**Legislation (-4.9)**	
||		
||		
Non-narrative		

Figure 5.2. *Comparison of factor scores for Dimension 2*

Figure 5.2. displays mean scores for the texts along Dimension 2 interpreted as *Narrative versus Non-narrative Discourse*. First, all the legal texts have negative scores, which means that overall they do not contain many features associated with the narrative mode. However, there appears to be considerable variation among legal genres. Textbooks are relatively the most narrative of all with only two standard deviations below the overall mean. At the opposite end are legislation and contracts as two categories of legal texts with the lowest concentration of narrative features. However, as the Duncan's test shows below (Table 5.2.), the mean scores for contracts and legislation are significantly different. Worth noting is that legislation has the largest negative score ever documented in MD studies for English registers (cf. Biber, 1988: 136).

Table 5.2. *The results of the Duncan's Test on Dimension 2*

	Mean	N	genre
A	- 1.8679	101	Textbooks
B	- 2.4773	114	Opinions
C	- 2.7790	63	Briefs
C	- 2.8639	100	Professional articles
D	- 3.1280	71	Academic journals
E	- 4.2227	177	Contracts
F	- 4.9410	60	Legislation

The subject matter has a role to play in the frequencies of narrative features. As Conrad documents in her study (2001: 103) and as shown in Figure 5.2, there is a clear distinction between the frequencies of history texts, where both textbooks and articles appear to have roughly the same concentration of narrative features as popular non-fiction or conversation, and ecology texts which are clearly towards the non-narrative end on Dimension 2 at the level close to that of contracts. There is a fairly straightforward explanation for this observation. After all, history is about narrating past events and referring to people. Conrad (2001: 104) compares a passage from a history research article to fiction because considerable parts of history texts entail telling a story, recounting of an event. A legal textbook seems to bear a striking resemblance in that respect as we can see in the following text sample:

Text Sample 6: Legal textbook (past tense forms underlined, third person pronouns capitalized, perfect aspect italicized, non-past tense verb capitalized and underlined)

> A counter-offer CANNOT constitute an acceptance of an offer; it AMOUNTS to a rejection of the offer, and so OPERATES to bring it to an end. In Hyde v. Wrench,for example:
> A offered to sell a farm to B for $1,000. B said that HE would give $950. A refused, and B then said he would give $1,000, and, when A declined to adhere to HIS original offer, tried to obtain specific performance of the alleged contract.
> The Court, however, held that an offer to buy at $950 in response to an offer to sell for $1,000 was a refusal followed by a counter-offer, and that no contract *had come* into existence. But an inquiry as to whether the offeror will modify his terms DOES NOT necessarily AMOUNT to a counter-offer. So in Stevenson, Jacques and Co. v. McLean, the offeree could still accept an offer of a certain quantity of iron 'at 40s. nett cash per ton', even though HE *had telegraphed* to the offeror requesting information as to possible terms of credit. It was held that this was not a counter-offer, but was a mere inquiry, which should *have been answered* and not treated as a rejection of the offer.'

In this passage from a legal textbook about rejection and counter-offer, the narrative mode is first used to describe what is in fact a landmark case (*Hyde v. Wrench* 1840 3 Beav 334) by providing a very succinct summary of events leading to the claim with the names of the litigants reduced to single letters. This is then followed by an account of the court's ruling providing the rationale behind the court's decision. Narrative is not the only mode employed in this passage. Worth noting is the first paragraph where a legal rule is formulated in the present tense. The third paragraph of this passage also contains a present tense verb form expressing another legal rule (*But an inquiry as to ....does not....amount to...*).

This is then again followed by a reference to another important case *Stevenson, Jacques and Co. v. McLean* rounded off with a judicial decision. It might be tentatively suggested that there is a discoursal pattern whereby legal rules formulated in present tense forms are stated in a definite succinct manner and such formulations are immediately followed by more elaborate and explanatory passages. Explanation is provided by narrating the details of a past judicial precedent. Linguistically, this pattern is realized by a discontinuous use of the narrative mode. Even though law and history textbooks seem to have a lot in common (i.e. frequent reference to human agents and specific events in the past), history textbooks seem to contain longer, more consistently narrative passages (Conrad, 2001: 105). They also tend to employ more narrative features, e.g. third person pronouns:

Text Sample 7: History textbook (from Conrad 2001: 105)

> The assembly's behavior only furthered angered the officers, and some of THEM decided to demonstrate THEIR resolve. On May 6 the brigade received orders to join John Sullivan's expedition against the Six Nations. That same day, officers in the First Regiment sent forth yet another petition. THEY again admonished the assembly about pay and supply issues. While THEY stated that THEY would prepare the regiment …

Conspicuous narrative concerns are also found in opinions. As may be recalled from Chapter 3, Section 3.4.6, the structure of a typical opinion given by the US Supreme Court includes a section devoted to the procedural history, i.e. the facts of the case and how lower-instance courts dealt with this case before it reached the appeal. Text Sample 8 illustrates how the frequent use of past tense forms used to summarize the procedural history of this case contributes to the overall narrative effect.

Text Sample 8: Opinion (USSC24-2004)

The petitioners, mothers of children eligible for EPSDT services in Texas, sought injunctive relief against state agencies and various state officials, claiming that the Texas program did not meet federal requirements. The claims against the state agencies were dismissed on Eleventh Amendment grounds, but the state officials remained in the suit and entered into a consent decree approved by the Federal District Court. In contrast with the federal statute's brief and general mandate, the decree required state officials to implement many specific proposals.

Finally, we now turn to consider an excerpt from a legal journal article. Figure 5.2. shows that, statistically, this type of legal texts has significantly fewer narrative features than law textbooks but at the same time, the narrative mode is stronger than in both ecology textbooks and research articles.

Text Sample 9A: Legal Journal Article

> On October 16, 1998, General Augusto Pinochet was arrested in London, England on charges contained in a Spanish provisional arrest warrant alleging that he was responsible for the murder of Spanish citizens in Chile while he was the ruler of that country.(1) A second provisional warrant was issued on October 22, 1998(2) and both were quashed by the Queen's Bench Divisional Court on October 28, 1998.(3) Next, on November 25, 1998, an appellate committee from the House of Lords issued an opinion reversing the lower court's decision, finding that General Pinochet could not benefit from head-of-state immunity and could potentially be extradited for crimes against international law.

This passage comes from the opening paragraph in an article about the extradition proceedings against general Pinochet as a case study in the emerging international system of criminal justice. It serves as an introduction to the ensuing discussion of the theory of universal jurisdiction for certain crimes under international law where many different, albeit related, concepts are dealt with (such as *ius cogens*, international ethics, head of state immunity, human rights crimes, universal jurisdiction, and extradition) on the basis of the general Pinochet case. As the following brief passage shows, the discussion of the concept of *ius cogens* is presented without any past tense verb forms.

Text Sample 9B: Legal Journal Article

> The system of international law is a tangled mass of bilateral and multilateral agreements between States that has grown steadily over the years.(10) However, the notion of jus cogens, fundamental social and legal norms, is superior to all treaties and any other customary law.

Thus, the narrative mode is not a consistent feature in legal journal articles. It is usually employed to provide a historical backdrop or to refer to past events or cases for the sake of analyzing a legal issue or problem. Unlike, in the case of law textbooks, where as can be seen, the narrative mode is more frequent in order to facilitate the understanding of legal concepts or principles, or the opinions, where it performs the important function of recounting the relevant facts and procedural history, the narrative concerns in journal articles are weaker, more marginal. However, even the brief examples shown above should suffice to signal an underlying similarity between the three types of legal writing. This similarity lies in the key feature of the common law system, i.e. the “doctrine of binding precedent" whereby precedents created by previously decided cases are the major source of law. This doctrine is universally regarded as "one of the oldest and most fundamental features of the English legal system" (Harris, 1988: 182). It is not surprising then that it is given so much prominence in legal education and scholarly work. What seems common to the three legal genres is the narrative focus used to refer and provide details about significant legal cases. Indeed, legal knowledge as embraced by law textbooks and journal articles seems to be structured around judicial precedents, the landmark cases, which give rise to the creation and emergence of legal principles under the common law system.

5.2.3. Dimension 3: Explicit[29] vs. Situation-dependent Reference

The presence of such features as "phrasal coordination" and "nominalizations" points towards discourse that is densely integrated and informational. More importantly, however, the relative clause constructions (*wh-* relative clauses on object position, *wh-* relative clauses on subject position, and pied-piping constructions) "explicitly identify reference or provide elaboration about referents" (Conrad, 2001: 33). This set of features represents a dimension that "distinguishes highly explicit and elaborated, endophoric reference from situation-dependent, exophoric reference " (Biber, 1988: 142). Texts which have positive scores on this dimension require "highly explicit, text-internal reference" as opposed to other genres (such as for instance broadcasts and conversation permitting extensive reference to the physical and temporal situation of discourse).

11
|| **Legislation (10.4)**
10
|| **Contracts (9.6)**
9
||
8 **Textbooks (8.0)**
|| *official documents*
7
|| **Professional Articles (6.8); Briefs (6.7)**
6 **Opinions (5.9)**
||
5

29 In some studies subsequent to 1988, for example, Biber (1995), this Dimension is referred to as Elaborated vs Situation-dependent Reference)

|| *academic prose*
4
||
3 **Academic journals (2.6)** *popular fiction*
||
2
||
1
||
0
||
-1
||
-2
||
-3
|| *general fiction*
-4 *conversation*
Situation Dependant

Figure 5.3. *Comparison of factor scores for Factor 3*

As Figure 5.3 shows all legal genres plot on the positive side of the factor. Thus, they should be viewed as representing a type of discourse that is complex, structurally elaborated, abstract and largely decontextualised. They are all more or less elaborate containing more or less explicit reference. Legislation and contracts are two text genres with the highest scores, while journal articles have by far the lowest score. Most legal genres fall somewhere in between these two extremes. However, textbooks, professional articles, briefs and opinions tend to cluster towards the higher end of the "Explicit versus Situation-Dependent Reference" continuum. It appears that legal discourse does not tend to vary substantially along this dimension. The only exception is journal articles. When set beside other, non-specialist genres marked in italics in Figure 5.3, legislation and contracts turn out to be the most elaborate of all with larger mean scores than even official documents. In fact, it appears that these two legal genres stand out from the other text genres on the three factors discussed so far. They are the most informational, non-narrative and elaborate texts. Interestingly, the mean score of legal textbooks corresponds to that of official documents. It is markedly higher than the one documented in Biber (1988) for academic prose (by almost four standard deviations). Finally, it is surprising to find that journal articles in law are not more explicit/elaborate than popular fiction, and markedly less than the academic prose.

Text Sample 9: (Legislation 2 - Tax)

> `(4) QUALIFIED VETERAN- For purposes of this subsection, the term "qualified veteran" means--
> `(A) in the case of the States of Alaska, Oregon, and Wisconsin, any veteran--
> `(i) **who** served on active duty, and
> `(ii) **who** applied for the financing before the date 25 years after the last date on which such veteran left active service, and
> `(B) in the case of any other State, any veteran--
> `(i) **who** served on active duty at some time before January 1, 1977, and
> `(ii) **who** applied for the financing before the later of--
> `(I) the date 30 years after the last date on **which** such veteran left active service, or
> `(II) January 31, 1985.'.

This text illustrates an unusually frequent use of *wh-* relatives on subject position. It shows how the *wh-* relatives are used to elaborate on the concept of "qualified veteran". The relative clauses are used to define the eligibility of potential applicants seeking to be granted the status of "qualified veteran". The structure of this excerpt in terms of its layout is typical for legislative provisions. Lines marked with (i) and (ii) begin with *who* and explicate the meaning of the term "qualified veteran". This excerpt shows that *wh-* relatives on subject positions are used heavily in the so-called legal definitions. Legislative provisions appear to be firmly anchored in time, especially, when this is connected with meeting certain specific requirements.

Text Sample 10A: (Legislation - Bankruptcy)

> (a) DEVELOPMENT OF FINANCIAL MANAGEMENT AND TRAINING CURRICULUM AND MATERIALS- The Director of the Executive Office for United States Trustees (in this section referred to as the `Director') shall consult with a wide range of individuals **who** are experts in the field of debtor education, including trustees **who** serve in cases under chapter 13 of title 11, United States Code, and **who** operate financial MANAGEMENT EDUCATION programs for debtors, and shall develop a financial MANAGEMENT training curriculum and materials that can be used to educate debtors **who** are individuals on how to better manage their finances.

This excerpt shows the unusually frequent use of *wh*-relatives combined with nominalizations (in the top capitalized line). It is interesting to note the consistent use of the relativizer *who* to elaborate on a range of persons addressed in this legislative provision (e.g. *individuals who are experts, trustees who serve in cases under chapter 13*). A different excerpt from the same document illustrates the use of pied-piping relative clauses:

Text Sample 10B: (Legislation – Bankruptcy)

> d) NOTICE- Section 342 of title 11, United States Code, is amended by adding at the end the following:
> `(d) In a case under chapter 7 of this title **IN WHICH** the debtor is an individual and **IN WHICH** the presumption of abuse arises under section 707(b), the clerk shall give written notice to all creditors not later than 10 days after the date of the filing of the petition that the presumption of abuse has arisen.'.

By way of digression, it is interesting to compare the frequency of relativizers in this genre. Surprisingly, *wh-* relative clauses are only slightly more frequent than *that*-relatives (with mean scores of 3.9 and 3.2 per 1000 words, respectively). As can be seen in the excerpt below, *that* can also be used in definitions to elaborate on the meaning of a particular term:

Text Sample 11: (Legislation)

> `SEC. 602. DEFINITIONS.
> `Except as otherwise provided, in this title:
> `(1) ASSISTIVE TECHNOLOGY DEVICE-
> `(A) IN GENERAL- The term `assistive technology device' means any item, piece of equipment, **or** product system, whether acquired commercially off the shelf, modified, or customized,**THAT** is used to increase, maintain, **or** improve functional capabilities of a child with a disability.
> `(B) EXCEPTION- The term does not include a medical device **THAT** is surgically implanted, **or** the replacement of such device.
> `(2) ASSISTIVE TECHNOLOGY SERVICE- The term `assistive technology service' means any service **THAT** directly assists a child with a disability in the selection, acquisition, or use of an assistive technology device. Such term includes--

Relative clauses are used for nominal identification and elaboration. They pack information into noun phrases instead of expressing the information as separate, independent clauses. As far as statutory language is concerned, it seems that linguistic features with positive loadings on Dimension 3 tend to be most readily found in the definition part of this type of texts.

Contracts have been identified as the second most "elaborate" genre. Below is an example of contractual language, selected from *Agreement of Lease*:

Text Sample 12: (Agreement of Lease)

> Provided that Landlord's right of full recovery under its ***policy or policies*** aforesaid is not adversely ***affected or prejudiced*** thereby, Landlord hereby waives ***any and all*** right of recovery **WHICH** it might otherwise have against *Tenant, its servants, agents and employees*, for ***loss or damage*** occurring to the ***Building and the fixtures***, ***appurtenances and equipment*** therein, to the extent the same is covered by Landlord's insurance, notwithstanding that such ***loss or damage*** may result from the ***negligence or fault*** of *Tenant, its servants, agents or employees*. Provided that Tenant's right of full recovery under its aforesaid ***policy or policies*** is not adversely ***affected or prejudiced*** thereby, Tenant hereby waives ***any and all*** right of full recovery **WHICH** it might otherwise have against Landlord, *its servants, agents and employees*, and against every other tenant in the Building **WHO** shall have executed a similar waiver as set forth in this Section 9.08(c) for ***loss or damage*** to, *Tenant's furniture, furnishings, fixtures and other property*
> removable by Tenant under the provisions hereof to the extent that the same is covered by Tenant's insurance, notwithstanding that such ***loss or damage*** may result from the ***negligence or fault*** of Landlord, its servants, ***agents or employees, or such other tenant and the servants, agents or employees*** thereof.

An example of a contractual clause taken from *Agreement of Lease*, shows, apart from the three *wh*-relative clauses (capitalized), a heavy concentration of phrasal coordination (in bold and italicized). There are usually noun phrases that are coordinated by either "and" or "or". Their use is highly repetitive, e.g.: *loss or damage, policy or policies, negligence or fault.* Note also, the presence of the coordinated verb phrases *affected or prejudiced.* This type of linking phrases is considered a typical feature of certain legal text genres. As Tiersma notes, such conjoined phrases have a long history and date from the "early Germanic times" (1999: 61). According to Gustafsson (1984), such binomial expressions are used five times as often in legal writing as in other prose styles. While, these statistics could vary depending on a particular text genre, binomial expressions appear to be characteristic of legal operative documents in general. It can be also safely assumed that legal drafters tend to employ a certain number of such expressions over and over again, as it is evident even in the above excerpt. Repetition can be seen in reproducing parallel structures, virtually identically worded, where the only variable is the party to the Agreement. The conditional clause *Provided that Landlord's right of full recovery under its* ***policy or policies*** *aforesaid is not adversely* ***affected or prejudiced*** *thereby,* is repeated at the beginning of the next sentence and *Landlord* is replaced by *Tenant,* but otherwise the clause is phrased in exactly the same way. The repetition of lexis and structure is continued in the next clause. The use of parallel structures reflects the symmetry of the legal relationship between the two parties to the agreement.

Noteworthy is also the frequent use of lists of words, usually nouns, as is illustrated by the following examples from this excerpt: *Tenant, its servants, agents and employees, Tenant's furniture, furnishings, fixtures and other property.* The use of such "word lists" is again commonly found in most operative documents since they are employed by legal drafters in order to anticipate and deal with "every possible future contingency" (Tiersma, 1999: 63). This consideration often encourages lawyers to come up with increasingly long lists of semantically related words in order to allow for ever more remote possibilities. The relative clauses introduced by *which* in both cases elaborate on the legal term *right of (full) recovery,* by specifying the possibility of having recourse to such entitlement, the category of persons affected by its exercise, and finally stating the reasons for claiming this right (loss or damage to the property). Interestingly, in the second sentence, the *which* clause is followed by another relative clause introduced by *who.* This clause elaborates on the somewhat general referent *every other Tenant [in the building]* by placing him or her in the same category of a legal act, i.e. waiving a right by tenants who give up their right to recover compensation for "any loss or damage" to their property.

The next two excerpts illustrate features linked to explicit/elaborated discourse featuring high in the legal definitions. Just as in the statutory language of legislation, nominalization, phrasal coordination, and *wh*-relative clauses are found in legal definitions placed in contractual provision:

Text Sample 13: (Agreement of Lease)

> The term "Taxes" shall <u>mean</u> all real estate taxes, assessments, governmental levies, business improvement district charges **and** assessments, municipal taxes, county taxes **or** any other governmental charges, general or special, ordinary **or** extraordinary, unforeseen as well as foreseen, of any kind **or** nature whatsoever, **WHICH** are **or** may be assessed, levied **or** imposed upon all **or** any part of the Land, the Building and the sidewalks, plazas **or** streets in front of **or** adjacent thereto, <u>including</u> any tax, excise **or** fee measured by **or** payable with respect to any rent, and levied against Landlord **and/or** the Land **and/or** Building, under the laws of the United States, the State of New York, **or** any political subdivision thereof.

Text Sample 14: (Asset Purchase Agreement)

> (l) "TAXES" <u>means</u> all taxes, however denominated, including any interest, penalties or other additions to tax that may become payable in respect thereof, (i) imposed by any federal, territorial, state, local **or** foreign government or any agency **or** political subdivision of any such government, for **WHICH** Buyer could become liable as successor to **or** transferee of the Business **or** the Purchased Assets **or** **WHICH** could become a charge against **or** lien on any of the Purchased Assets,

> **WHICH** taxes shall <u>include</u>, without limiting the generality of the foregoing, all sales **and** use taxes, ad valorem taxes, excise taxes, business license taxes, occupation taxes, **real and personal** property taxes, stamp taxes, environmental taxes, real property gains taxes, transfer taxes, payroll and employee withholding taxes, unemployment insurance contributions, social security taxes, and other governmental charges, and other obligations of the same or of a similar nature to any of the foregoing, **WHICH** are required to be paid, withheld or collected, or (ii) any liability for amounts referred to in (i) as a result of any obligations to indemnify another Person.

Text Samples 13 and 14 come from two sections in two different contracts which deal with definitions. Contracts contain a lot of specific definitions which are the fundamental way of determining the precise meaning of a lexical unit As Alcaraz and Hughes (2002: 30-31) observe, "many legal texts, such as statutes, contracts, deeds and warranties commonly contain clauses, appendices, riders (additional clauses) or schedules (annexes) that provide definitions of the main terms involved or representative lists of the principle items caught by the agreement". There is a classic distinction between "intension" and "extension". The former may be roughly defined as the class of objects to which a sign or term refers, or "the range of a term as measured by the number of objects to which it applies" (Alcaraz and Hughes, 2002: 31). Intension is equivalent to the sum of the attributes subsumed in the concept. In the two excerpts above, there are two definitions of the term 'taxes'. These are definitions which combine both extension and intension. The relativiser *which* tends to be employed in intension definitions to specify specific attributes of the defined term. Coordination appears in definitions by extension whereby a term is defined by providing a class of objects to which this term refers. This is realized textually through lists of coordinated nouns or adjectives as in:

> The term "Taxes" shall mean all real estate taxes, assessments, governmental levies, business improvement district charges **and** assessments, municipal taxes, county taxes **or** any other governmental charges, general or special, ordinary **or** extraordinary (…).

Taxes are defined by providing a long list of various types of charges. In both statutes and contracts, elaborate discourse is predominantly (albeit not exclusively) found in sections devoted to legal definitions. This is in keeping with the essential function of this type of legal writing which involves explicit identification of referents and providing elaboration about referents. The link between the relativizers and the construction of definitions in normative texts is further corroborated after examining the relevant corpus material.

In contracts, *who* appears 782 times while *which* 5312. The top ten nouns that immediately precede *who* include:

- employee (57), person (64), employees (51), partner (36), directors (19), persons (49), participant (30), director (17), party (18), partners (14)

and make up for half of all the occurrences of *who.* If we combine the singular and plural forms and place the word forms in the order of frequency, the following rank list emerges:

- person(s) – 113; employee(s) – 108; partner(s) – 50; director(s) – 36; participant – 30; party – 18

If we look at the collocates that immediately follow *who,* then an interesting observation can be made. Two forms of the verb BE are, by far, the most frequent collocates: *is* – 140 occurrences and *are* – 108. What is interesting is the consistent use of the verb BE in the *wh*-relative clause. This might be indicative of the descriptive mode employed to provide detailed elaboration about legal terms. There seems to be a restricted set of head nouns (antecedents), i.e. persons, employees, partners, etc. are the most frequently elaborated nouns.

The text sample (15) provided below comes from a textbook and illustrates the frequent use of *wh-clauses* (*kinds of difficulty which arise..., an acceptance which is equivocal*) employed to elaborate on the concept of 'acceptance'. In addition, the text shows relatively frequent use of nominalization stressing its informational and nominal content (*acceptance, rejection, reference, addition, arrangement*). Noteworthy is also the use of coordinator 'or' to mark contrast between the different types of 'acceptance'. The text is well structured and carefully planned.

Text Sample 15: Textbook (5-001)

> The kinds of difficulty **WHICH** arise in determining whether or not an acceptance is conclusive may be said to be three. The alleged acceptance may be (a) a rejection and counter-offer; (b) an acceptance with some variation **or** addition of terms; **or** (c) an acceptance **WHICH** is equivocal, **or** **WHICH** is qualified by reference to the subsequent arrangement of terms.

These features are further illustrated by the following text taken from another textbook which deals with the concept of 'contract':

Text Sample 16: Textbook (5-002)

CONTRACTS FOR **WHICH** WRITING IS REQUIRED

We have now dealt with the contract **which** is valid by reason of its form alone, and we pass to the contract **which** depends for its validity upon the presence of consideration.

Here, the above sentence marks a transition in the discussion of various types of contracts. The title of the section uses a pied-piping construction (*contracts for which writing is required*). The *WH*-relative clauses serve the purpose of distinguishing between the two types of contracts. They carry information necessary to define either type. A very formal, nominal nature of text can be noticed in the use of *validity, presence* or *consideration.*

Finally, we provided below a slightly longer example from yet another textbook on contract law. It also presents and discusses various types of contracts.

Text Sample 17: Textbook (5-003)

Contract specifically enforceable

The contract must be one **which**, if it were properly evidenced by writing, would have been specifically enforceable. This condition arises from the history of the doctrine, **which** is wholly the creation of the Courts of Equity; and although, since the Judicature Acts, it may be administered in any Court, it still has the limitations **which** were impressed upon it by the nature of equitable jurisdiction over contracts before the amalgamation of the Courts.

In comparison with contracts, coordination in textbooks does not seem to be frequently employed. This may be due to the fact that elaboration and explicitation are no longer used to construct legal definitions or otherwise define legal persons or entities, as is usually the case with contractual provisions. As we noticed above, coordinating a number of predominantly nominal forms is very frequent in legal definitions. Also, in the above excerpt, *WH*-relative clauses greatly contribute to sentence length. The second sentence in Text Sample 17 contains 56 words, which is twice as long as the average sentence length reported by Barber (1985) and almost exactly the length documented by Gustafsson (1975) for his corpus of English legal texts (see also the discussion on sentence length in specialized discourse in Gotti (2003: 85). Unlike the other text samples, this one contains two time expressions, however, by and large, the occurrence of place and time adverbials tends to be infrequent. At the same time, it should be emphasized that law textbooks, when elaborating on legal concepts often include references to the past in order to show the concept from a historical perspective by describing its evolution. As we will see in the next chapter, this textual practice has been found to be one of the most characteristic features of this text genre.

The next two text genres with almost the same scores on Dimension 3 are professional articles and briefs (6.8 and 6.7 respectively). Professional articles are a relatively new text category without an established genre structure. Individual texts can therefore display considerable variation. In the following sample, an endophoric reference is made to the standards provided by the Financial Accounting Standards Board, a US organization that establishes financial accounting and reporting standards for the private sector:

Text Sample 18: (Professional Article)

> Under FASB guidelines, the lease term includes, among other things, any periods during **WHICH** the lessee provides or guarantees the lessor's debt or any periods in **WHICH** the lessee is subject to an economic **penalty** for **failure** to renew the **base lease** such that **renewal** of the **lease** appears reasonably assured at its **inception**

This excerpt in fact illustrates the so-called "genre nesting", where there can be several layers of genre type within a particular discourse structure. The above excerpt sampled from a professional article contains a stretch of text exhibiting features commonly associated with the text genre of legislation or contractual provisions. This occurs when an extensive reference is made to a normative act in order to provide a legal basis and a source of authority for statements made in the text. In other words, the relatively frequent occurrence of the positive features on this dimension may result from the inclusion of language characteristic of a different genre.

Text Sample 19: (Professional Article)

> Make sure the record is clear on **WHO** proposed **WHICH** special verdict form, **WHO** proposed the changes adopted, and any objections you have to the form used.

Text Sample 19 seems to be more representative of this text genre. Professional articles serve the purpose of giving advice either to potential clients or other lawyers. The relativizers help to focus on the kind of information that should be obtained and/or confirmed in the course of the proceedings. Many texts in this category are relatively short and sometimes employ "telegraphic" and direct style.

Text Sample 20: (Brief 00-507(2))

> Section 4401 of the Internal Revenue Code imposes an excise tax, in this case equal to .25% of every amount wagered, on "[e]ach person **who** is engaged in the business of accepting wagers" or "**who** conducts any wagering pool **or** lottery." 26 U.S.C. 4401(a) and (c). Section 4411 of the Code imposes an occupational tax, in this case equal to $50 per person, on "each person **who** is liable for the tax imposed under section 4401 or **who** is engaged in receiving wagers for **or** on behalf of any person so liable." 26 U.S.C. 4411(a).

The above text excerpt sampled from a brief written for the proceedings before the Supreme Court provides another illustration of features associated with the elaborate type of discourse occurring in this text genre due to the inclusion of references from a different genre of legislative provisions, this time found in the Internal Revenue Code. In much the same way as in the previous genre of professional articles, lawyers constructing their arguments refer to external legal sources.

Text Sample 21: (Brief 00-1073)

> FERPA also requires a school to make "education records" of students available to their parents for inspection and review. Thus, FERPA specifies that *"[n]o funds shall be made available under any applicable program to any educational agency or institution which has a policy of denying, or which effectively prevents, the parents of students who are or have been in attendance at a school of such agency or at such institution . . . the right to inspect and review the education records of their children.*" 20 U.S.C. 1232g(a)(1) (A); see also 20 U.S.C. 1232g(a)(1)(B) (applying inspection and review requirements to State educational agencies).

This excerpt comes from another brief, this time filed by the Solicitor General representing the United States of America as amicus curiae in support of the petitioners, the Owasso independent school district. It comes from a section of the document described as "statement" and a subsection of "statutory framework". This part of the brief serves to indicate the legal basis for any legal argumentation subsequently put forward. It shows the extent to which briefs rely on literal quotations of normative acts relevant for the case at hand. FERPA stands for the Family Educational Rights and Privacy Act, and it is of fundamental importance in light of the case brought before the Supreme Court. It is clearly the disciplinary practice of law to include direct citations from legislative acts. It seems that both professional articles and briefs contain relatively high scores of positive features on this dimension due to a large degree of "intertextuality". This textual practice is further demonstrated in the text sample below:

Text Sample 22: (Brief 00-1073)

> The term "education records" in FERPA, 20 U.S.C. 1232g(a)(4)(A), refers to materials that are preserved **or** retained by an educational agency **or** institution, **or** someone acting for such agency **or** institution, as an institutional **or** official record of a student. That term does not include student work that is created, used, **or** kept in the classroom and is not made part of a student's institutional record.

The excerpt provided above illustrates a very frequent use of coordination in a portion of text that does not constitute a citation from a normative act. The coordinated elements include verbs (*preserved or retained*), nouns (*agency or institution*), and adjectives (*institutional or official*). This text refers to and elaborates on a term previously defined by a legislative enactment. The original wording of the normative provision is provided below for comparison[30]:

> **(4)**
> **(A)** For the purposes of this section, the term "education records" means, except as may be provided otherwise in subparagraph (B), those records, files, documents, and other materials which—
> **(i)** contain information directly related to a student; and
> **(ii)** are maintained by an educational agency or institution or by a person acting for such agency or institution.

In light of the above, it is clear now that the text in Sample 22 (Brief 00-1073) employs genre nesting and depends on intertextuality to make sense for its intended audience. It seems highly characteristic for a good deal of legal writing to rely substantially on external sources. For example, in quantitative terms, this document consists of 12,077 words, while all verbatim quotations from the FERPA only, amount to almost 500 words, which is over 4% of the entire document and this does not include quotations from the petitioners statements and the holdings of lower courts which heard the case earlier. The last source seems especially prominent in briefs where a great deal of space is devoted to reporting previous judicial decisions.

Finally, we turn to opinions, which, as Figure 5.3 shows, have their mean score only marginally lower than briefs and professional articles.

30 This provision comes from Title 20, Chapter 31, Subchapter III, Part 4 § 1232g (Family, educational and privacy rights of the US Code accessed from the Cornell University Law School webpage.

Text Sample 23

> Souter, J., delivered the opinion of the Court, **in which** Rehnquist, C. J., and O'Connor, Kennedy, and Breyer, JJ., joined. Ginsburg, J., filed a dissenting opinion, **in which** Stevens, Scalia, and Thomas, JJ., joined.

Prepositions preceding relativizers appear relatively frequently in certain fixed formulas such as the one above, which is routinely placed at the end of a judicial opinion to indicate the stance taken by each judge with respect to a particular decision. They can be found there because of the highly formal and formulaic nature of such text. Interestingly, the combination of *in which* accounts for as much as 20% of all instances when *which* occurs in the judicial opinions. The unusually frequent use of preposition plus *wh*-relatives is illustrated by the following snapshot generated by the Cluster feature of the *WordSmith* 4 programme:

N	Word	With	elation	Total	otal Left	al Right	L5	L4	L3	L2	L1	Centre
1	WHICH	which	0,000	3 691	16	16	9	3	2	2	0	3 659
2	THE	which	0,000	2 833	1 409	1 424	254	303	682	170	0	0
3	OF	which	0,000	1 373	1 006	367	173	299	246	87	201	0
4	IN	which	0,000	1 334	1 047	287	82	105	87	33	740	0
5	TO	which	0,000	1 138	588	550	115	145	77	36	215	0
6	A	which	0,000	975	547	428	82	173	183	80	29	0
7	AND	which	0,000	627	334	293	80	88	80	57	29	0
8	IS	which	0,000	541	123	418	53	50	14	5	1	0
9	THAT	which	0,000	369	148	221	45	29	30	15	29	0
10	FOR	which	0,000	301	185	116	23	23	28	9	102	0
11	ON	which	0,000	289	225	64	12	38	21	5	149	0
12	COURT	which	0,000	283	148	135	18	5	13	101	11	0
13	WAS	which	0,000	271	19	252	7	6	6	0	0	0
14	BE	which	0,000	258	32	226	12	14	3	3	0	0
15	NOT	which	0,000	258	80	178	36	24	14	4	2	0
16	IT	which	0,000	245	54	191	32	10	5	1	6	0
17	BY	which	0,000	233	114	119	24	21	19	13	37	0
18	OR	which	0,000	221	129	92	27	40	36	16	10	0
19	ARE	which	0,000	219	30	189	7	6	11	5	1	0
20	OPINION	which	0,000	183	178	5	77	8	1	82	10	0

Figure 5.4. *Top twenty collocates of the word "which".*

The top twenty collocates include as many as six prepositions. *In* appears 740 times directly preceding *which.* Other prepositions appearing within one word of *which* include *of* (201), *to* (215), *for* (102), *on* (149) and *by* (37). In all, prepositions directly precede *which* 1444 times, which accounts for almost 40% of all instances when this relativiser appears. Otherwise, elaboration is usually provided with reference to various normative acts:

Text Sample 24

> Respondents emphasize the fact that §252(c)(1), **which** requires state commissions to assure compliance with the provisions of §251, adds "including the regulations prescribed by the Commission pursuant to section 251," whereas §252(c)(2), **which** requires state commissions to assure compliance with the pricing standards in subsection (d), says nothing about Commission regulations applicable to subsection (d).

Such acts are routinely referred to in a rather succinct form by way of symbols (as for instance *§252(c)(1)* as illustrated by means of the following concordance lines (except for the first line):

N	Concordance
1	outstanding debt, approximately $430,000, which was secured by a mortgage on
2	Federal Rule of Criminal Procedure 7(c)(1), which provides that an indictment "must be a
3	pursuant to 42 U. S. C. §7607(b)(1), which lodges jurisdiction over challenges to
4	review scheme established by Order No. 1, which "provides that appeal of a review
5	orders under 42 U. S. C. §7607(b)(1), which renders reviewable in the appropriate
6	States itself. The text of Article III, §1, which extends federal judicial power to
7	emphasize the fact that §252(c)(1), which requires state commissions to assure
8	are not contemplated by Rule 7(c)(1), which provides that an indictment "shall be a
9	op., at 1-2). The literal text of §3731(b)(1), which uses an event that is not an element of
10	differences between §2255 and §2244(d)(1), which governs petitions for federal habeas
11	review statute, 26 U. S. C. §7482(a)(1), which instructs courts of appeals to review
12	and Representatives,' Art. I, §4, cl. 1, which power is matched by state control over
13	the Government relies on §1512(e)(1), which states that an official proceeding "need
14	Government relies heavily on §1512(e)(1), which states that an official proceeding "need
15	§1977A(a)(1), 42 U. S. C. §1981a(a)(1), which provided that "[i]n an action brought by
16	part. Military Commission Order No. 1, which governs the military commission
17	statutory provision, 28 U. S. C. §2244(d)(1), which governs petitions for federal habeas
18	Order No. 1 (Commission Order No. 1), which was issued by the President on March
19	are set forth in Commission Order No. 1, which was amended most recently on
20	procedures. Subsection (e) of §1005, which is entitled "Judicial Review of

Figure 5.5. *Top twenty concordance lines of the node word "which".*

A certain regularity can be easily noticed. Various normative acts, such as, for instance, *Federal Rule of Criminal Procedure, Military Commission Order*, or those simply identified by reference to specific paragraphs, sections or subsections are called upon to provide a legal basis for the argumentation and these instruments are then further elaborated by means of *which.* The elaboration consists in indicating the "regulatory" function(s) of a given provision. This is realized through a number of verbs, usually in the Present Simple tense, for instance, *provides, extends, governs, requires, instructs, states,* etc. The first line is interesting because it shows a different use of *which*. As can be seen below, it details property needed to provide security for a debt. It does so by coordinating a number of nouns, each of which constitutes a particular type of property:

Text Sample 25: (sc 14-03)

> On December 10, 1999, the parties executed new loan documents encompassing Alafabco's entire outstanding debt, approximately $430,000, **which** was secured by a mortgage on commercial real estate owned by the individual respondents, by Alafabco's accounts receivable, inventory, supplies, fixtures, machinery, and equipment, and by a mortgage on the house of one of the individual respondents. Id., at *2.

Opinions are the last legal genre where the features associated with elaborated (explicit) reference plays a significant role. With the mean score of 2.6, journal articles are similar to popular fiction in that these features do not load strongly for these two genres.

Unlike, in studies dealing with variation along written and spoken genres, one should not expect to see dramatic differences among the genres. For example, a sports broadcast reporting events in progress is bound to contain lots of direct references to the physical and temporal situation of the discourse coupled with the absence of the linguistic features such as relative clauses, nominalization, phrasal coordination, "pied-piping" constructions. As already stated above, all legal genres included in this analysis have been found at the positive end of the elaborate vs. situation-dependent cline. The differences are a matter of degree captured by the statistical analysis but sometimes difficult to account for qualitatively. Two legal genres, legislation and contracts, contain an unusually frequent concentration of such features that can be mostly found in a specific part of these legal instruments – legal definitions. Given the considerable space devoted to defining terms and concepts in normative texts, it is not surprising that these two genres have the largest scores on this dimension.

5.2.4. Dimension 4: Overt Expression of Persuasion/Argumentation[31]

Just as in the case of Dimension 2, this dimension groups features with positive weights only. The features with positive weights include, infinitives, prediction modals, suasive verbs (e.g. *command, demand, instruct*), conditional

31 In studies done after 1988, Dimension 4 has been referred to both as "Overt Expression of Persuasion" and "Overt Expression of Argumentation".

subordination, necessity modals, split auxiliaries, and possibility modals. After analyzing how these features function in texts Biber (1988) proposed the interpretive label of "overtly persuasive vs. not overtly persuasive discourse". Using the example of a professional letter, Conrad and Biber (2001: 35) illustrate how these linguistic features are utilized in texts with large positive scores on this dimension.

Text Sample 26: Professional Letter (Conrad and Biber, 2001: 35)

> Furthermore, it really would be inappropriate for me to put words in your mouth. In short, you should really take the format of the resolution and put in your own thoughts… the association is already sampling opinion on a number of other matters and it may be possible to add this one. If it is not possible to add your concern this year, it would certainly be possible to add it next year.

First, there is an extensive use of modals. Prediction modals are used to speculate about future possibilities and/or to discuss hypothetical situations. Possibility modals indicate the likelihood of certain events. Necessity modals (e.g. *should*) are used to express obligation for the addressee. Conditional subordination specifies the conditions under which certain events can take place. In Sample 26, there is a frequent use of infinitives as adjective complements, where the adjectives refer to the writer's attitude or stance. In addition, there is a frequent use of the so-called "suasive" verbs (although not in this sample) employed in order to encourage certain actions proposed by an author.

So far, the configuration of genres in relation to the dimensions has been fairly unequivocal. All the legal genres have been informational, relatively non-narrative and they have been marked for explicit reference. They tended to occupy extreme points on the previous dimensions, especially with regard to the non-legal genres. This time, legal genres cluster around with more moderate score means alongside other genres. This dimension is the first that shows a clear split between the legal genres, with only textbooks and professional articles having positive scores, contracts being unmarked for this dimension (a mean score of 0), while all the other legal genres have similar, moderately negative scores.

6 =
5 =
4 =
3 =

2 **Textbook (2.2)**
||
1 **Professional article (1.2)** *general fiction*
||
0 **Contract (0.6)** *official documents*
|| *academic prose, conversation*
-1 *popular non-fiction*
|| **Academic journals (-1.5) Legislation (-1.5) Opinions (-1.6)**
-2 **Briefs (1.9)**
||
-3
||
-4
||
-5
||
-6
Not overtly persuasive

Figure 5.6. *Mean Scores of Legal Genres along Dimension 4*

As shown above, two legal genres have clear positive mean scores on Dimension 4. It is somewhat surprising to note that textbooks are one of them, especially if we bear in mind that academic prose is reported as unmarked for this dimension (Biber, 1988: 149).

Text Sample 27: (Textbook: Introduction to English Law)

> It **would be impossible** to **persuade** anyone to act as trustee **unless** the discretion entrusted to him were very liberally conferred, and it is now possible for a trustee to delegate to an agent, not merely pieces of business requiring especial skill, but the whole business of the trust, and escape liability long as he acts in good faith. In cases of doubt, a trustee **may** protect himself by obtaining, at the cost of the trust property, the direction of the court, and the Trustee Act 1925, s. 61, had enabled the court to relieve a trustee, who has acted honestly and reasonably and ought fairly to be excused, from liability for breach of trust.

Text Sample 28: (Textbook)

> No one can say what the next century **will** bring. Most recently the Law Commission in 1989 recommended replacement of the dual system of trusts for sale and Settled Land Act settlements by a new trust machinery applicable to all trusts of land. Trustees **would** hold the legal estate on trust with a power (though not a duty)

> to sell and a power to retain. As at present, they **would** be able to overreach equitable interests; and the **Law Commission** considers that the simplicity of such a new system **would** outweigh any possible disadvantages. **It remains to be seen** whether this suggestion **will** become law, but the only really confident prediction **must** be that long as capitalism remains, trusts **will** continue to change and develop so as to meet changes in social conditions and the tax structure.

First of all, the texts above sampled from legal textbooks tend to be considerably less author-centred than, for example, the professional letter provided earlier. This means that persuasion or argumentation conducted in textbooks is much less direct and personal, very much in keeping with the conventions of the genre that call for objectivity and absence of any emotive statements. This is, for instance, manifested in the complete absence of the second person pronoun used in conjunction with the necessity modal and the use of impersonal constructions. The modal *would* is used to discuss a hypothetical situation, more specifically, the consequences of introducing a proposed reform of the legal institution of "trustees". The expression of stance shifts from the authority of a legal body, the Law Commission (*the simplicity (...)* ***would*** *outweigh any possible disadvantages*) to that of the author (*It remains to be seen whether this suggestion* ***will*** *become law, (...) the only really confident prediction* ***must*** *be that trusts* ***will*** *continue to change and develop (...).* The presence of these features can be accounted for by the attempt of the author to present the proposed new system and its possible consequences. The prediction modal *will* is used to express the knowledge status of the information included in the propositions.

Text Sample 29: (Professional Article: "Petitioning and Opposing Certiorari in the U.S. Supreme Court")

> Studies have found that the filing of amicus briefs in support of a petition increases the likelihood of a grant, so **you should actively seek ou**t amici to help you persuade the Court that the issue presented is of broad concern. You have a little extra time to mount this effort, since amicus briefs are due not when the petition is filed but "within the time allowed for filing the brief in opposition," which is 30 days after the petition is filed, barring an extension. S. Ct. R. 15.
> **If** the question raised in your petition is of consequence to the federal government, the Court **may** ask the Solicitor General to file a brief expressing the views of the United States before voting on your petition. **If that occurs**, you **would do well** to contact the Solicitor General's office and the relevant federal agencies to discuss the position the United States will take in its brief. **If you can persuade** the SG that your case deserves further review, the battle is more than half won.

Predictably, given that professional articles primarily aim to dispense advice directed at both other lawyers and the general public, they also contain a relatively large number of features associated with overt persuasion. The sample provided above comes from an article which considers the pros and cons of taking a case before the Supreme Court, which is usually more technically phrased as "filing a petition for certiorari". Since it is extremely difficult to obtain a permission to have the case heard, any advice from someone who have actually argued before the Court is definitely invaluable. Essentially, in this excerpt, the authors attempt to persuade the reader what advantages there are if a petition for a certiorari is accompanied by filing amicus briefs, which are additional petitions filed by interested 'third' parties (not parties to a particular case) in appeals concerning matters of a broad public interest. Unlike in the previous sample from a legal textbook, persuasion is rather direct in terms of addressing the target audience by combining the second person pronoun with the necessity modal (and the additional split auxiliary as in *you should actively seek out*), or employing the second person pronoun with conditional subordination (*If that occurs, you would do well to contact..., If you can persuade...*). Conditional subordination is used along with a possibility modal to discuss a hypothetical course of events (*If the question raised in your petition is of consequence... the Court may ask the Solicitor General* (...). In sum, all the features taken together are employed to structure an argument, present advisable, desirable scenarios, and encourage certain courses of action. However, Figure 5.6 shows that most legal genres are unmarked for this dimension. Interestingly, among them, opinions tend to employ few Dimension 4 features. One reason for this could be that opinions are not expressed by means of overt argumentative features, rather by stating them in a factual manner or employing lexical items charged with evaluation.

5.2.5. Dimension 5: Impersonal vs. Non-impersonal Style

Originally, Biber (1988: 152) interpreted this dimension as "abstract versus non-abstract information". In subsequent studies, this dimension was referred to as "abstract versus non-abstract style" and "impersonal vs. non-impersonal style". In this study, the last label was adopted as best interpreting the features grouped along this dimension.

Most of the features associated with this dimension are passives (agentless passives, passives with *by*-phrases, past participial (passive) adverbial clauses and past participial (passive) postnominal clauses (also called past participial *whiz* deletions). Other features include conjuncts (such as *thus, however*) and other adverbial subordinators (i.e. those with multiple functions, not consistently causative, concessive or conditional).

Impersonal		
8	**Contracts (8.1)**	
‖	**Textbook (7.8)**	
7		
‖	**Legislation (6.4)**	
6		
‖		*academic prose*
5	**Professional Article (5.0)**	
‖	**Briefs (4.7)**	*official documents*
4	**Opinions (4.1)**	
‖	**Journal Articles (3.9)**	
3		
‖		
2		
‖		
1		
‖		
0		*popular non-fiction*
‖		
-1		
‖		
-2		
‖		*general fiction*
-3		
‖		*conversation*
-4		
Non-impersonal		

Figure 5.7. *Comparison of Mean Scores along Dimension 5*

As can be seen in Figure 5.7, all legal genres are marked for this dimension. Contracts, textbooks and legislation have the largest scores, in fact the largest ever found using the MD methodology. This reinforces the stereotypical perception of legal language as highly impersonal. For instance, Tiersma (1999: 205) links frequent impersonal constructions in legal documents with problems in understanding; Alcaraz and Hughes (2002: 18) mention "abundant use of the passive voice" among the leading features of the morphology and syntax of legal English). However, if we consider this dimension against a wider backdrop of other non-legal registers, important differences among the legal genres can be noticed. Three genres (contracts, textbooks and legislation) have scores larger than other non-legal genres, such as academic prose or official documents.

Text Sample 30: (Agreement of Lease)

> (l) The termination of this Lease during the original term of this Lease shall also terminate and render void all of Tenant's options or elections under this Article 43, whether or not the same shall have **been exercised**; and nothing **contained** in this Article 43 shall prevent Landlord from exercising any right or action **granted** to or **reserved** by Landlord in this Lease to terminate this Lease. None of Tenant's options or elections **set forth** in this Article 43 may be **severed** from this Lease or separately **sold**, **assigned** or **transferred**.

Contracts, the most "impersonal" or "abstract" of all the legal genres, are an interesting case. For one, they are somehow not really expected to be so impersonal given that their major function is to specify parties' duties and obligations. Put differently, it should be stated clearly who does what in a contract and an extensive use of passives does not facilitate this. The reasons for this can be, to some extent, accounted for by examining the passive structures in isolation (Table 3.5 below). Contracts rank high in all three categories. Their mean score for agentless passives is almost as large as that of textbooks, however, they have the largest score for *BY*-passives and one of the highest scores for "postnominal modifier plus past participle forms". The large score for *BY*- passives is clearly motivated by the need to mention the agent of the described actions. In the text sample above, we find ***granted*** *to or* ***reserved*** *by Landlord.* The agentless passives are used when human agents are largely unimportant. In the sample above, agentless passives can be found in the last sentence. It protects the Tenant's rights by explicitly prohibiting certain activities (***none*** *of Tenant's options or elections (...)* ***may*** *be severed (...), sold, assigned or transferred*). The focus is on prohibition without specifying the addressee. In fact, such specification is inferable from the conceptual content of the verbs. There is an implicit reference to a potential agent entitled to participate in the legal act of *selling*, *assigning* and *transferring* already, as it were, encoded in these terms.

The frequent presence of postnominal modifiers undoubtedly contributes to the overall large score on this dimension and marks contracts as a highly informational type of texts where information is tightly packaged in the most economical manner by eliminating *WH*-relative clauses. It should be pointed out that, in many cases, the use of the postnominal clauses does not necessarily obscure the agent. In phrases such as *nothing* ***contained*** *in this Article,* or *options or elections* ***set forth*** *in this Article,* the modifiers are followed by a prepositional phrase with a deicitic function that make the proposition unambiguous. The use of postnominal modifiers is strongly patterned and highly formulaic. The word form *contained* provides a good example. It appears an overall of 547 times in the contracts . It functions as a past participle passive postnominal modifier in all but 4 cases! Its overall pattern could be formulated as follows: **nouns(s)** + *contained*

+ **place adverb,** where the nouns can be subsumed under a very specific semantic group of CONDITIONS (e.g. *conditions, covenants, provisions, terms, warranties, etc.*), and the place adverbs refer to contractual instruments or their parts (e.g. *section(s), paragraph, Article, Agreement, contract, Lease, document, Plan, etc.*) as in the following example sentences:

Example sentence from *5-year Credit Agreement* (emphasis added in bold)

> **the representations and warranties contained in Section 4.01 of the Credit Agreement** (except the representations set forth in the last sentence of subsection (e) thereof and in subsection (f) thereof (other than clause (ii) thereof)) are correct,

Example sentence from *Operating Agreement* (emphasis added in bold)

> **Nothing contained in this Agreement** will, or will be deemed to, convey any title or ownership interest in all or any portion of the Database, the Licensed Data and/or CD-EXPORT regardless of whether any portion thereof is used by Retailer or other users.

Noteworthy is also the occurrence of *contained* with *nothing.* The two words appear as a contiguous pair 54 times, and indeed 66 times, if we include the intervening *herein* as illustrated in the following 5 random concordance lines:

N	Concordance
57	provided, however, that nothing contained herein shall be construed as
58	the cost of such Advance. Nothing contained herein shall, however, obligate
59	a director. Provided that nothing herein contained shall authorised a director or
60	in the shares; but nothing herein contained shall release the estate of the
61	provided, however, that nothing contained herein shall be construed as

In fact, it is possible to notice an emerging phraseological pattern of "nothing" plus *contained* plus *shall.* In light of the above, it seems that a large proportion of passives (at least of the postnominal past participial type) does not effectively obfuscate the agent and its frequent use may be accounted for in terms of recurrent formulaic phrases.

Table 5.3. *Mean scores for three types of passive structures. The frequencies are per 1,000 words*

Genre	Agentless passives	*BY*- passives	Postnominal clauses
Academic journals	11.1	1.6	3.1
Legislation	13.4	**3.7**	**13.45**
Briefs	11.6	1.8	4.6
Contracts	**19.2**	**3.8**	**9.6**
Professional articles	14.5	2.2	3.97
Opinions	10.5	1.5	4.3
Textbooks	**20.3**	3.6	3.08

It is somewhat surprising to find that textbooks' mean score on this dimension puts them in the same league as the two operational legal genres, especially that, when we recall the distribution of legal genres along Dimension 1, textbooks are the least informational, unlike contracts and legislation. The relatively low score of textbooks for postnominal clauses (see Table 5.3 above), which I interpret as contributing to an informational character of a given genre or register, tends to confirm this. The impersonal/passive constructions used in textbooks seem to serve a different function.

Text Sample 31: (Textbook 6-041)

> Since capital costs and costs of necessaries **are incurred** in order to earn the lost revenue the deduction of these items **may be designed** to avoid double recovery. Certainly the case is not authority for denying recovery of overheads in all cases.
> Support for recovery **can** also **be found** in Re Vic Mill Ltd. #145. Although the claim was for loss of profit Hamilton LJ thought that if the creditors' works **were** wholly or partially **stopped** in consequence of their not manufacturing the machines **ordered by** the buyer, due to the buyer's repudiation, 'there might **have been** a claim for some proportion of the overhead charges attributable to the period when the works were at a standstill, when charges were running on and nothing **was being made** against them, because the appellants, the buyers, would not perform their contract.

The passage, provided above, opens with an adverbial clause introduced with the subordinator *since* to mark reason. The entire sentence, and in fact, this whole sample, presents information with little emphasis on the agent (*costs of necessaries* ***are incurred,*** *items* ***may be designed***) because it is either incidental to the purpose of the text or inferable. The first paragraph (in fact, an entire sentence) uses passives in keeping with the generic conventions of academic prose. They are used to conduct a consistent and objective line of argumentation.

In the next paragraph, the second sentence starting with *although the claim was (...)* appears perhaps more typical of legal style, not only in terms of length, but also in terms of an almost complete absence of anaphora in the case of nouns referring to parties in the dispute. In one instance, *the machines* are modified with past participial passive modifier *ordered* followed by the prepositional phrase *by the buyer*. This use of a *BY*-passive is strategic and serves to create an explicit link between failure to carry on a desired activity (*not manufacturing the machines*) and one of the parties (*by the buyer*). On the purely linguistic level, the use of *by the buyer* strikes one as redundant, especially that we find *due to the buyer's repudiation* directly following it. Such use becomes more understandable and justified in light of the conventions operating in the legal genres. One final observation concerns agents specified in a *by-* phrase. Unlike in academic prose (Biber, 1988: 153) , such agents tend to be animate in legal prose.

Finally, we turn to examine an excerpt from a legislative provision (Title 17 from the USC on copyrights).

Text Sample 32: (Legislation)

> (f) Effect of Errors. - (1) Error in any statement or assertion as to the utility of the useful article **named** in the application under this section, the design of which **is sought to be registered**, shall not affect the protection **secured** under this chapter.
>
> (g) Design Made in Scope of Employment. - In a case in which the design **was made** within the regular scope of the designer's employment and individual authorship of the design is difficult or impossible to ascribe and the application so states, the name and address of the employer for whom the design **was made** may **be stated** instead of that of the individual designer.

Legislation is similar to contracts in the dense use of past participial WHIZ deletions (*article named, protection secured*). Characteristically, in both genres, the postnominal modifiers are followed by a text deictic reference to a legal instrument or its part: *in the application under this section, under this chapter.* This excerpt does not indicate human agents for the activities mentioned in the propositions. The prime reason for such use is that the agent can be easily inferred (e.g. *was made within the regular scope of the designer's employment*) or it is not important (e.g. *may be stated*).

5.3. Conclusions

The groups of linguistic features identified along each dimension provide an interesting insight into the detailed linguistic composition of the discourse, which is not normally seen in qualitative observations. By identifying and isolating these groups of linguistic features, it is possible to define further both the internal and external qualities that form the building blocks of the discourse. Biber's multi-feature, multi-dimensional analytical framework has been applied in the analysis of a range of written legal genres using the 1988 model of variation in the broader context of other specialized genres (history and biology textbook textbooks and research articles on the two first dimensions) and other less specialized genres whose dimension scores had been computed using the same procedure in Biber (1988). This analysis has described legal genres relative to other disciplines, and genres. It turns out that, in respect of some dimensions, the interpretation of legal genres' mean scores is quite straightforward and it confirms earlier observations or perception of legal texts. For example, all legal genres (albeit to a varying degree) emerge as clearly informational with little concern for affective or interactive features. They are all relatively non-narrative and they marked by explicit reference and abstract or impersonal style. Interestingly, their mean scores often by far exceed those computed for other genres or registers. They are thus not only informational and impersonal but also they are *the most* informational and *the most* impersonal in terms of the MD analysis. However, on some dimensions, the picture can be an altogether more complex one. The way mean scores are plotted along some of the dimensions suggests considerable variation *within* legal discourse For example, while all the legal genres tend to be non-narrative, law textbooks have a relatively large concentration of narrative features similar to that of history textbooks, research articles and popular non-fiction. On the other hand, legislation and contracts have been found to be the least narrative genres in law.

In fact, a regular pattern can be noticed along the first two dimensions, where legislation and contracts plot on the negative side of the factor scores with the largest scores, while textbooks and opinions have the lowest scores. On Dimension 3, legislation and contracts have the largest positive scores but this time, it is the academic journals that are the least marked for explicit or elaborate reference. As already indicated, Dimension 4 is an exception in that it splits the legal genres on both positive and negative sides of the continuum. It also shows that legal genres tend to cluster around the nil mean score without radical differences among them. On Dimension 5, contracts and legislation are found towards the top end of the positive side with the intervening textbooks between them.

Dimensions 1 and 2 provide interesting observations on the three disciplines of law, history and ecology. In terms of their respective mean scores, legal texts tend to be more 'scattered' along these two dimensions while the other genres tend to cluster. This could suggest there is considerable linguistic variation within legal discourse between different legal genres. Informational content in law textbooks and opinions is not as tightly packaged as in the other disciplinary genres. Irrespective of genre, research or journal articles are generally more informationally dense than textbooks. This could be attributed to their different goals, audiences and conventions that cut across disciplines. Journal articles are expected to provide state-of-the-art, highly specialized content directed at experts. Some difference between the disciplinary texts are motivated by the subject matter. For example, history texts, irrespective of genre are more narrative than the other disciplines precisely because history as a discipline involves narrating past events. This comparative study signals the need for more extensive analysis of similarities and differences between specialized texts in terms of discipline, register or genre.

CHAPTER VI: MULTI-DIMENSIONAL PATTERNS OF VARIATION ACROSS LEGAL GENRES

6.1. Introduction

We saw in the previous chapter that the 1988 Model of Variation can be extremely useful in characterizing legal genres relative to dimensions identified for general, non-specialist use of language. This type of analysis enables one to make comparisons among various specialist as well as non-specialists genres and registers outside the legal discourse. Most importantly, it affords the possibility of adding another level of description to this by going beyond the legal discourse. It provides useful and insightful points of reference, thus leading to a better understanding of legal writing as set against the backdrop of other language varieties. However, as Biber points out in his study of university registers, this type of analysis cannot be used to identify and describe dimensions "that are actually most important in a particular domain of use" (Biber, 2006: 181). The co-occurrence of linguistic features is unique to a particular discourse domain. It reflects "the specialized functional priorities of those domains" (ibid.). A new MD analysis involves carrying out a new factor analysis in order to identify the co-occurrence patterns relevant and actually present in a collection of texts under examination. In this study, the two types of multi-dimensional analysis are treated as complementary. This time, we focus on studying multi-dimensional patterns of variation only *within* legal discourse. By conducting a new MD analysis (its methodology is provided in Section 2.8.1 in Chapter 2), we hope to identify the co-occurrence patterns unique to the domain of legal texts. Individual legal genres can be then compared in terms of the new dimensions.
The new dimensions are then interpreted in order to describe the patterns of variation among legal genres.

6.2. Interpretation of the legal (ALC) dimensions of variation

6.2.1. Dimension 1: Narrative, Stance-focused vs. Informational and Normative discourse

A total of twenty-four features comprise Factor 1 with seventeen features on the positive and seven on the negative side of the factor. Only two features have larger loadings on other factors (marked in brackets in Table 6.1). These are *indefinite pronouns* (.38 on Factor 2) and *THAT relatives* (-.33 on Factor 3). Such features are regarded as of secondary importance in the factor analysis.

Table 6.1 *Summary of the linguistic features extracted on Factor 1*

Features with positive loadings		*Features with negative loadings*	
demonstrative pronouns	*.35*	*prepositions*	*-.62*
pronoun IT	*.44*	*phrasal coordination*	*-.42*
adv. subordinator: causative	*.62*	*nominalizations*	*-.35*
indefinite pronouns	*(.32)*	*modal shall*	*-.69*
past tense	*.83*	*quantity noun*	*-.48*
third person pronoun	*.53*	*BY passives*	*-.36*
perfect aspect verbs	*.58*	*postnominal passives*	*-.36*
downtoners	*.36*		
THAT relatives	*(.32)*		
THAT cl. with communication verbs	*.74*		
THAT cl. with factive verbs	*.63*		
THAT cl. with likelihood verbs	*.49*		
THAT cl. with all adjectives	*.37*		
THAT cl. with all nouns	*.69*		
all stance adverbs	*.39*		
cognitive nouns	*.63*		
mental verbs	*.47*		

A number of positive features on this dimension suggest a narrative orientation. At .83, past tense forms have the largest positive loading on Factor 1. Past tense forms have been traditionally regarded as an indication of narration (Schiffrin, 1981). Biber (1988: 223) lists other studies which used frequency counts of past tense forms in order to analyze possible differences and similarities (cf. Blankenship. 1962; Marckworth and Baker, 1974; Biber, 1986). The narrative concerns are further illustrated by the relatively large positive loading of the third person pronouns (.53) and perfect aspect forms (.58). These are also typically associated with narrative or descriptive texts. Some scholars have long concluded that "perfect aspect forms can frequently co-occur with past tense forms as markers of narrative" (Biber, 1988: 224; Biber, 1986; Marckworth and Baker, 1974). As can be recalled from the previous chapter, these three features are documented on Dimension 2 as contributing to the narrative focus in discourse in Biber (1988) study. They co-occur with public verbs in Biber's study. The category of public verbs was used after Quirk et al (1985: 1181-2) but it was abandoned in subsequent studies in favour of the class of communication verbs in keeping with the classification adopted in LGSWE, p. 360. In the present study, on Factor 1, a large occurrence of *that*-clauses are controlled by communication verbs. Communication verbs are 'a special subcategory of activity verbs that involve communication activities (which do not necessarily involve speech)'

(LGSWE, pp.362, 368, 370). Examples include *describe, claim, offer, deny, propose, challenge, declare, inform*, etc.

Apart from the above features associated with a narrative orientation, there are a number of other features which typically convey epistemic stance (cf. Chapter 4, Section 4.5.3; see also LGSWE, Chapter 12) These include *that*-clause controlled by *likelihood verbs,* i.e. verbs typically expressing uncertainty, such as *assume, believe, doubt, gather, guess, imagine, etc.*, see Biber, 2006: 195); *mental verbs* (e.g. *think, know, understand,* see LGSWE, p. 362-363); *cognitive nouns* ("nouns referring to mental and cognitive processes or perceptions" (Biber, 2006: 249, such as *analysis, assessment, conclusion, consequence, assumption, possibility, etc.*). These features (3rd person pronouns, *that*-clauses controlled by communication verbs, past tense verbs, *that*-clause controlled by likelihood verbs and cognitive nouns) resemble the grouping in the dimension 'reconstructed account of events' identified by Biber (2006).

In addition, the positive features also include *stance adverbs,* which cover four subcategories of *certainty adverbs* (e.g. undoubtedly, obviously, certainly), *likelihood adverbs* (e.g. evidently, predictably, roughly), *style adverbs* (e.g. frankly, mainly, truthfully) and *attitude adverbs* (e.g. surprisingly, hopefully, wisely; (cf. Appendix A in Biber, 2006: 245). At this point, worth noting is also the relatively frequent occurrence of *pronoun IT.* Obviously, it can refer to a wide range of referents; it is said to be "the most generalized pronoun" (Biber, 1988: 225). As demonstrated in Text Sample 2, and discussed below, *pronoun IT* is primarily used in extraposed *that*-clauses to signal a stance or attitude which is not directly attributed to a particular person. This is evidenced by a number of adjectival predicates found in Text Sample 2, for example, *it is likely that, it is natural to assume that, it has therefore been forcefully argued that, etc.*

Interestingly, there are six types of *that*-clauses found on this factor (or five, if we discount *that*-relatives because of their larger loading on a different dimension). Their discourse functions are roughly related to reporting "the speech, thoughts, attitudes, or emotions of humans" (Biber, 1999: 660). A large loading of causative subordination (.62) can also be regarded as a marker of stance, i.e. a way to explain one's actions or beliefs (*because*). Finally, we note a moderately large loading of *demonstrative pronouns.*

In contrast, there are seven negative features identified on this factor: *prepositions, phrasal coordination, nominalizations, modal "shall", quantity nouns, BY passives and postnominal passives.* Their interpretation is fairly straightforward. Virtually all these features mark informational density (except for *modal "shall"*). In comparison with previous multidimensional studies, the six features are listed as features with negative loadings and characteristic of "literate discourse" in Biber's study of university registers (2006: 184). In the present analysis, these features appear to serve as primary markers of a high informational focus, a careful integration of information. *Phrasal coordination* is indicative of the strong presence of complex noun and prepositional phrases. As we saw in the previous chapter, Dimension 3 showed that *phrasal coordination* is linked to the phenomenon of *binomial expressions* and a heavy concentration of mostly *coordinated noun phrases* is found in the 'operative' type of legal discourse. Coordination has been recognized as one of the two linguistic features (besides subordination) which greatly contributes to the complexity of legal syntax (see Klinck, 1992: 270-276).

In my study, none of the negative features has larger weights on other factors. Interestingly, a specific type of nouns, *quantity* or *quantifying nouns* occurs indicating a highly specialized, informational content. *Nominalization* signals the tendency to package maximum information in as few words as possible. It is usually found in discourses that strive to achieve maximum precision and accuracy of expression. Nominalization is traditionally listed as one of the most typical features of legal English (see, e.g. Tiersma, 1999). However, the distribution of this feature might be a matter of degree. Nominalization is certainly very frequent in some legal genres. We might expect to find a strong presence of grammatical metaphor in this type of discourse because its use permits the dense packaging of information, particularly in the noun phrase. Interestingly, it co-occurs with other "informational" features. The modal *shall* signals the deontic use of *shall* to express obligation, promise, etc., as it is commonly associated with legal English (see Tiersma, 1999:104-106, or, more recently, Witczak-Plisiecka, 2007:181-199). In virtually all the instances where *shall* was found, it was used in keeping with the conventions of legal texts. Interestingly, as we will see later, this modal verb has an unusually high frequency in just two legal genres of legislation and contracts to the extent that it can be effectively considered a genre marker for the *normative* and *operative* types of texts. *Postnominal passives* are also associated with the informational focus and contribute to the density of information packed by modifying the nouns. Finally, the other type of *passives, by-phrase*, signals an impersonal style but at the same time, one, where agent is explicitly mentioned. In the context of legal discourse, Gibbons (2003: 20-21) refers to passives as one of many features characterizing more literate discourse.

Table 6.2. *Duncan's Multiple Range Test for seven legal genres: Factor 1 (Means with the same letter are not significantly different).*

	Mean	**N**	**Genre**
A	11.4232	101	Textbooks
B	9.5162	114	Opinions
C	7.4355	71	Academic journals
C	6.8846	63	Briefs
D	5.0679	100	Professional articles
E	14.7712	177	Contracts
F	18.2091	60	Legislation

The configuration of features on this factor is extremely interesting for a number of reasons. First, as can be seen in the previous chapter, all legal genres tend to be non-narrative in comparison with other genres in English, which might have suggested that narrative concerns play a somewhat marginal role in legal texts. However, Figure 1 indicates a great deal of variation with respect to this dimension. Legal genres fall at both ends of this linguistic parameter. The Duncan's Multiple Range Test (Table 6.2) shows that only journal articles and briefs have mean scores which are not significantly different. Five legal genres are marked for positive features on this dimension (textbooks, opinions, journal articles, briefs and professional articles) while two (contracts and legislation) have large negative scores. This seems to suggest that features associated with narrative concerns (although not exclusively) do play a crucial role in characterizing legal genres. The configuration of genres in respect of this new dimension resembles the distribution on Dimension 2 (Narrative vs. non-narrative concerns) in the 1988 model. Both types of MD analysis point to textbooks and opinions as the most narrative legal genres (although, in the former, the values are *relative* to those of other legal genres). At the same time, in both cases, contracts and legislation have the largest negative scores. In between, there are three 'intermediary' genres of briefs, professional articles and journal articles with relatively small differences in terms of their respective mean scores on these two dimensions. It is equally interesting to consider the issue of "informationality". In the previous chapter, we saw that all legal genres are marked for being highly informational (along with other non-legal disciplinary texts) with contracts and, especially legislation having the largest loadings. If we look at Figure 6.1, an altogether more complex picture is emerging. Only two genres (contracts and legislation) have markedly large negative loadings on Factor 1, which prompts one to conclude that in the case of the non-operative genres, narrative and stance-focused concerns prevail.

12
‖ TEXTBOOK
11
‖
10
‖ OPINIONS
9
‖
8
‖ ACADEMIC JOURNALS
7
‖ BRIEFS
6
‖
5 PROFESSIONAL ARTICLES
‖
4
‖
3
‖
2
‖
1
‖
0
‖
-1
‖
-2
‖
-3
‖
╫
-13
‖
-14
‖ CONTRACTS
-15
‖
-16
‖
-17

||
-18 LEGISLATION

Figure 6.1. *Mean scores for legal genres along Dimension 1 (Narrative, Stance-focused vs. Informational and Normative discourse)*

Thus, to a large extent, it appears that the findings obtained by means of the new factor analysis on Dimension 1 tend to corroborate and complement the results obtained by means of the 1988 MD analysis with regard to informational and narrative concerns. At the same time, they offer a hope of providing a more delicate, fine-grained picture.

We now turn to examine texts on this Dimension 1 in the hope of providing an effective illustration of the features and their discoursal functions. The computer program (the SAS system) enables one to select texts with the highest scores on a given factor thus making it a lot easier to identify the relevant features in the texts. We will start with textbooks because they have the largest loadings on Dimension 1. Clearly, it is not realistic to find a portion of text that would contain all the relevant features listed in Figure 1. However, in order to provide ample textual evidence, in some cases, one genre category is represented by more than one text sample, as is the case below.

Text Sample 1 deals with the legal concept of *consideration.* Put simply, consideration in common law is an essential element in the formation of a contract. It is the price (but not necessarily money) paid by one person in exchange for another person's promise to do something (Blacks, 1990). The extract below refers to one important principle, a well-known "maxim" which states that "consideration must move from the promise". It basically means that only someone who actually paid the price, i.e. provided consideration, can enforce contractual provisions, e.g. by suing the other party on breach of contract. The excerpt contains a number of relevant features identified with positive loadings on Dimension 1 and associated with strong narrative concerns.

Text Sample 1: Textbook 6-001 (past tense forms [in bold], perfect aspect forms [in bold], third person pronouns [italicized], IT pronouns [italicized], THAT clauses [*that* plus controlling verb or noun capitalized])

> *It* is one of the best-known axioms of the common law of contract THAT consideration must move from the promisee. Expanded, this means that no person can in contract enforce a promise for which ***he*** has not provided consideration. As a principle, it has on its side the highest authority and a reasonable degree of antiquity. Ten years ago, however, the High Court of Australia **came up with** a formula which, while purporting to respect the principle, would, if accepted, have the effect of reducing its impact in a potentially important group of cases. In Coulls v. Bagot's

> Executor and Trustee Co. Ltd. four of the five High Court judges EXPRESSED the view THAT a joint promisee, if she were party to a contract, could sue to enforce it notwithstanding that ***she* had not *herself* furnished** any part of the consideration. The case **concerned** a widow whose late husband **had contracted** to grant a licence to a quarrying company for the extraction of metal from a quarry which the husband **owned**. Under the contract royalties **were to be paid** to the husband and wife jointly while they both **lived**, and thereafter to the survivor of them. The wife's only part in the proceedings **had been** to append **her** signature to the contract document. Barwick C.J. and Windeyer J. (dissenting) HELD THAT the plaintiff **was** a party to the contract and, as a joint promisee, could enforce ***it*** notwithstanding THAT her husband alone **had provided** the consideration. McTiernan, Taylor and Owen JJ. HELD THAT the wife **was not** a party but Taylor and Owen JJ. **agreed** THAT if ***she* had been** a party the FACT THAT *it* **was** her husband who **had** provided the consideration would not have been an impediment to her.

The central issue, i.e. the explanation and description of the basic legal maxim in contract law, is introduced right at the beginning by means of three sentences in the Present Tense. What follows is, as we will see, highly characteristic of legal academic texts; it is a switch to the narrative mode in order to provide an illustration, by reference to an actual legal case, of how this principle works in practice. First of all, this lengthy example helps to account for the large mean score of the past tense forms. The general phrasing of the principle is followed by a detailed account of a landmark case. Noteworthy are frequent references reporting judicial decisions, e.g. *held that*, *agreed that*, *expressed the view*. The account of the case itself is reminiscent of narrating a story (*the case concerned a widow...*). The presence of a narrative mode was already identified in the previous chapter, when Dimension 2 (Narrative v. Non-narrative Discourse) is discussed. We also noted that in legal texts, especially textbooks, the use of the narrative is somehow discontinued by the use of the present tense forms. This is also the case in the above excerpt as demonstrated in another example from a legal textbook (Text Sample 2). In this excerpt, the narrative mode is employed to describe the evolution of the concept of "consideration" (e.g. *the lawyers evolved, they decided, it was decided that assumpsit was not to be used...*) . Characteristically, this follows some general statements about the enforceability of contracts. There seems to be the prevalent pattern whereby statements expressing principles or legal rules, "universal truths", are followed by a more detailed account drawing upon past cases or providing a historical background to these general issues. Unlike, the previous sample, this excerpt also contains a number of *extraposed that-clauses* which introduce the argument through the use of stance adverbs (*it has therefore been forcefully argued that, it has been said, so it has been persuasively argued that*). Examples in brackets also illustrate the use of anticipatory *it* in extraposed structures with passive verb predicates. Indeed, there are more examples of anticipatory *it* in this type of structure but with predicative adjectives: *it is likely that,* or *it is natural to assume that.*

Text Sample 2: Textbook 5-058 (Past tense and perfect aspect forms in bold, IT pronouns and third person pronouns in italics, *that* clauses with controlling adjectives and nouns capitalized, extraposed *that*-clauses underlined, stance adverbs underlined,)

> In the previous chapter we **saw** THAT agreement, or at least the outward appearance of agreement, **was** an essential ingredient of a contract. But *It* is LIKELY THAT few legal systems treat all agreements as enforceable contracts. In early systems the distinction between unenforceable and enforceable agreements is often one of form and signs of that can be found in English law in the survival of the RULE THAT a promise under seal is legally binding.
> In developed English law, that is, since the sixteenth century, the crucial factor is the presence or the absence of "consideration". *It* is natural to assume THAT the adoption of this test is related to some underlying theory about why agreements are enforced. *It* **has** therefore **been forcefully ARGUED** THAT "consideration" is a word long rooted in the language of English law and denotes its fundamental attitude to contract and THAT when, in the middle of the sixteenth century, the lawyers **evolved**, through the action of assumpsit, a general contractual remedy, **they DECIDED** at the same time THAT *it* would not avail to redress the breach of any and every promise, whatever its nature. In particular, *it* **has been said** THAT *it* **was decided** THAT assumpsit **was** not to be **used** to enforce a gratuitous promise so that the plaintiff must show that the defendant's promise, upon which **he was** suing, **was** part of a bargain to which **he himself had contributed**. So *it* **has been persuasively ARGUED** THAT the doctrine of consideration represents the adoption by English law of the NOTION THAT only bargains should be enforced.

The use of the present perfect forms in the extraposed *that*-clauses additionally accentuates the prevalent academic attitudes towards the legal concept. The many passive structures contributing to the sense of objectivity in the expression of stance are combined with more emphatic adverbs (*forcefully, persuasively*), which in turn are used with the verb *argue*. This verb indicates a consistent line of argumentation. However, the presence of these features seems to signal the existence of at least some degree of controversy surrounding the origin of *consideration*. Note also the indefiniteness expressed through the use of *some* as in:

> (...) the adoption of this test is related to some underlying theory about why agreements are enforced.

It is interesting to note that the explanation of a legal term in a textbook is not formulated in terms of a precise, clear-cut definition, as one might expect from legal discourse, but through a descriptive historical account. In addition, the first sample also explains the notion of a *joint promise*, albeit in an indirect way, through a reference to a legal case (Coulls v. Bagot's Executor and Trustee Co. Ltd.), which serves not only as a very practical illustration of the principle introduced at the beginning, but it also develops the point by showing two possible ways in which judges approached this case. It seems that such short synopsis or case summaries are an inseparable part of legal textbooks. They might be considered as discipline-specific. Bhatia (2004: 41) contrasts this textbook approach to the explanation of concepts with the way in which legal definitions are presented in legislation. As Swales (1981, 1982) and Bhatia (1983, 1993, 1994) assert, in legislative texts, legal definitions tend to be formulated in a clear, precise and unequivocal way to ensure the all-inclusiveness of legal provisions. Apparently, in this case, discursive practices may vary depending on the genre rather than the discipline. The reason for this is that it is commonly accepted in legal education that in order to fully grasp the meaning of legal concepts or institutions, it is important to understand how the concept has originated and evolved over time. Legal textbooks tend to be concerned with descriptions of human conduct in a given socio-legal context. Textbooks are marked by a high degree of intertextuality and interdiscursivity. This is frequently achieved by referring to past cases as we saw in Text Sample 1. This textual practice reflects the central importance of judicial precedent in common law generally and in legal education in particular. [32] We will return to this point in the next section devoted to the interpretation of Factor 2.

Let us now, however, turn to examine an excerpt from Supreme Court opinion. This is the second most narrative/argumentative genre identified on this dimension. Text Sample 3 has been conveniently divided into two paragraphs. They both illustrate a very frequent use of past tense forms, IT pronouns and *that*-clauses.

Text Sample 3: Opinion SC 29-05 (past tense forms in bold, IT and third person pronouns in italics, *that*-clause capitalized)

Paragraph 1

Justice Kennedy **delivered** the opinion of the Court.

32 Bhatia (2004) provides an interesting account of disciplinary differences between legal and economics textbooks. It seems that the two disciplines differ in their use of discursive practices with respect to the rhetorical strategies that are employed.

The United States Court of Appeals for the Ninth Circuit, convening en banc, **granted** habeas relief to respondent William Payton. *It* **held THAT** the jury instructions in the penalty phase of his trial for capital murder **did not permit** consideration of all the mitigation evidence Payton **presented**. The error, the court **determined, was THAT** the general mitigation instruction **did not make** it clear to the jury **THAT** *it* could consider evidence concerning Payton's postcrime religious conversion and the prosecutor **was allowed** to urge this erroneous interpretation. We **granted** the petition for certiorari, 541 U. S. 1062 (2004), to decide whether the Ninth Circuit's decision **was** contrary to the limits on federal habeas review **imposed** by 28 U. S. C. §2254(d). We now reverse.

Paragraph 2

In 1980, while spending the night at a boarding house, Payton **raped** another boarder, Pamela Montgomery, and then **used** a butcher knife to stab her to death. Payton **proceeded** to enter the bedroom of the house's patron, Patricia Pensinger and to stab her as *she* **slept** aside her 10-year-old son, Blaine. When Blaine **resisted**, Payton **started** to stab him as well. Payton's knife blade **bent**, and *he* **went** to the kitchen to retrieve another. Upon the intervention of other boarders, Payton **dropped** the second knife and **fled.**
Payton **was arrested** and **tried** for the first-degree murder and rape of Pamela Montgomery and for the attempted murders of Patricia and Blaine Pensinger.

One striking similarity between the textbook samples and the excerpt from the opinion lies in the extensive use of past tense forms. Text sample 3 provides ample evidence to support the claim that the narrative mode is also commonly employed in judicial opinions. In fact, this particular text sample contains perhaps even more past tense forms than the previous example. However, statistically, their use of past tense forms is very similar, with 22.4 forms in the case of opinions and 23.6 in textbooks (normalized count per 1,000 words). Still, the narrative forms seem to be used in different ways. As it can be seen in the excerpt above, two major uses of the narrative mode can be identified in opinions. First, it serves to provide a summary of the legal proceedings (and their outcome) carried out by courts of lower instance, prior to the appeal heard by the Supreme Court. In the first paragraph of Text Sample 3, we can learn what measures were taken by the court of lower instance (*Court of Appeals for the Ninth Circuit granted habeas relief to respondent* (…), what constituted the grounds for the appeal and the reasoning behind this court's decision (*the error, the court determined, was that* (…) . The use of the past tense of *hold* marks the lower court's decision (*it held that*). It contrasts with the decision of the US Supreme Court at the end of the first paragraph expressed in the present tense (*We now reverse*).

The second major use of the narrative mode consists in providing an account (quite detailed sometimes as in the example above) of a person's wrongdoing. In Paragraph 2, we have a narrative account of a violent act committed by the defendant, where the dense use of the past forms of verbs followed frequently by *to-infinitive* (underlined in paragraph 2 for ease of reference) clauses adds to the highly dynamic, probably unintended, dramatic effect. It is worth noting, in passing, that the sentences are relatively short in this passage. One sentence has only ten words (*When Blaine resisted...*), which is relatively rare for legal prose, especially when compared with the average of 45-55 words reported in various studies on legal language (see the discussion in previous chapter p. 21). Consider also the use of personal pronouns. Apart from the characteristic first person plural pronoun *we* to refer to the court *en bloc*, *it,* unlike in textbook examples, is used as a third person pronoun to refer collectively to the court (*it held that*) and the jury (*it could consider evidence*). In both cases, the tone is one of utmost objectivity, there is no room for the slightest indication of attitude or evaluation. Our findings confirm the highly narrative nature of judicial opinions at least in the section devoted to "facts". Le Cheng and King Kui Sin (2007: 334) in their genre analysis of American opinions reveal an elaborate structure with several segments that serve different functional and rhetorical functions. Essentially, a typical opinion consists of a label, heading, introduction/summary, context/facts, analysis and decision/solution. The narrative features are usually found in the introduction/summary and context/facts sections. In terms of size expressed by means of word count, these two sections account for 27% of the total number of words of an average opinion (Le Cheng and King Kui Sin, 2007: 350). Thus, the way the narration is used in this opinion depends on its location in the generic structure. The significance of narrative in law has been noticed and examined. For example, Klinck notes that the narrative mode employed in judicial discourse by a judge need not necessarily be done in a neutral manner. He gives the example of Lord Denning as the most famous (or notorious) case of the judicial tendency to "marshall the facts so as to lead inevitably to the desired legal conclusion" (p. 296). Moreover, Klinck continues "frequently, of course, as is the case with any narration, a judicial recounting of facts will be determined by the point to which the judge wishes the facts to conduce" (ibid.). Noteworthy are also examples of how the description of the facts of a case can be a technique of argumentation. Klinck again suggests that the entire judicial opinion could be seen as a story with the judgment being its part and the inevitable conclusion. Given, the elaborate structure of a legal opinion with a number of different elements, we would expect to see considerable variation within this text genre. So far, we have only seen a very frequent use of narrative features but this is only partly related to Dimension 1. We would expect to see some textual evidence indicating the presence of features attributed to argumentation and, perhaps, stance.

Text Sample 4: Opinion SC22-05 (past tense forms in bold, *that*-clause capitalized)

> The State Department's position with respect to waters surrounding fringing islands on both coasts **was** THAT the sovereigns of those islands **could** only claim a territorial sea of three miles from the coast of each island. Secretary Bayard **explained** THAT, in asserting the 3-mile belt of territorial sea, the United States **denied** neither "the free right of vessels of other nations to pass, on peaceful errands, through this zone" nor the right "of relief, when suffering from want of necessities, from the shore." Id., at 720-721.
>
> According to Secretary Bayard, the State Department's position **was** a well-considered one, rooted in principles of reciprocity and consistent practice.

This excerpt was selected because it effectively shows how the narrative mode is applied in the "Analysis" section of a legal judgment to indicate and elaborate on the position of one of the litigants (*the State Department's position with respect to waters surrounding (...) was that the sovereigns (...) could only (...).* Unlike in Text Sample 4, the narrative is not used as a factual account of an incriminating event but it is an integral part of the legal reasoning, constituting its background. Noteworthy is also an explicit expression of stance through the use of an adjective (*the State Department's position was a* <u>*well-considered*</u> *one* (…) [my emphasis]. In the same opinion, another passage can be found illustrating the frequent use of nouns controlling *that*-clauses.

Text Sample 5: Opinion SC22-05 (past tense forms in bold, nouns plus *that* capitalized]

> The principal PROBLEM with Alaska's ASSERTION is THAT the 1824 Treaty by its terms did not address navigation for the purpose of innocent passage, but rather addressed only navigation "for the purpose of fishing and trading with the natives." Even on the questionable ASSUMPTION THAT the Treaty's reference to "interior seas" included all the waters of the Alexander Archipelago and not just waters within three nautical miles of the coast of the mainland or any particular island, but see Report 27-28 (refuting this assumption), the Treaty <u>simply</u> does not provide EVIDENCE THAT Russia asserted a right to exclude innocent passage.

This passage is characteristic of legal argumentation where there is a careful and detailed presentation of arguments of opposing parties and then their subsequent refutation or acknowledgement. The case in this opinion involves the State of Alaska, appearing as plaintiff against the United States of America. In the example above, the position taken by the State of Alaska comes under close scrutiny. The nouns (capitalized) are in fact used as labelling noun phrases in order to "encapsulate" a preceding stretch of text containing the concept or arguments (*Alaska's assertion, questionable assumption*).[33] This is a very useful device as it enables the author to indicate and locate an argument and then deal with it by exposing its weaknesses (*the Treaty simply does not provide evidence that (...)*. It is also a vehicle for expressing stance through a value-laden word choice, as can be observed in the modification of the noun *assumption.*

We can now move on to examine a sample from an academic journal. Journal articles and briefs have their mean scores not significantly different on Dimension 1 (7.4 and 6.8 respectively). However, this is where the similarity ends. Journal articles belong to the so-called "expository" legal writing. They typically focus on a certain legal issue (a point of law) and discuss it objectively. As Tiersma observes: "Expository genres tend to conform to a traditional structure, but it is usually less rigid than that of operative documents. Their style resembles formal everyday language, although use of legal terminology is almost unavoidable" (1999: 139). Journal articles are supposed to provide state-of-the-art, highly specialist information, for the kind of audience where considerable prior knowledge is already assumed. The excerpt below comes from an article that deals with ineffective assistance of counsel, i.e. inadequate representation rendered by an attorney in legal proceedings before a court of law. Such conduct can give rise to legal claims and the article reviews the relevant case law in an attempt to trace the evolution of both state and federal decisions over, approximately, the past fifteen years (from the time when the article was written) in an attempt to demonstrate the manner in which such claims are resolved.

Text Sample 6: Journal Article 00-1 (past tense forms in bold, pronoun IT and third person pronouns capitalized,

> In two cases **decided** in the mid-eighties, the Supreme Court of the United States **elaborated** on the appropriate standards for judging claims of ineffective assistance of counsel. United States v. Cronic **involved** a conviction for mail fraud which **was reversed** by the Tenth Circuit on the grounds that a young attorney who **was** inexperienced in criminal law **was given** only twenty-five days to prepare a complex matter for trial. While ineffectiveness **was found** by the Tenth Circuit on the basis of these factors alone, the Supreme Court **reversed** this judgment and **required** a finding of actual prejudice to the defendant.
>
> In Strickland v. Washington, where IT **was held** THAT the defendant **was** not denied effective assistance of counsel because HE **failed** to affirmatively prove prejudice, the Supreme Court **went** on to define this prejudice as a "reasonable

33 See Partington 1998: 96-101 for a useful overview and a brief corpus-based analysis of selected labeling noun phrases. See also Francis 1994.

> probability sufficient to undermine confidence in the outcome, that, but for counsel's unprofessional errors, the result of the proceeding would have been different".

As can be seen in the Text Sample 4, the narrative features (mostly past tense forms) have been utilized to provide a concise summary of two judicial decisions (e.g. *in two cases decided, the Supreme Court (...) elaborated on the appropriate standard, a conviction (...) was reversed,* etc.). This bears a close resemblance to what we saw in textbooks where the clarification of concepts and legal rules frequently involves having recourse to landmark cases. However, here, the purpose for citing past rulings is to present the recent legal (judicial) practice in that respect and, at the same time, to show the prevalent attitude to this problem (a significant point given the "judge-made" nature of common law). Such references form the background to the discussion of a particular legal problem.

Conflicting attitudes to the issue of counsel ineffectiveness can be noticed in the succinct description of judicial decisions encapsulated in single lexical items such as *reverse, find* and *hold* as in *a conviction (...) was **reversed**, ineffectiveness was **found**, it was **held** that.*

Summarizing judicial decisions given in a particular landmark case is clearly a recurring feature of legal writing that cuts across different legal genres. Resolution of the conflict is usually sought by citing a Supreme Court ruling, verbatim which equals invoking the highest legal authority. Journal articles obviously vary in their focus. The excerpt provided above comes from an article that purports to give an overview of a problem rather than advancing any argument that would call for defending a potentially controversial point. However, the concerns could be different as in another sample from a journal article:

Text Sample 7: Journal Article ALR-3 (past tense forms and perfect aspect forms in bold, pronoun IT and third person pronouns capitalized)

> Recently, courts **have begun** applying the 1948 definition of Indian country to recognize tribal sovereignty and preempt state jurisdiction. They are using the twentieth century test, but giving it a nineteenth century meaning. General <u>confusion</u> about Indian law, **abetted** by an authoritative treatise in this area, **has led** the courts <u>to overlook</u> <u>critical</u> changes made to the meaning of "Indian country" at the beginning of this century.
>
> While the initial results of this <u>misunderstanding</u> **were** <u>unremarkable</u>, that **has begun** to change.

In the excerpt above, the author does not stop at providing a purely factual account of historical backdrop to the case in question. In the article, the concepts of the Indian country and tribal sovereignty are indeed traced over the years by referring to past judicial decisions, the discursive practice already identified in virtually all the examples of legal writing analysed so far. However, in this case, the tone becomes more polemical. In terms of surface linguistic features, there is not a great deal of change in comparison with Text sample 4. But this excerpt uses value-laden word choice to put forward an argument. There is an overt criticism of the stance taken by courts with respect to the issue of Indian country, which the author attributes to "general confusion about Indian law" and an institutional factor, i.e. "authoritative treatise". Evaluation is achieved by using labelling nouns (*misunderstanding*), adjectives (*unremarkable, critical*) and the verb (*overlook*). This is all done in order to establish the author's point, which is to argue that the use of the Indian country statute to recognize sovereignty directly conflicts with other United States Supreme Court standards for defining the scope of Indian government, and that it runs afoul of principles of state sovereignty. In sum, the aim of citing past judicial decisions is subordinate to the argument advanced by the author.

The next excerpt comes from a legal brief. As can be recalled from previous chapters, a legal brief is a written legal argument, usually in a format prescribed by the courts, stating the legal reasons for the suit based on statutes, regulations, case precedents, legal texts, and reasoning applied to facts in the particular situation. A brief is submitted to lay out the argument for various petitions and motions before the court (sometimes called "points and authorities"), to counter the arguments of opposing lawyers, and to provide the judge or judges with reasons to rule in favour of the party represented by the brief writer. This is a highly structured document, i.e. it consists of clearly designated parts. It is also a highly argumentative type of writing where the counsel makes every possible attempt to convince the judge. However, a section of a legal brief is routinely devoted the summary of a case (the so-called "legal history", which is also realized through the narrative mode as can be seen below:

Text Sample 8: Brief 00-9285 (past tense forms and perfect aspect forms in bold)

> In March 1992, Timothy Hall's body **was discovered** beneath an abandoned construction site along the James River in Newport News, Virginia. It **was covered** with stab wounds and **was naked** from the waist down with the legs splayed. There **were** bloody "transfer" stains on the outside of Hall's thighs and other signs of an attempted sodomy. The medical examiner **concluded** that Hall **had bled** to death from 143 separate "sharp force injuries," and that Hall **could have survived** in a conscious state for as long as 30 to 45 minutes after the last wound **was inflicted**.

It is similar to paragraph 2 of Text Sample 3 which also contained a factual account of a crime. Just as in opinions, such accounts of wrongdoings are only an introduction to the presentation of legal arguments. They are intended as exhaustive and objective descriptions of indisputable facts[34]. Briefs are probably the most polemical, given their nature and purpose. They aim to be most persuasive and authoritative. Thus, there is no room for uncertainty or equivocating. The following excerpt illustrates this point:

Text Sample 9: Brief 00-1519 (past tense forms and perfect aspect forms in bold, all stance adverbs underlined, cognitive nouns italicized, demonstrative pronouns in bold and italicized, that-clauses capitalized, signalling noun in bold and capitalized)

(1) The court of appeals **has departed** fundamentally from this Court's totality-of-the-circumstances test for determining whether reasonable suspicion exists. By declaring as a matter of law that law enforcement officers may not consider certain facts when forming a suspicion of illegal activity, the court of appeals **has created** a direct conflict with decisions of ***this*** Court and other courts of appeals, <u>incorrectly</u> **excluded** critical evidence in this case, and **undermined** effective law enforcement in the Ninth Circuit.

(2) The court of appeals also **erred** by substituting its own *assessment* of the facts for the *inferences* drawn by the officer on the scene and the local district court. For example, the district court **agreed** with Stoddard THAT the seemingly coached waving by the children in respondent's vehicle (which Stoddard demonstrated at the suppression hearing, see 12/7/98 Tr. 20) **was** suspicious; the court of appeals should **have accorded** ***that*** finding "due weight." Ornelas, 517 U.S. at 699, 700; see App., infra, 25a. <u>Yet</u> the court of appeals **excluded** ***that*** factor from its analysis without discussing the district court's finding. Id. at 13a-14a. <u>Similarly</u>, the federal judge sitting in the District of Arizona **was** well-positioned to determine, in light of "[t]he background facts," Ornelas, 517 U.S. at 700, THAT respondent's vehicle was not following a logical route to any established recreation area. App., infra, 22a. The court of appeals <u>erroneously</u> **ignored** ***that*** finding, and **relied** instead on the general proposition that "the road in question is used for a number of entirely innocuous purposes." Id. at 17a-18a. Such **DISREGARD** for the "inferences drawn from th[e] facts by resident judges and local law enforcement officers" <u>directly</u> contravenes ***this*** Court's holding in Ornelas, 517 U.S. at 699;

First of all, this brief was drafted in the name of the Solicitor General acting on behalf of the United States of America who petitions for a writ of certiorari to the Supreme Court to review the judgment of the United States Court of Appeals for the Ninth Circuit. In other words, the Government, represented by the Solicitor

34 At this stage of the legal proceedings before the Supreme Court, facts are never disputed. It is however their interpretation that can be hotly debated.

General lost on appeal and it is now seeking to have the unfavourable decision overturned. First, however, in order to comply with the formalities of the judicial process, the Solicitor General must convince the Supreme Court to grant the petition, i.e. to agree to hear the case. It should be borne in mind that the Supreme Court does not *have to* hear cases. In fact, it is totally at the discretion of the court to accept or reject a petition for writ of certiorari. Thus, lawyers, no matter which party they represent, are at pains to find the most powerful, logical and convincing arguments. In terms of discourse functions, this results in briefs being probably one of the most persuasive and argumentative types of legal discourse. In the excerpt above, the Solicitor General explicitly and directly points out to what she perceives as errors made by the court of appeals. In terms of surface linguistic features, this is chiefly achieved by combining past (or as in the last example, present) tense verbs and stance adverbs (*incorrectly excluded, erroneously ignored, directly contravenes*) which, from the petitioner's perspective, negatively evaluate the way in which the court of appeals acted in this case. Sometimes, the negative evaluation can be inferred as in *the court of appeals has departed fundamentally* (...). The actions of the court of appeals are contrasted with those of the district court (which obviously found for the petitioner, the United States of America). The court of appeals is thus criticized for failing to take into account a legal point established by the district court (*the court of appeals* ***should have accorded*** *that finding "due weight."*). This excerpt (as many others we examined so far) does have strong narrative concerns because it refers to past rulings but, strikingly, it is also marked by several value-laden lexical choices. Apart from the adverb plus verb combinations we saw above, there are verbs such as *undermine, err, contravene,* or even *exclude*. There is one signalling noun, *disregard,* which (apart from forming a cohesive link with the preceding stretch of text) also serves the purpose of providing a succinct negative evaluation of the court of appeals actions. The criticism is even made more scathing by asserting that the court of appeals disregarded a past holding of the Supreme Court. This excerpt is a fine example of a unique blend of strong narrative and argumentative concerns that characterize much of expository legal discourse. The proportions between the narrative and argumentative elements seems to vary from genre to genre. The argumentative, stance-focused element has a very strong presence in briefs due to their highly adversarial nature. At the same time, briefs are the last legal genre with positive loadings in Factor 1. At the other extreme, there is the textual category of legislation exemplified by legislation.

Legislation has scored highest on the negative features. It will be recalled that the seven negative features (prepositions, nominalizations, quantity nouns, BY-passives, phrasal coordination, postnominal passives and the modal "shall") are commonly associated with informational density. Below is perhaps a rather extreme example:

Text Sample 10: Legislation 2 (tax) illustrating certain negative features on Factor 1 such as (prepositions capitalized, phrasal coordination and nominalizations in bold, postnominal passives underlined).

TITLE I--**EXTENSION AND MODIFICATION OF** CERTAIN **PROVISIONS**

Sec. 101. Increased **expensing for** small **business**.

Sec. 102. **Capital gains and dividends rates**.

Sec. 103. Controlled foreign **corporations**.

TITLE II--OTHER **PROVISIONS**

Sec. 201. **Clarification** OF **taxation** OF certain **settlement funds**.

Sec. 202. **Modification OF** active **business definition** UNDER **section** 355.

Sec. 203. **Veterans' mortgage bonds**.

Sec. 204. **Capital gains treatment** FOR certain self-created musical **works**.

Sec. 205. **Vessel tonnage limit**.

Sec. 206. **Modification** OF special **arbitrage rule** FOR certain **funds**.

Sec. 207. **Amortization** OF **expenses** <u>incurred</u> IN **creating or acquiring music or music copyrights**.

Sec. 208. **Modification** OF effective **date** OF **disregard** OF certain **capital expenditures** FOR **purposes** OF qualified small **issue bonds**.

Sec. 209. **Modification** OF **treatment** OF **loans** to qualified continuing **care facilities**.

The text in Sample 10 aptly accounts for the exceptionally large loadings of negative features in this genre. The excerpt provided above consists in listing different sections and reflects the way in which legislative acts are organized. This is also an example of a highly specialized text, where the focus is on conveying the maximum amount of information in the most economical way irrespective of any stylistic considerations. Consider, for instance, Section 208. There is a sequence of nouns and nominalizations with the prevalent **n *of* n** pattern plus a prepositional phrase (*for purposes* of). Section 205 consists of nouns only (*Vessel tonnage* limit). Nominalization is certainly not unique to legal language. Obviously, it is also found in general language. What is distinctive in its use is its frequency and extensive pre- and postmodification involved (e.g. *vessel tonnage limit*). Nominal density, by far greater in specialized than in general texts, was documented in Sager *et al* (1980). It is the preferred choice made by experts even though there are often other syntactic options available. Gotti notes the ubiquity of grammatical metaphor in specialized discourse irrespective of discipline (Gotti, 2003: 77) and ascribes its popularity to specific textual constructions which call for thematizing information by means of nominalization. Interestingly, the entire excerpt provided above does not contain a single verbal construction. The underlying purpose of this passage is to package maximum information in as few words as possible even at the expense of any aesthetic value. The economy of expression is of utmost importance. It is an example of language used for purely informative, technical purposes. Our findings confirm Bhatia's (1994) observation about legislative provisions:

> The use of [...] nominalized expressions helps the writer to bring in a greater degree of precision and all-inclusiveness in his legislative statements. Nominalisation certainly helps a legal drafter to make his provisions more compact and yet precise and all-inclusive (Bhatia 1994: 142)

It should be pointed out that even though no single, isolated feature can adequately account for linguistic variation across the different text genres, in this case, nominalization, unlike nouns, is a fairly good indicator of variation found in legal genres.

Table 6.3. *Nouns and nominalization across the legal genres (normalized counts per 1,000 words)*

Genre	Nouns	Nominalization
Academic Journals	338.9	**20.9**
Legislation	**357.4**	**101.0**
Briefs	334.4	76.9
Contracts	312.5	86.5
Professional articles	332.6	78.3
Opinions	332.0	70.0
Textbook	**252.6**	64.0

Table 6.3 shows that, except for textbooks, nouns are distributed fairly evenly across the legal genres. Legislation has the largest score but there is not a great difference between their mean score and that of academic journals, briefs, professional articles and opinions. Somewhat surprisingly, contracts do not have an unusually large score. However, the mean scores of the six genres remain basically in the same range. By far greater variation can be observed in the case of nominalization. This time, legislation are clearly well above the other genres with 101 nominalized forms per 1,000 words. They are followed by contracts with a markedly lower mean score of 86.5 forms. At the other end, academic journals have a very low score of 20.9 forms. In between, there are professional articles (78.3), briefs (76.9) opinions (70.0) and textbooks (64.0). Except for academic journals, the mean scores for nominalization correspond to how the overall scores on Dimension 1 are spread. More evidence of highly informational and normative features can be found in Text Sample 9. The negative features on this Factor (nouns, nominalizations, prepositions, phrasal coordination) package the sentence with information about specific referents. Nouns are one of the means by which

writers can refer to entities or concepts, and their high frequency reflects a high density of information.

Text Sample 11: Legislation 17 (modal *shall* capitalized, prepositions, nouns and nominalizations in bold)

> (a) **Establishment**- The **Secretary**, **in consultation with** the **Administrator of** General **Services**, SHALL establish an Advanced Building **Efficiency Testbed program for** the **development**, **testing**, and **demonstration** of advanced engineering **systems, components, and materials** to enable **innovations in building technologies**. The **program SHALL** evaluate **efficiency concepts for government and industry buildings,** and demonstrate the **ability of** next **generation buildings** to support individual and organizational **productivity** and **health** (including by improving **indoor air quality**) as well as **flexibility** and technological **change** to improve environmental **sustainability**. Such **program** SHALL complement and not duplicate existing national **programs**.

Text Sample 11 representing a legislative provision spells out the nature and scope of the duties assigned to the post of the Secretary. Apart from the density of nominal forms and prepositions observed already in the previous excerpt, we note the presence of the modal *shall* typical for stipulating provisions in legislative instruments. The narrative or argumentative concerns are absent in this type of texts. The focus is also on transmitting information in the most precise and concise manner. As we could see in Figure 6.1 and then Table 6.2 (the Duncan's Test), legislation stands out as a category of legal writing with the largest score for negative features on this dimension. The other category of contractual writing has its scores significantly smaller but still relatively large in comparison with the other five genres.

Finally, we consider a text sample from the category of contracts:

Text Sample 12: Contract US 01 (nouns, nominalizations, prepositions, prepositional phrases underlined, *shall* capitalized, passive forms italicized, phrasal coordination in bold and italicised)

> (a) **In lieu of** the **payment of** the **Exercise Price**, the **Warrantholder** SHALL have the **right** (but not the **obligation**) to require the **Company** to convert this **Warrant**, ***in whole or in part***, **into shares of Common Stock** (the "**Conversion Right**") as provided for **in** this **Section** 1.2. **Upon exercise of** the **Conversion Right**, the **Company SHALL** deliver to the **Warrantholder (without payment by the Warrantholder of** any **of** the **Exercise Price**; provided, however, that the **Warrantholder** SHALL *be required* to pay the **par value for** any **shares of Common Stock** so *delivered*) that **number of shares of Common Stock** equal to

> the **quotient** *obtained* **by** dividing (x) the **value of the Warrant at the time** the **Conversion Right** *is exercised* (*determined* **by** subtracting the aggregate **Exercise Price in effect** immediately prior to the **exercise of** the **Conversion Right** from the aggregate Fair **Market Value** for the **shares of Common Stock** issuable **upon exercise of** the **Warrant** immediately prior to the **exercise of** the **Conversion Right**) by (y) the Fair **Market Value of** one **share of Common Stock** immediately prior to the **exercise of** the **Conversion Right**.

Sample 12 seems to share a great deal of similarity with Text Sample 11. In fact, one observation is that, as far as the negative features on Factor 1 are concerned, the two categories are not at all dissimilar. The excerpts provided above show how the two categories are characterized by the frequent occurrence of nominal forms, prepositions and *shall* modals. At the same time, there is a complete absence of the positive features (e.g. past tense forms, perfects, third person pronouns, downtoners, *that*-clauses etc.). Prepositional phrases in contracts are used to make temporal and deictic references (e.g. *upon exercise of, prior to the exercise of, in this Section,* etc.). The legislative text (at least in Text Sample 11) projects a more generalized universal principle. The contract seems to be marked for a greater degree of specificity. It contains more technical details and certainly a greater focus on referring to time and textual space. It should be also noted the fundamental difference in the way *shall* is used in the two texts. In the legislative provision in Text Sample 11, it serves to create a duty (e.g. *the Secretary (...) shall establish (...) the program*), while in the contractual instrument, apart from fulfilling this function (*the Warrantholder shall be required to pay*) *shall* is used to confer a right (e.g. *the Warrantholder shall have the right (...)*). As shown in Table 3.3 in Chapter 3, both legislation and contracts are characterized by an unusually high frequency of *shall.* The two genres are clearly marked for the presence of this modal. Its frequency is unusually high even for legal texts. Given the functions fulfilled by *shall,* we believe there are sufficient grounds to interpret the co-occurrence of features with negative loadings on Dimension 1 as informational and normative.

To sum up, all the legal genres under examination appear to be polarized along Dimension 1. At one extreme, we have categories which can be characterized as having largely narrative concerns but combined with a frequent marking of personal stance and evaluation. In the two genres of textbooks and opinions, the narrative mode is utilized to achieve a different more strategic goal. In textbooks, the narrative goal is used as a discursive practice to elaborate on previously introduced concepts, principles or legal institutions. This is done by providing narrative accounts which describe the evolution or historical development of the concepts. The uninterrupted evolution of English legal system lends itself easily to this type of discourse. It should also be stressed at this point that the type of narrative concerns found in legal genres differs from the stereotypical fictional narrative. In genres placed at the positive end of Factor 1, especially textbooks, there is a greater emphasis on explanation and exemplification. This corresponds to the considerably lower density of traditional informational features. In the case of textbooks, the audience level of background knowledge of law and training in law must be considered. Unlike in the case of academic articles, textbooks are not expected to contribute new knowledge to the discipline. Textbooks and opinions probably differ in respect of stance expression. This issue goes, however, beyond the scope of this book but our analysis seems to suggest that judges are less likely to overtly project their attitude. The narrative parts in opinions are at the same time meant to be highly objective, chiefly by focusing on the factual aspect and avoiding any form of overt projection of stance. In contrast, as we saw in Sample 1, narrative account in textbooks is interlaced with present perfect forms which are used to convey the 'state-of-the-art' received and universally accepted opinion on a particular issue. As Hyland (2000: 105) asserts, textbooks are perceived as "repositories of codified knowledge". This is often augmented by the presence of stance expressions. On the basis of the above analysis, Dimension 1 in the present analysis can be interpreted as representing Narrative, Stance-focused vs. Informational and Normative discourse.

6.2.2. Dimension 2: Instructive and advisory discourse

There are markedly fewer features on Dimension 2 (ten as compared with twenty-four on Factor 1). Only two of them are negative and they can be considered as weak because they appear on Dimension 3 with larger loadings. Thus, they do not count as very important features in the interpretation of Factor 2. In the absence of negative features, this dimension will be interpreted in terms of a continuum rather than a binary opposition. Unlike on Dimension 1, non-past tense forms are prominent here. The strong presence of BE as the main verb and predicative adjectives suggests that there are in fact many subject predicatives. In academic prose, claims are often framed by means of predicative adjectives (Biber et al, 1999: 518). Conditional subordination is another salient feature and given the presence of second person pronouns, one might expect to see them combined to produce the effect of giving advice or convey some instructive content. The moderately common use of second person pronouns is in itself quite surprising since this feature is typically associated with informality, while legal language is stereotypically perceived as a rather formal type of discourse, which is to a large extent devoid of personal pronouns. Avoiding pronouns and repeating nouns is viewed as an attempt made by legal drafters to achieve greater precision (see Tiersma, 1999: 71-73). Thus, it will be interesting to see how such presence of second person pronouns can be accounted for textually. Personal pronouns are naturally very common in conversation because the interlocutors are in immediate contact (Biber, 1999: 333). The frequent use of the second person pronoun is usually interpreted as indicating a high degree of involvement with the addressee and there must be the assumption of a specific audience (Chafe, 1985). Biber (1988) points out that second person pronouns have been used as a marker of register differences, for example in Hu (1984), Finegan (1982) and Biber (1986). Conditionals as such are a frequent and even stereotypical features of legal language (cf. Klinck, 1992). For instance, Finegan (1982) reports a fairly frequent use of conditional clauses in legal wills. He attributes this to the possible conditions existing when the will is executed. Noteworthy are also the relatively large loadings of two types of modal verbs. As Biber et al (1999: 494) document, *should* for instance, is relatively common marking personal obligation. Interestingly, in academic prose, *must* tends to be more frequently used to mark personal obligation than logical necessity. Possibility modals are marked for different use preferences depending on particular registers. Biber et al (1999: 491-492) report that, for instance, in academic prose as well as in conversation *could, may* and *might* are used primarily to mark logical possibility. The linguistic features grouped on Dimension 2 seem to suggest at least some degree of textual interaction present in at least some genres. We will examine several samples to see how and to what extent these features are realized textually.

Table 6.4. *Summary of the linguistic features identified for Dimension 2:*

Features with positive loadings		Features with negative loadings	
non-past tense	.74	Word length	(-.31)
second person pronouns	.40.54.38	nouns	(-.38)
BE as main verb	.65		
indefinite pronouns	.68		
possibility modals	.55		
adv. subordinator: condition	.48		
necessity modals			
predicative adjective			

The Duncan's test (Table 6.5) and Figure 6.2 show that the distribution of genres in terms of their overall mean scores is the opposite of what we saw on the previous dimension. Now, there are only two genres, textbooks and professional articles that score positively. The other genres have negative scores, however, in the case of four cases, these are moderate and not significantly different (opinions, journal articles, contracts and briefs). Legislation stands out by having the largest negative scores.

Table 6.5. *Duncan's Multiple Range Test for seven legal genres: Dimension 2 (Means with the same letter are not significantly different)*

	Mean	N	Genre
A	9.1431	101	Textbook
B	2.7041	100	Professional Articles
C	1.1025	114	Opinions
C	1.2320	71	Academic journals
C	2.2585	177	Contracts
C	2.5814	63	Briefs
D	6.9722	60	Legislation

We first turn to textbooks which, just as on Dimension 1, have the highest score on this Dimension.

13
||
12
||
11
||
10
||
9 TEXTBOOKS
||
8
||
7
||
6
||
5
||
4
||
3
|| PROFESSIONAL ARTICLES
2
||
1
||

0
||
-1 OPINIONS
|| ACADEMIC JOURNALS
-2 CONTRACTS
|| BRIEFS
-3
||
-4
||
-5
||
-6
||
-7 LEGISLATION
||
-8

Figure 6.2. Mean scores for legal genres along Factor *2*

An excerpt from the textbook demonstrates how four of the linguistic features are employed in textbooks:

Text Sample 13: Textbook (excerpt from *Introduction to English Law*): (non-past forms (bold), second person pronouns (capitalized) , BE as main verb (bold and underlined), adv. subordinator: condition (bold and italicized).

> ***If*** a Chancellor has decided that certain conduct in one case **is** against conscience, he **is** likely to decide that similar conduct **is** against conscience in another: the chances **are** that another Chancellor **will decide** the same. YOU **get** what in reality **is** a new set of rules of law -- rules which YOU **can** rely on as likely or certain to be applied uniformly in the future. And **YOU get** a new set of rights – rights which **can** be enforced in the Chancellor's Court side by side with the Common
> Law rights, which alone **can** be enforced in the Common Law Courts, the former in effect, though not in theory, overriding the latter. **YOU** even **get** to think of two sorts of ownership.

Here, the use of the second personal pronoun serves to engage the reader. Effectively, the tone of this passage strikes one as rather informal, which is further strengthened by the combination of *you* and *get.* Indeed, it is surprising to see the presence of the phrase *you get* in what appears to be a fairly formal written type of English. This use of language could be interpreted in terms of the intended audience, which in this case, most likely, are the undergraduate law students. Conspicuously, there are a number of BE verbs (admittedly though, not always as the main verb). Note also the use of the modal *can* to signal ability. The reader is presented with a certain amount of information that pertains to the principle of stability and predictability of law. The relationship between the writer and reader is not equal. The information is conveyed in a way that does not admit of any possibility to dispute it or discuss its merits, despite the air of informality created by the pronouns. Incidentally, worth noting is also the informal expression *the chances are.* The information is imposed on the reader in the form of statements. There are hardly any downtoners or hedges. In fact, referring to someone as *you* puts him in the position of a passive receiver not an active participant in an intellectual debate. Finally, noteworthy is the somewhat atypical form of the *if*-clause found at the start of the passage above. The present tenses in both the main and subordinate clauses express a principle, which the author believes to be universally true. This form of discourse is understandable given that it is found in an undergraduate textbook. Another excerpt provided below confirms that the linguistic characterization just described is not accidental. This is a short piece which deals with the form required to ensure the validity of a certain class of contracts, the so-called "contracts under seal".

Text Sample 14: Textbook 5-002
(non-past forms (bold), second person pronouns (capitalized) , BE as main verb (bold and underlined), possibility modals (bold and capitalized), IT pronouns, adv. subordinator: condition (bold and italicized),

> *If* YOU **can** spell out of the document a reference in it to some other transaction, YOU **<u>are</u>** at liberty to give evidence as to what that other transaction **is**, and, *if* that other transaction **contains** all the terms in writing, then YOU can get a sufficient memorandum within the statute by reading the two together.

From the legal point of view, all the essential, material terms of a contract should be in writing but not necessarily in one document. The same device of addressing the reader directly is in place and the present tenses are employed to deal with certain rules concerning the written form a contract, namely that memorandum can consist of several documents. The conditionals are used to show what requirements must be met in order to comply with the legal rules. The use of the second person pronoun makes the content more personal and explanatory. The reader is expected to feel more involved and treat the situation as potentially highly relevant in their own professional practice. More importantly, in this passage we begin to notice a specific type of instruction which aims to familiarize students with a set of legal rules. The exposition of legal rules and principles is then made more understandable by frequent references to precedential law, the case law. Such textual practices were already demonstrated in the previous chapter. In excerpt 1 of Text Sample 15, provided below, however, is yet another passage from a textbook provided to show *if*-clauses used for making speculative, hypothetical claims in response to the question posed at the beginning of the paragraph and the use of possibility modals to speculate about the way in which a court could decide under specific circumstances described earlier (e.g. *they may find that the third party* is (…)). This is not pure speculation as, in each case, the prediction is firmly grounded in the actualities of a particular (e.g. *as in Olley v. Marlbrough Court Ltd.*).

Text Sample 15: Textbook 6011 (non-past forms (bold), BE as main verb (bold and underlined), possibility modals (capitalized), adv. subordinator: condition (bold and italicized)

Excerpt 1

> Consideration must move from the promisee
>
> Should the consideration rule be abolished? ***If*** it were, it would allow a court to award damages to a person who provided no consideration but who was a party (that is, a person to whom a promise was made) and who suffered loss or damage as a result of breach of that promise. The courts **strain** to provide a remedy, ***if*** they **think** the third party deserves one. They MAY find that the third party **is** actually a personally contracting party, as in Lockett v. A. and M. Charles Ltd. Or they MAY hold that a contracting party was acting as agent for the third party, as in Olley v. Marlbrough Court Ltd.

Excerpt 2

> *If* A **fails** to perform his promise at all, he **will** not be entitled to retain the consideration provided by B and thereby obtain a windfall at B's expense. B **will** in such a case be able to recover as on a total failure of consideration. *If* B **has** not yet **paid** the consideration, A **will** not be able to claim it. However, *if* A partially or defectively **performs**, he **will be entitled** to retain the consideration and unless substantial damages MAY be recovered (leaving aside for a moment the question of by whom they are recoverable), he **will** escape liability and to the extent that he **has** defectively **performed** (less any nominal damages he MAY have to pay) he WILL obtain a windfall.

Excerpt 2 from the same text sample provides a very good example of how law textbooks use conditional clauses to build hypothetical cases in order to illustrate and aid the reader in the understanding of legal concepts and processes. Excerpt 2 contains a number of examples of *if*-clauses which are primarily used as a discourse frame for describing hypothetical cases in order to clarify and exemplify a legal problem. The use of symbols such as "A", "B" and "C" further underscores the hypothetical nature of this case. It is worth noting that instruction in law textbooks is invariably done through purely textual means, without having recourse to more visual, graphic representation, as seems to be in the case, for example, in business textbooks (cf. Bhatia, 2004).

Text Sample 16: Textbook

> In order to ascertain the rights to which any given set of facts **give rise**, we **must** always ask what **is** the rule of Common Law? What difference (if any) **is** made in the working of this rule by the existence of some rule of Equity applying to the case? Like the Common Law, the rules of Equity are judicial law, i.e. to find them we **must** look in the first instances to the decisions of the judges who **have administered** Equity.

This short excerpt from yet another sample of legal textbook has been selected solely to illustrate the fairly frequent use of necessity modals in texts that have a high score on Dimension 2. The modal *must* serves as a rhetorical, discourse-organizing device which signals the sequence in which certain points are discussed.

In the text sample, the professional form of instruction is exemplified by the Text Sample 17 taken from the category of "professional articles". As can be recalled, apart from textbooks, this is the only legal text genre with a positive mean score on Dimension 2. Indeed, many of the linguistic features with large positive loadings can be found in this type of texts. Features identified in this passage include *if*-clauses frequently combined with second person pronouns and possibility modals, such as *might, may, could* and *can,* present tense forms and BE as main verb.

Text Sample 17: Professional Article 90 (non-past forms (bold), second person pronouns (capitalized) BE as main verb (bold and underlined), possibility modals (bold and capitalized), adv. subordinator: condition (bold and italicized)

> Should You Refinance Your Home?
>
> By Digiacomo and Jaggers, L.L.P.
>
> ***If*** YOU bought your home a few years back when annual interest rates hovered around 11 and 12 percent, refinancing now **can** save YOU a great deal of money over the term of the mortgage. Or YOU **MIGHT** be able to switch from a 30-year

mortgage to a 15-year, so YOU **can** pay off your loan in half the time with roughly the same monthly payments.
Especially **if** YOUR loan **is** fairly recent, YOU **MAY** be able to go back to the lender who wrote your original mortgage and sign a few papers. Savings and loans and small town banks, which often **keep** mortgage loans in their portfolios, <u>**are**</u> often willing to modify a recent existing loan rather than lose your business. Instead of refinancing, which **means** paying off the loan and replacing it with a new one, YOU **can** cut a deal with the lender to bring the existing loan in line with the market. The new rate **MIGHT** be slightly higher than what YOU could get **if** YOU refinanced, but the costs **COULD** be significantly lower because the lender **knows** your payment history. For loans originated within the past few years, some lenders **require** only a one-page loan modification form and a fee that **MIGHT** be under $1,000. Ask your lender **if** a loan modification **is** feasible.

Professional articles texts are intended to provide legal advice to the general public. The texts are preceded by the names of the authors, usually practicing lawyers, and the name of their law practice. These articles aim to address the common legal needs of average American citizens in a condensed, highly matter-of-fact way. It is difficult to determine the extent to which they might also constitute a covert form of advertising the law firm's legal services.

The frequent use of second person pronoun *you* and the conditional clauses are used to sketch the likely scenario relevant for the reader (*if you bought your home a few years back*). The combination of *you* and the possibility modals show the benefits the reader could attain if they followed the advice (e.g. *you might be able to switch from a 30-year mortgage to a 15-year, you may be able to go back to the lender*). The text is highly instructive, its chief function is to impart advice. The non-past tense forms are used to provide minimum background information necessary to make an informed decision (e.g. *Savings and loans and small town banks, which often keep mortgage loans in their portfolios, are often willing to modify a recent existing loan rather than lose your business*). There is quite a wide range of modals employed for such a relatively short chunk of text. Their frequent presence is probably due to the characteristic tendency on the part of lawyers to avoid making strong, unequivocal claims. They can be thus considered a form of hedging to eschew any form of liability for giving an incorrect or misleading decision. Similar strongly advisory concerns can be found in another excerpt from a different article entitled "How to File an Appeal Regarding Your Pension Benefits".

Text Sample 18: Professional Article (Appeal 15) (non-past forms (bold), second person pronouns (capitalized) BE as main verb (bold and underlined), possibility and necessity modals (bold and capitalized), adv. subordinator: condition (bold and italicized)

> YOU **Do Not Need** an Attorney to Represent You.
> YOU **MAY** act on your own behalf during the appeals process or YOU **MAY** have someone else represent you. YOU do not need an attorney to file an appeal. However, ***if*** YOU do select a representative and that person is not an attorney, YOU **MUST** send the Appeals Board a notarized power of attorney signed by YOU that specifically **states** the scope of his or her authority to act for YOU.

In this excerpt we find the same strong interpersonal focus. The title of the section provides a factual information on the legal principle whereby one does not need to be represented by an attorney in the course of this type of appeal. This provides the background to the subsequent act of giving advice. The possibility modal *may* is used to advise the reader on the available options (acting on one's own or being represented by a lawyer). The subordinator *if* signals the consequences resultant from choosing one particular course of action (*if you do select a representative* (...)). The necessity modal guides one to take the necessary steps to satisfy existing legal requirements (*you must send the Appeals Board a notarized power of attorney* (...)). The modals tend to have extrinsic meaning whether indicating possibility or necessity. This type of legal texts appears to be dominated by one central goal of instructing or providing legal advice. Interestingly, the strong interpersonal focus present in the person marker *you* is not restricted to this type of text. There is compelling evidence suggesting that it can also be found in other legal genres. The frequent use of second person pronoun in the professional articles could be accounted for by their intended audience, i.e. the general public. The titles of the articles from which the extract had been taken suggest that the authors intend to attract readers by dealing with everyday issues relevant to large sections of the society (mortgage, pensions, etc.).

Below is an interesting excerpt from the category of journal articles showing the frequent presence of the second person pronoun. In that respect, this text is by no means an exception. The *Plot* feature of the WordSmith Concord tool shows that there are twenty-three different texts that contain at least one instance of *you*. Of course, this does not necessarily indicate much except for perhaps a certain tendency to make legal texts more accessible, reader-friendly, a practice somehow akin to that found in consumer documents and influenced by the plain language movement. Textbooks, professional articles and journal articles all depend for their existence upon a possibly wide readership. This is reminiscent of one the plain language guidelines which explicitly urges legal drafters to use personal pronouns when referring to the parties to the contract.

Text Sample 19: Academic Journal (03-03) (non-past forms (bold), second person pronouns (capitalized) BE as main verb (bold and underlined), predicative adjectives underlined.

> Aristotle's discussion of the voluntary in Ethics III.i **is** largely a discussion of what **is** not voluntary,[18] it **is** primarily concerned with exculpatory claims.[19] But from what exactly do such claims **exculpate**? Suppose I **break** my promise to take YOU to the train because I was kidnapped. When I later **explain** to YOU why I broke my promise, I **will hope** that my explanation (which **takes** the form of 'I was forced not to keep it; I couldn't help it') will (1) **keep** YOU from being or feeling angry with me; (2) **convince YOU** not to blame or find fault with me for my failure; (3) **persuade YOU** not to resent my failing; and (4) **give YOU** reason not to judge me a bad person. Of course these reactions **are** all related, but they **are** nonetheless distinguishable.

Overall, academic journals do not have many positive features on this dimension. In this excerpt, there are no possibility or necessity modal verbs. There is a mix of past and non-past forms. However, apart from the above-mentioned frequent use of second person pronouns, BE as main verb combines with predicative adjectives. This is not surprising in light of earlier findings according to which copula *be* + adjective occurs over 5,000 times per million for all registers and this pattern has been found to be particularly common in academic prose and fiction (Biber et al, 1999: 437). Additionally, the first and last sentences demonstrate that this passage contains multiple predicative adjectives employed as a useful device to frame intellectual claims. There seems to be another similarity that lies in the use of conditional subordinator. It has been demonstrated above how conditional clauses are used to build a hypothetical case illustrating a particular point discussed in the text. This was particularly conspicuous in textbook samples where the principle of consideration was discussed. In one excerpt from a professional article, this strategy was employed to highlight the pros and cons of financing a home. In the above excerpt, this is signalled by *suppose* which introduces an imaginary, hypothetical situation in which the author breaks her promise to the reader. This is a useful strategy whereby the reader is directly engaged in the author's argumentation and the philosophical concept of voluntary vs. non-voluntary is clarified by reference to an everyday situation.

Table 6.6. Necessity modals (frequency per 1000 words)

Academic journals	2.8
Legislation	0.4
Briefs	2.2
Contracts	0.4
Professional articles	**4.9**
Opinions	2.4
Textbooks	**4.6**

The distribution of necessity modals to a large extent reflects the mean scores for the seven legal genres on Dimension 2. Necessity modals are most often used in professional articles and textbooks while they appear very seldom in legislation and contracts. Academic journals, briefs and opinions display similar and relatively moderate scores.

Table 6.7. Possibility modals (frequency per 1000 words)

Academic journals	5.0
Legislation	2.1
Briefs	4.0
Contracts	3.0
Professional articles	**6.2**
Opinions	4.4
Textbooks	**9.5**

A similar quantitative trend can be noticed in respect of possibility modals. Again, textbooks and professional articles have the highest scores while contracts and legislation contain the lowest number of possibility modals per 1000 words. It appears then that these two modals had a considerable impact on the overall factor loading.

Finally, below is an excerpt from an opinion, a textual category with a mean score similar to that of academic journals. Similarly, Text Sample 20 shows a limited number of features identified for Dimension 2. Most notably, we do not find the co-occurrence of second person pronouns and necessity and possibility modals so characteristic of the instructive/advisory style discussed above. The non-past tense forms are used to introduce certain legal facts (*the Act grants the Attorney General authority*). Present tense forms tend to be appear in conditional *if*-clauses as passives (e.g. *if the action is commenced, if the actions is launched*). The main clause contains a necessity or possibility modal. The necessity modals have an extrinsic meaning. They specify obligatory steps in legal procedures on condition that certain requirements are met (*the United States must be substituted as the defendant*). Alternatively, *must* is used to express logical necessity that results from following the legal procedure (*if the action is commenced, and the Attorney General certifies that (...) the United States **must** be substituted (...). May* expresses the discretionary powers vested in a legal person or entity (*the Attorney General **may** remove the case to the appropriate federal court*).

Text Sample 20: Opinion (SC46-06) (non-past forms (bold), possibility and necessity modals (bold and capitalized), adv. subordinator: condition (bold and italicized).

As earlier noted, see supra, at 1, the Act **grants** the Attorney General authority to certify that a federal employee named defendant in a tort action was acting within the scope of his or her employment at the time in question. §2679(d)(1), (2). **If** the action **is commenced** in a federal court, and the Attorney General **certifies** that the employee "was acting within the scope of his office or employment at the [relevant] time," the United States **MUST be** substituted as the defendant. §2679(d)(1). **If** the action **is launched** in a state court, and the Attorney General **makes** the same certification, the action "shall be removed" to the appropriate federal district court, and again the United States **MUST** be substituted as the defendant. §2679(d)(2). Of prime importance to our decision, §2679(d)(2) concludes with the command: "Th[e] certification of the Attorney General shall conclusively establish scope of office or employment for purposes of removal." (Emphasis added.)
This directive markedly differs from Congress' instruction for cases in which the Attorney General "refuse[s] to certify scope of office or employment." §2679(d)(3). **In that event**, the defendant employee **may** petition the court in which the action was instituted to make the scope-of-employment certification. **If** the complaint was filed in a state court, the Attorney General **may** remove the case to the appropriate federal court, but he is not obliged to do so. Ibid.

The co-occurrence of conditional clauses, present tense forms and necessity and possibility modals represents a different version (from that found in textbooks and professional articles) of instructive legal discourse. As can be seen in the passage above, judges state certain facts and on such factual basis formulate and prescribe rules. Obviously, this type of instruction, unlike in the case of previously discussed legal genres is legally binding.

6.2.3. Dimension 3: (Abstract, Elaborated and Operative v. Content-focused Lexically Specific Discourse)

Table 6.8. Summary of the linguistic features for Factor 3

Features with positive loadings		*Features with negative loadings*	
prepositions	(.37)	Type token ratio	-.50
phrasal coordination	(.34)	Word length	-.46
third person pronouns	(.32)	nouns	-.66
perfect aspect verbs	(.34)	attributive adjectives	-.54
adv. subordinator: other	.50	THAT relatives	-.33
all conjuncts	.46		
agentless passives	.64		
all WH relatives	.36		
activity verbs	.47		
communication verbs	.35		

As Table 6.8 shows, *agentless passives* have the largest score. Previously, passives (*BY-passives* and *postnominal passives*) appeared on Dimension 1 as features with negative scores. They turned out to be an important feature contributing to the informational and normative type of legal discourse exemplified, in our analysis, by the text genres of legislation and contracts. On this Dimension, contracts are also one of the genres which has been found to contain a relatively large number of passives with no indication as to an agent. Initially, this may strike one as interesting given that contracts should, in principle, be precise in defining the agents or recipients of particular actions. The tag *adverbial subordinator: other* refers to subordinators or subordinating conjunctions other than *causative* (which already appeared on Dimension 1) and *condition* (Dimension 2). They clearly are indicative of a considerable degree of syntactic complexity since we are concerned with clausal forms rather than with single words and phrases. Subordinators are used to introduce adverbial clauses. This aspect of complexity is further accentuated by the relatively large score of conjuncts. *All conjuncts* label stands for the distinctive category of adverbials which perform the function of "conjoining two utterances or parts of an utterance, and they so by expressing at the same time the semantic relationship (e.g. of time or contingency) obtaining between them" (Greenbaum and Quirk 1990: 184). In the previous chapter, it was noted how the use of *wh*-relative clauses helps to explicitly identify referents and provide further elaboration about different referents. Thus, the four features of agentless passives, subordinators, conjuncts and *wh*-relatives point towards an abstract, elaborated type of discourse. Finally, there are two types of verbs present. The label *activity verbs* comes from the LGSWE (pp. 361 – 362, 367-368, 370) to denote "actions and events that could be associated with choice, and so take a subject with the semantic role of an agent". Also, some activity verbs could be used to mark non-volitional actions, events or static relations (LGSWE p. 362). According to the same source, *communication verbs* are classified as a subcategory of activity verbs which are simply linked to various types of communication activities (chiefly speaking and writing). The nature of these two categories of verbs seems to be in stark contrast to the abstract and somehow impersonal features mentioned above (most notably agentless passives). Finally, there are five features with fairly large negative loadings. Interestingly, all the features with negative loadings (except for *that*-relatives) are associated with informational production (cf. Conrad and Biber 2001: 30). In that, the features display considerable similarity with the informational and normative discourse identified on Dimension 1 of this study.

Table 6.9. Duncan's Multiple Range Test for seven legal genres: Factor 3 (Means with the same letter are not significantly different).

	Mean	N	Genre
A	9.4472	101	Textbook
B	4.4712	177	Contract
C	-2.8815	100	Professional Article
C	-3.7184	114	Opinion
B	-4.9877	60	Legislation
C	-5.3720	63	Brief
C	-5.5750	71	Academic journals

Table 6.9 summarizes the factorial structure along Dimension 3. It shows that only textbooks and contracts display positive mean scores. Interestingly, other genres do not tend to vary much along this Dimension. They have negative scores but these are not markedly different. Figure 6.3 illustrates conveniently how these genres tend to cluster. In what follows several samples from textbooks and contracts are scrutinized in an attempt to interpret the findings provided above.

Sample Text 22 from a textbook (divided for ease of reference into two excerpts) employs most of the features with positive scores to introduce the basic distinction between two types of contracts (*express or implied*). The dichotomy is posited by means of coordination. These two types of contracts represent abstract legal concepts defined using passive forms of communication verbs where the agent can be inferred or it is not important (*the consent (...) is manifested, terms are not ...stated*). Note also the subordinators marking time adverbials which indicate the conditions necessary to determine membership in either category (e.g. *when their terms are not so stated*).

Sample Text 21: Textbook (5-012) (agentless passives (underlined), communication verbs and activity verbs italicized, phrasal coordination in bold, adverbial subordinator and relativizers capitalized,)

Excerpt 1

> **Express and implied** contracts. Contracts may be either **express or implied.** The difference is not one of legal effect but simply of the way in WHICH the consent of the parties is manifested. Contracts are express when their terms are stated in words by the parties. They are often *said* to be *implied* WHEN their terms are not so *stated*, as, for example, WHEN a passenger is permitted to *board* a bus.

Excerpt 2

> CLAIMS AGAINST INTERMEDIATE ASSIGNEE. WHERE a debt which **has been assigned** to one person **is** then **assigned** by him to another, the question may arise whether a claim or defence WHICH the debtor has against the first assignee can **be set up** against the second assignee. Such a claim or defence should be available against the second assignee, if it arose_after the first assignment, but before notice of the second assignment **had been given** to the debtor.

Excerpt 2 shows the combination of agentless passives and activity verbs (e.g. *had been* given). The complexity of this type of discourse can be illustrated by considering the sentence started by *Where a debt* ... and finishing with ... *against the second assignee.* Worth noting is the use of the subordinator *where* which, in this context, tends to set the stage for the hypothetical situation the implications of which are discussed in the main clause.

13
||
12
||
11
||
10
|| TEXTBOOKS
9
||
8
||
7
||
6
||
5
|| CONTRACTS
4
||
3
||
2
||
1
||

0

||

-1

||

-2

||

-3 PROFESSIONAL ARTICLES

|| OPINIONS

-4

||

-5 LEGISLATION

|| BRIEFS

-6 ACADEMIC JOURNALS

||

-7

||

-8

Figure 6.3. Mean scores of legal genres along Dimension 3

More evidence of this type of elaborate and abstract discourse can be found in Text Sample 22. This excerpt summarizes a court ruling and uses it to expound a principle related to the legal concept of "ratification". We can again notice the use of *where* to introduce a clause that appears to signal condition (e.g. *where an agent purports to accept* (…). This is highly typical of expositional legal discourse found, where statements are accompanied by numerous qualifications to achieve maximum precision of expression.

Sample Text 22: Textbook 5-010

> It was held that the defendant was bound. The ratification related back to the time of the agent's acceptance and so prevented the defendant's subsequent revocation. But there can be no true ratification WHERE an agent *purports* to *accept* an offer 'subject to ratification', or WHERE the other contracting party has intimation of the limitation of the agent's authority. In such a case the so-called ratification would merely be an acceptance of the offer of the other party, WHICH may be withdrawn at any time BEFORE the so-called ratification takes place.
> The rules which govern ratification may be summarized as follows

Some of the positive features on Dimension 3 are frequently found in the so-called 'operative documents' (i.e. those that create or modify legal relations), more specifically in the category of standard consumer documents.

Text Sample 23: Contract - *Quitclaim Bill of Sale* (agentless passives (underlined), activity verbs in bold , phrasal coordination italicized), all WH relatives – bold and capitalized)

> BE IT KNOWN, for good consideration, and in consideration of the payment of__________, the receipt and sufficiency of **WHICH** **is acknowledged**, the undersigned______________________(Seller) hereby **sells**, **transfers**, **assigns** and **conveys** unto_____________ and its successors and assigns forever with quitclaim covenants only, the following described property:

In this textual category, it is verbs rather than nouns that appear to play a more significant role. Statistically, this is reflected in the large negative mean score for nouns and relatively large positive mean scores for communication and activity verbs. These two semantic categories of verbs were proposed for analyzing non-specialist registers. In legal texts, as we can see in the text samples, "activity verbs" should be understood as terms denoting certain acts performed in the course of commercial transactions. Some sound fairly familiar (*selling, paying, delivering*), while others can have a more technical legal meaning (*transferring, assigning, conveying*, etc.). Such verbs typically appear in fixed coordinated sequences (e.g. *transfer and deliver* in Text Sample 24). A detailed analysis of all the instruments grouped as "contracts" revealed that the highest mean scores on Dimension 3 are found in short (usually 1-3 page long) standard formulaic contracts such as the ones from which the samples had been taken (*Contract for Sale of Goods, Quitclaim Sale of Goods*). Interestingly, such texts also contain instances of agentless passives despite the relatively frequent presence of BY passives as documented on Dimension 1. This is motivated by the fact that the agent in such instances can be inferred precisely because of the frequent occurrence of formulaic, highly repetitive contractual clauses (e.g. *the receipt and sufficiency of which is acknowledged*). For example, the expression *shall not be deemed to* found in Text Sample 24 is a fixed five-word lexical bundle that appears 52 times in the ALC:

Text Sample 24: Contract for Sale of Goods

> Seller hereby agrees to **transfer** *and* **deliver** to buyer, *on or before* [date], the following goods:
>
> Buyer agrees to **accept** the goods and **pay** for them in accordance with the terms of the contract.
>
> Buyer and Seller agree that identification shall not **be deemed** to **have been made** until both parties have agreed that the goods in question are to **be appropriated** and *fulfill* the requirements of performance of said contract with the buyer.

In Chapter 3, Section 3.4.4 documents the phraseological patterns in which the keyword *deem* is found. In 21 cases, it is followed by the verb *be,* eight times by *have* (which is, as in our text sample, part of another passive construction). Other verbs that are found in this structure include *bind, constitute, create, exclude, limit, mean.* Similarly, the four word bundle *shall be deemed to* appears as many as 336 times. The statistical information is provided to demonstrate that the use of the agentless passives (at least in the case of the verb *deem*) is not accidental. Instead, it is found in certain fixed patterns that have a genre-specific function. As noted in Chapter 3, multi-word strings with *deem* tend to be found in the definition sections of contractual instruments. For anyone familiar with the genre conventions of contracts, the meaning of this phrase is clear even if the immediate co-text might appear somewhat obscure to the uninitiated.

So far, it has been demonstrated that the interpretation of Dimension 3 hinges upon verbal forms, which, crucially, are the major vehicle for carrying the specialist information. It is interesting to look at the statistics for the single category of verbs across the seven genres. Textbooks are the most 'verbal' category with 118 words per 1000 words, while legislation appears to have the smallest average number of verbs. In this respect, there seems to be a rift between the expository and persuasive genres on one end and the operative ones on the other.

Table 6.10. Mean scores for the category of "all verbs"

Genre	**All verbs (mean) per 1,000 words**
Academic articles	101.3
Legislation	78.0
Briefs	99.4
Contracts	94.5
Professional articles	110.2
Opinions	104.0
Textbooks	118.0

However, the situation looks markedly different if we look at the statistics for more specialized verb categories.

Table 6.11. Mean scores per 1,000 words for "activity" and "communication" verbs

Genre	Activity verbs	Communication verbs
Academic journals	14.6	6.6
Legislation	14.8	4.0
Briefs	13.4	6.9
Contracts	19.7	7.5
Professional articles	18.0	7.6
Opinions	14.8	8.4
Textbooks	21.3	6.4

Table 6.11 shows mean scores for the two semantic groups of activity and communication verbs. In light of the overall findings on Dimension 3, activity verbs seem to play a crucial role. In this respect, there is a clear gap between textbooks and contracts (with professional articles in close proximity) and the rest of the genres which display a shared range of scores clustered around 14. The situation is not as unequivocal with communication verbs but one should bear in mind that activity verbs have a loading considerably larger than the other verb category.

Table 6.8 shows that nouns have a large negative mean score on Dimension 3. However, such figures should be approached with caution. They merely indicate the extent to which a given features participates in the overall pool of shared variance accounted for by the factor analysis. This does not mean that we are not going to find any nouns in texts that have positive and large mean scores on this Dimension. Instead, this figure signals that nouns do not tend to be prominent on this Dimension because of their decreased frequency in comparison with the other positive features. This dimension has revealed that there are substantial parts of contractual instruments that are not so much informational as documented on Dimension 1. In other words, nominal forms are not the main carriers of specialist information. The density of verbal forms signals a procedural discourse. Some of them are typical peformatives, i.e. verbs performing operative legal acts. They are often marked as such by *hereby* as for example in Text Samples 23 and 24, provided above.

As may be recalled, features with large negative loadings include word length and type/token ration associated with lexical specificity (cf. Conrad and Biber, 2001: 219) and nouns and attributive adjectives linked to 'increased complexity" (Biber and Conrad, 2001: 219). The remaining *that*-clauses signal the presence of dependent clauses. As shown in Figure 6.3, academic journals and briefs have the largest negative score on this Dimension.

Text Sample 25: Journal Article 99-1 (nouns in bold, attributive adjectives in italics)

> Rather, utilizing the **market forces** at **work** in the *private* **sector** would represent an *expanded* **view** of the **responsibilities** and **abilities** of *regulatory* **agencies**. In an **era** of *dwindling* **resources**, *educated* and *empowered* **consumers** should allow *regulatory* **agencies** to focus their *limited* **resources** on dealing with truly *bad* **actors**.

A short extract from a journal article about legal aspects of environment protection shows an unusually large concentration of different nouns qualified by equally frequent attributive adjectives. Interestingly, the nouns in this excerpt are fairly general and the attributive adjectives are used to limit their scope or application (e.g. *regulatory agencies*) or they tend to carry authorial evaluation, i.e. they are used to express stance (e.g. *educated and empowered consumers, dwindling resources, bad* actors). A similar aspect in the use of attributive adjectives can be also found in briefs.

Text Sample 26: (Brief 98-822)

> First, the **Court** has erred in its *prior environmental standing* **cases** by relying on a *formalistic* **understanding** of the *American political* **system** that ignores the *significant* **barriers** in the *political* **process** to **expression** of the *broad public* **interest** in *environmental* **protection**.

The relatively large negative score for word length and type-token ratio are reflected in the long (e.g. *understanding, protection*) and varied nouns, i.e. there is comparatively little lexical repetition. Just as in the previous sample, this one contains numerous examples of premodification used for both first and subsequent mentions. The high frequency of occurrence of premodifying adjectives in expository legal genres ties in with extremely large frequencies of premodifying adjectives in academic prose documented in Biber et al (1999: 589). The presence of negative features on this dimension signals discourse focused on providing additional or descriptive details through specific and precise modification of nouns.

6.3. Conclusions

This chapter demonstrated the applicability of a new factor analysis in describing the most significant co-occurrence of linguistic features in legal genres. The approach adopted is exploratory which means that the new factor analysis was employed in order to identify a set of co-occurrence patterns corresponding closely to the available data. Unlike in the previous chapter, there are no previously-identified dimensions that could be adopted as useful and expedient reference points. The role of the human analyst is then to interpret such patterns. Thus, it should be stressed that there are hardly any previous MD studies of legal discourse which could be used as a basis or prompts to facilitate the interpretation of the results. Indeed, the present analysis is to date the first attempt to analyze variation within one disciplinary domain encompassing a range of different genres. The new factor analysis has led to the identification of a three-dimensional model of linguistic variation across legal discourse. Despite some points of similarity between the 1988 model of register variation and the MD analysis of legal genres, most conspicuous with regard to (non) narrative concerns, Dimensions 2 and 3 of the latter have no direct counterparts in the former. Methodologically, these patterns demonstrate the utility of conducting a new factor analysis for a specific discourse domain. The ALC factor analysis identified important patterns of linguistic variation among legal genres, realized by specific configurations of linguistic features that were not captured by in the general 1988 model of variation. The first dimension has shown a clear split between genres associated with narrative and stance-oriented discourse characteristic of legal academic genres (textbook, academic journals), expository genres (opinions) and persuasive genres (briefs, professional articles) and legal discourse that is highly informational and normative (legislation and contracts).

The second dimension represents a continuum linked to instructive and advisory legal discourse. It focuses on the pragmatic aspect of legal texts whereby there are specific linguistic patterns employed to facilitate the dissemination of specialist knowledge by direct reference to the text recipients and offering realistic hypothetical scenarios. Interestingly, the two genres with largest positive mean scores (textbooks and professional articles) address non- or semi-experts and the extensive use of such linguistic patterns could be attributed to the particular communicative need of negotiating the transfer of knowledge with non-specialists.

The third dimension cuts across the so far fundamental distinction between operative and expository/persuasive genres. This dimension indicates the presence of legal discourse that is elaborate, abstract and dependent upon verbal forms to convey specialist content. Textbooks show what and how legal acts should be performed to achieve specific legal effects and conform with legal rules and regulations. Contracts reflect the performativity of actual legal acts. Features grouped along this dimension seem to reflect the influence and corresponding constraints of the sub-domain of contract law (realized in textbooks and contracts). At the same time, the excerpts show that textbook is a relatively complex type of discourse with different linguistic patterns employed depending on particular functions envisaged by textbook authors. While retaining its explanatory character, there are different discursive practices at work. In other words, textbooks display a variety of ways in which their discoursal goals can be realized. It is possible that this genre permits a relatively high degree of variation in the linguistic form of its texts. Also, textbooks represent a relatively unrestricted genre (cf. Hatim and Mason, 1990: 53). Clearly, no individual text can adequately represent a given genre. Certain genres could have both narrative and interactive/persuasive goals and these two concerns can be weighted quite differently from one text to another. This may also reflect internal variation in the text genres. Genres with negative loadings on this dimension use varied specialized and relatively rare vocabulary to convey carefully integrated information.

The analysis of Dimension 3 raises the issue of complexity in legal discourse. Discourse complexity and the way in which it is manifested linguistically has attracted a great deal of attention from scholars working from various perspectives (e.g. linguistic, educational, psychological, etc). In his 2001 study, Biber demonstrated the applicability of the multi-dimensional methodology in approaching the complexity of discourse. He provides a list of 33 surface linguistic features associated with linguistic complexity. The first six are linked to a reduced complexity. In this analysis, only two features (pronoun IT and demonstrative pronouns) can be classified as contributing to "less specified reference" (Biber, 2001: 219). The remaining 27 features on Biber's list are associated with increased complexity. Twenty-two of them can be found across the three dimensions identified in the present analysis. For example, all the features linked to integrated structure such as nouns, prepositions, attributive adjectives, nominalizations and phrasal coordination are found as features with negative loadings on either Dimension 1 or 2. The same applies to the entire categories of "lexical specificity" (word length and type/token ratio) and "passive constructions" (agentless passives and *by*-passives). Also, most of the features grouped under the "dependent clauses" category are scattered across the three dimensions. Thus, linguistically, legal texts represent a highly complex type of discourse. It is one of the most important conclusions drawn in Biber 2001 that discourse complexity should not be viewed as "a single unified construct; rather the results [of the analysis] indicate five separate but interrelated dimensions of complexity based on surface structure features, and consideration of linguistic features associated with information packaging, cohesion, and rhetorical organization will likely reveal additional dimensions" (p. 227).

CHAPTER VII: SYNTHESIS AND FINAL CONCLUSIONS

Despite the widely-held perception of legal language as constituting a relatively homogenous and uniform linguistic phenomenon, the situation appears to be much more complex. The analyses presented in this book are to date the first attempt to demonstrate variation within the disciplinary discourse of law encompassing a range of different genres. The preceding chapters have documented many important linguistic characteristics of legal genres. Table 7.1 below summarizes the most important features identified for individual legal genres. The findings obtained from the analyses demonstrate that there exist highly systematic patterns of use occurring across legal genres. Especially noteworthy are the following patterns:

1. The crucial importance of the distinction between operative or "language of the law" genres and the other legal genres, especially the expository and persuasive genres. Linguistically, legislation and contracts share more similarities than differences. They both have the most limited sets of different words but they contain the greatest range of different lexical bundles. This marks them off as the most formulaic and lexically restricted legal genres. This fundamental distinction between operative and expository genres is projected on the first two dimensions of the 1988 Model of Variation and the first dimension of the new MD analysis, where they are polar opposites. Thus, operative genres are by far more informational, normative and non-narrative than expository and persuasive genres. To a lesser extent, operative genres are more structurally elaborate and complex (Dimension 3 of the 1988 study). In terms of lexical diversity (discussed in Chapter 3), there is a clear divide between operative genres, which rely on a fairly restricted word choice and other legal genres, which contain a substantially richer and more varied vocabulary as reflected in the use of a larger set of different low-frequency word types.
2. The central importance of narrative concerns and stance in **all** expository and persuasive genres, as exemplified most conspicuously by the judicial recounting of facts in legal opinions, and the discursive practice of explaining legal concepts in textbooks.
3. The distribution of features associated with informational production and normative focus (e.g. heavy nominalization, passives, phrasal coordination, modal *shall*) and commonly perceived as contributing to the opacity of legal language restricted primarily to operative genres.
4. Each legal genre has its own set or sets of distinctive lexical categories found virtually exclusively within a particular genre. Such genre specificity is not

necessarily related to subject matter. At the same time, there is evidence of a small set of "core" legal vocabulary shared by all the genres.

5. The importance of multi-word combinations in discriminating between different legal genres. As a result, it is argued that legal genres can be described and differentiated in terms of their preferred phraseologies and that the phraseological preferences correlate strongly with the different communicative priorities and epistemological precepts of the legal genres.
6. More specifically, the varying degree of formulaicity found among legal genres and indicated by the lexical bundle frequency information. It emerges that all legal genres use lexical bundles. However, the genres use bundles to differing extents, and for different functions. Operative genres are structured around lexical bundles to a greater extent than any other genre.
7. The differences among legal genres are best viewed in terms of a cline. The degree of variation observed across the range of legal genre prompts one to view language used in legal contexts in terms of a system of related domain-specific genres rather than as a unitary phenomenon commonly referred to as "legal language".

Table 7.1. Summary of linguistic characteristics of legal genres

Academic journals	diversified vocabulary; a wide range of rare (low-frequency) words; most high-frequency verbs are shared by other genres; frequent occurrence of general language keywords; relatively few genre-specific keywords (e.g. keywords linked to legal reasoning); very limited use of lexical bundles; relatively few high- frequency bundles; few referential bundles but significantly larger proportions of stance and text-oriented bundles (e.g. largest proportion of transition bundles, also marked for high occurrence of framing bundles); relatively few features related to explicit/elaborated reference and impersonal style; relatively strong presence of narrative and stance-oriented concerns
Briefs	moderate use of different word types and rare (low-frequency) words; high-frequency verbs shared with opinions; numerous salient highly specific keyword categories (e.g. crime and incarceration keywords); relatively low use of lexical bundles; a moderate use of legal reference bundles (largest proportion of institutional bundles), relatively even distribution of stance and text-oriented bundles (a substantial proportion of framing bundles); absence of features related to overt expression of persuasion; moderate use of explicit/elaborated reference; relatively strong presence of narrative and stance-oriented concerns
Contracts	recurrent use of a relatively small set of different word types; the smallest number of rare (low-frequency) words; high-frequency words include many specialist terms, terminologically denser and lexically more genre-specific than other genres; a few distinctive, largely genre-specific keyword categories (e.g. participation keywords, the keyword "deem"); greatest range of different lexical bundles, the largest number of all

	bundles and the highest proportion of texts comprised of words in bundles; focus on legal reference (largest proportion of procedure-related bundles and time bundles but very few location bundles), with relatively few bundles expressing stance and a moderate number of text-oriented bundles (a large proportion of structuring bundles); a strong presence of informational and normative features; highly explicit and elaborated, endophoric reference; highly impersonal style; non-narrative; abstract and elaborated discourse; reliance on verbal forms to convey specialist content
Legislation	recurrent use of a relatively small set of different word types the smallest number of rare (low-frequency) words; some genre-specific high-frequency verbs (e.g. insert, strike); numerous salient keyword categories, most are genre-specific (e.g. keywords related to modification of legislative provisions, some overlap with those found in contracts (time/place/text deixis), a considerable proportion of general language keywords; greatest range of different lexical bundles, the largest number of all bundles and the highest proportion of texts comprised of words in bundles; focus on legal reference (largest proportion of procedure-related bundles and time bundles but very few location bundles, with relatively few bundles expressing stance and a moderate number of text-oriented bundles (largest proportion of structuring bundles); strong presence of informational and normative features, highly explicit, elaborated, and endophoric reference, highly impersonal style; non-narrative
Opinions	moderate use of different word types; some high-frequency verbs overlap with those in briefs, while some are genre-specific (e.g. concur, dissent); relatively small (albeit frequent) number of different lexical bundles, especially high-frequency bundles; few referential bundles but significantly larger proportions of stance and text-oriented bundles (largest proportion of framing bundles); absence of features related to overt expression of persuasion; moderate use of explicit/elaborated reference; strong narrative and stance-oriented focus
Professional Articles	diversified vocabulary; a wide range of rare words; most high-frequency verbs shared by other genres; most keywords include terms; relatively low use of lexical bundles; smallest proportion of high-frequency bundles, focus on legal reference (largest proportion of attributive bundles) with relatively few bundles expressing stance and a moderate number of text-oriented bundles (a fair proportion of framing bundles); relatively large occurrence of explicit and elaborated reference; moderate use of overt expression of persuasion/argumentation, relatively strong presence of narrative and stance-oriented concerns; a moderate use of features related to instructive and advisory discourse
Textbooks	Moderate use of different word types; many high-frequency verbs shared by other genres; most keywords include terms; a relatively wide range of different lexical bundles but relatively few high- frequency bundles; a moderate use of legal reference bundles (largest proportion of terminological bundles),

	relatively even distribution of stance and text-oriented bundles; strong narrative and stance-oriented concerns; explicit and elaborated reference; moderate use of overt expression of persuasion/argumentation; a large concentration of features related to instructive and advisory discourse; abstract and elaborated discourse; reliance on verbal forms to convey specialist content

The consideration of the findings has led to the inevitable conclusion that the term "legal language" is a misnomer. It merely indicates the shared subject matter but it hides the bewildering variety of diverse linguistic forms and their functions found across various legal genres. The 1988 Model of Variation has shown that in many respects, legal genres share important linguistic characteristics with other specialised genres as well as other general varieties of English. Features stereotypically associated with opaque legalese are found almost exclusively in the operative genres. At the same time, most of such features linked to informational production have been found to have large frequencies in the disciplinary genres of biology and history. The fundamental distinction between genres with narrative and stance-oriented concerns versus the genres with an informational and normative focus precludes treating them as belonging to the same category of 'legal language'. The distinction between the operative genres and the expository genres has been found to exist at the other levels of description, i.e. the lexical and phraseological levels. Some degree of relatedness is manifested in certain shared co-occurring linguistic characteristics. For example, briefs and opinions overlap to some extent in the use of certain lexical items, which reflects their shared institutional framework of appeal proceedings. As a result, I propose that language in legal contexts should be viewed in terms of a system of related albeit distinct genres.

This study has attempted to fill, what the author perceived as a major gap in studies of legal discourse. The recent advancement in corpus linguistics and computational analytical procedures had not resulted in comprehensive, large-scale, multi-genre descriptions orientated towards measuring variation within legal discourse. The early 1960s "register" variation research (e.g. Crystal and Davy, 1969; Gustaffsson, 1975; Spencer, 1975;) was bound to be produce very limited findings due to their severely limited scope and depth. Not surprisingly, this trend progressed from textualization of selected, surface lexico-grammatical features towards the explorations in discourse organization and rheorical patterns (e.g. Swales, 1981; Bhatia,1983) and finally towards detailed genre studies in disciplinary and institutional contexts (e.g. Bhatia, 1999, 2000, 2005)[35]. The advent of sophisticated computer technology and large corpora has opened up new lines of argumentation, based on the perception of stretches of text as repeated events, and the ability to compute frequencies and use statistical

35 See Bhatia 2005 for an overview of historical development of written discourse analysis.

measures. For example, the relatively recent methodology of Keyword Analysis has proved to be a useful resource for mapping genre-specific lexical characteristics. The present study is the first to employ the perspective of corpus-linguistics and the computational tools to analyze a wide range of legal genres.

This study of variation within the legal discipline echoes a growing interest in variation among texts from different academic disciplines. It is increasingly argued that the diversity among disciplines is so great that the adequacy of using the general term "academic prose" could be questioned (see for example Brodkey, 1987; Crowley, 1991; Russell, 1991). Both theorists and practitioners in English for Specific Purposes acknowledge the value of studying variation for understanding how different disciplines create and negotiate the transfer of knowledge through written texts. As Conrad (2002) argues the deficiency in variation studies does not concern only disciplinary texts but also comparisons between specialised texts and texts from other registers. This gap in language studies means that it is virtually impossible to determine the extent to which features found in a given disciplinary genre or genres are characteristic of this discipline or perhaps are shared by other genres or registers.

The advent of Multi-Dimensional methodology and the analytical potential it holds has made it possible to rekindle interest in variation studies within legal discourse. Equally important has been the extensive research into multi-word expressions, especially clusters and bundles. Of all the many types of multi-word expressions, lexical bundles appear most suitable for the study of legal texts. The reason for this lies in the formal characteristics of lexical bundles, i.e. the inflexibility of an unbroken sequence of word forms. What can be perceived by some as a limitation turns out to be particularly useful for investigating legal texts, where their wording is often constrained by the institutional pressures of the legal system. Biber et al. (e.g. 1999; 2004) find major differences between bundles identified in two markedly different genres (academic writing and conversation). Chapter 4 compares seemingly similar legal genres. Yet even there, the types of bundles are distinctly different. This part of analysis presented in the present book started with the general assumption that high frequency patterns are by no means accidental. The results have provided a wealth of descriptive facts requiring subsequent explanation. Legal genres are no different from other written academic genres in that multi-word expressions form important building blocks of discourse. They differ in terms of their functions, which in legal discourse, are primarily used as vehicles for conveying legal reference.

The results of the linguistic descriptions are important in developing effective training programmes, teaching materials and assessment instruments. The comprehensive descriptions of similarities and differences among legal genres point towards the crucial importance of linguistic knowledge and the value of contextual evidence in ESP training. In didactic terms, it seems as if more emphasis should be placed upon the linguistic component in teaching legal

English, and especially legal terms. Having recourse to specialised data set enables one to gain access into the phraseological behaviour of legal terms. This approach goes well beyond the simple co-occurrence of two word forms (e.g. verb plus noun or noun plus noun combinations) by drawing students' attention to significant multi-word combinations and their sentential and/or textual positions.

There is still insufficient understanding of the relationships between the language component (language as communication) and language as vehicle for conveying disciplinary knowledge (Bhatia, 2004: 204). The view adopted in this study is that these two should not be treated as discrete components. Rather, research and teaching efforts must focus on demonstrating how different interactants in different legal settings create and understand meanings through patterns and phraseological items. Considerable research in corpus linguistics (e.g. Robinson 2006:8) has shown that various multi-word strings can "give shape to our beliefs and values, and social and cultural structures". The findings presented in this book have shown that legal writers tend to employ patterns or phraseological items that are highly structured, well-organized and that serve specific discoursal purposes in the specialised contexts of various legal settings.

The findings presented in this book can be extended in several ways. First of all, future linguistic descriptions could go beyond the limitations and frequency criteria adopted in this book. For example, Chapter 3 provides the results of a Keyword Analysis for one hundred keywords extracted from each genre. Future studies could incorporate a greater range of keywords perhaps leading to the identification of other lexical categories. Similarly, apart from lexical bundles, other types of multi-word expressions should be explored. Chapter 3 contains several detailed analyses of phraseological profiles identified for individual terms. Such profiling includes collocational, colligational and textual aspects. It seems that this type of analysis of legal terms in contexts, especially across different textual/genre categories would be especially beneficial to studies in legal terminology.

It would also be useful to expand the range of legal texts by considering genres created and utilized in different settings and intended for different, also non-specialist audiences. Incorporating descriptions of spoken legal language would paint a more complete picture of language used in legal contexts. Given the role English plays in the legal systems of the English-speaking world, it could also be quite revealing to study legal genres in other jurisdictions. Even more importantly, one direction in further research could involve comparing legal English used in national legal systems and legal English employed in institutionalised expressions of supranational laws, rules and procedures. By synthesizing the results of the present study with future research on global legal English should enable one to build a comprehensive description of legal genres across different legal contexts. The present study, by focusing on a selection of written legal genres utilized in the US federal jurisdiction, has provided a first step towards this goal.

REFERENCES

Abbot, K. and N. Pendlebury (1996) *Business Law*. London: DP Publications.

Abraham, H. J. (1998) *The Judicial Process,* New York, Oxford: Oxford University Press.

Aijmer, K. (1996). *Conversational Routines in English: Convention and Creativity*. London: Longman.

Alcaraz, E. and B. Hughes. (2002) *Legal Translation Explained.* Manchester: St.Jerome Publishing.

Altenberg, B. (1993). Recurrent Word Combinations in Spoken English. In: D'Arcy, J. (ed.). *Proceedings of the Fifth Nordic Association for English Studies Conference.* Reykjavik: University of Island.

Altenberg, B. (1998). 'On the Phraseology of English: The Evidence of Recurrent Word-combinations'. In: Cowie, A. (ed.) *Phraseology*. Oxford University Press', 101-122.

Atkinson, D. (2001). 'Scientific discourse across history: A combined multi-dimensional/rhetorical analysis of the "Philosophical Transactions of the Royal Society of London". In Conrad and Biber (eds.), 45-65

Atkinson, D. and D. Biber (1994). 'Register: A review of empirical research'. In: D. Biber and Finegan, E. (eds.) *Sociolinguistic perspectives on register*. New York: Oxford University Press, 351-385.

Barber, C. (1985). 'Some measurable characteristics of modern scientific prose.' In Swales, (1962) *Gothenburg Studies in English* 14, 21-43.

Badger, R. (2003). 'Legal and general: towards a genre analysis of newspaper law reports'. *English for Specific Purposes* 22, 249-263.

Baker, P. (2004). 'Querying keywords: Questions of difference, frequency and sense in keywords analysis'. *Journal of English Linguistics,* 32 (4), 346-359.

Barnbrook, G. (1996). *Language and Computers: A Practical Introduction to the Computer Analysis of Language.* Edinburgh: Edinburgh University Press.

Bell, A. (1997) 'Language style as audience design.' In Coupland, A. And Jaworski, A. (eds.) *Sociolinguistics: A reader and coursebook*, 240-250. Basingstoke, UK: Macmillan.

Bennett, J. M. (1989). 'In Defence of 'Shall'. *Australian Law Journal* 63, 522-25.

- (1990). 'Final Observations on the Use of "Shall"'. *Australian Law Journal* 64, 168-69.

Berezowski, L. (2009). *Jak czytać i rozumieć angielskie umowy?* Warszawa: Wydawnictwo C.H. Beck.

Berk-Seligson, S. (1992). *The Bilingual Courtroom. Court Interpreters in the Judicial Process.* Chicago: University of Chicago Press

Berkenkotter, C. and T. N. Huckin (1995). *Genre Knowledge in Disciplinary Communication – Cognition/Culture/Power.* Hillsdale, NJ: Lawrence Erlbaum Associates

Bhatia, V.K. (1983). 'Simplification vs. easification: the case of legal texts'. *Applied Linguistics* 4/1, 42-54.
- (1993). *Analysing Genre: language use in professional settings.* London:Longman.
- (1994). 'Generic integrity in professional discourse'. In: Gunarsson, B. L., Linell, P. and Nordberg, B. (eds.). *Text and Talk in Professional Contexts.* Uppsala, Sweden: ASLA, Skriftserie nr. 6, 61-76.
- (2002). „LSP and Professional Practice: Negotiating Disciplinary Conflicts. In: Gotti et al (eds.), 41-57.
- (2004). *Worlds of Written Discourse. A Genre-based View.* Continuum International Publishing Group.
- (2006). Discursive practices in disciplinary and professional contexts. *Linguistic and Human Sciences*, 2(1), 5-28.

Biber, D. (1984). A model of textual relations within the written and spoken modes. Unpublished doctoral dissertation, University of Southern California.
- (1985). 'Investigating macroscopic textual variation through multi-feature/multi-dimensional analyses. *Linguistics* 23, 337-360
- (1986). 'Spoken and written textual dimensions in English: Resolving the contradictory findings'. *Language* 62, 384-414
- (1987). 'A textual comparison of British and American writing'. *American Speech* 62, 99-119
- (1988). *Variation across Speech and Writing,* Cambridge University Press
- (1990). 'Methodological issues regarding corpus-based analyses of linguistic variation', *Literary and Linguistic Computing, 5,* 257-269.
- (1993) 'Representativeness in corpus design'. *Literary and Linguistic Computing, 8,* 243-257.
- (1995) *Dimensions of Register Variation: A Cross-Linguistic Comparison.* Cambridge: Cambridge University Press.

Biber, D. and E. Finegan (1994). *Sociolinguistic Perspectives on Register,* Oxford University Press

Biber, D. Conrad, S. and R. Reppen (1998). *Corpus Linguistics: Investigating Language Structure and Use.* Cambridge: Cambridge University Press.

Biber, D., Johansson, S., Leech, G., Conrad, S. and E. Finegan (1999). *The Longman Grammar of Spoken and Written English.* London: Longman.

Biber, D., and S. Conrad (eds.) (2001) *Variation in English: Multidimensional Studies,* Longman

Biber, D. and E. Finegan (2001). 'Register variation and social dialect variation: The register axiom'. In Eckert, P. and Rickford, J. R. (eds.), *Style and Sociolinguistic Variation*, 235-67. Cambridge: Cambridge University Press.

Biber D, Conrad S. and V. Cortes (2003). 'Lexical Bundles in Speech and Writing: an Initial Taxonomy', In Wilson, P., Rayson P. and McEnery T, *Corpus Linguistics by the Lune*, Peter Lang.

Biber, D. and S. Conrad (2003) 'Register variation. A corpus approach', In Schiffrin, D., Tannen, D. and Hamilton H. (eds) *The Handbook of Discourse Analysis,* Blackwell Publishing, 175-196

Biber, D. (2004). Lexical bundles in academic speech and writing, In Lewandowska-Tomaszczyk, B (ed.) *Practical Applications in Language and Computers PALC 2003,* Peter Lang, 165-178.

Biber, D., Conrad, S. and V. Cortes (2004). '*If you look at...*: Lexical bundles in university teaching and textbooks', *Applied Linguistics, 25,* 371-405.

Biber, D. (2006). *University Language. A Corpus-based Study of Spoken and Written Registers.* Amsterdam/Philadelphia: John Benjamins Publishing Company.

Biber, D. and F. Barbieri (2007). 'Lexical bundles in university spoken and written registers', *English for Specific Purposes* 26, 263-286.

Biber, D. and S. Conrad (2009). *Register, Genre, and Style.* Cambridge: Cambridge University Press

Black, H. L. and H. C. Black (1990). *Black's Law Dictionary with Pronunciations.* New York: West Publishing Company.

Blankenship, J. (1962). 'A linguistic analysis of oral and written style'. *Quaterly Journal of Speech* 48, 419-22.

Bowker, L. and J. Pearson (2002). *Working with Specialized Language. A Practical Guide to Using Corpora.* London: Routledge.

Brostoff, T. K. and A. Sinsheimer (2003). *Legal English. An Introduction to the Legal Language and Culture of the United States.* New York: Oceana Publications, Inc.

Brown, P. and Fraser (1979). 'Speech as a marker of situation', In Scherer, K. R. and Giles, H. (eds.), *Social Markers in Speech,* 33-62. Cambridge: Cambridge University Press.

Butler, C. S. (1997). 'Repeated word combinations in spoken and written text: Some implications for Functional Grammar.' In Butler et al (eds). *A fund of ideas: Recent develpments in Functional Grammar.* Amsterdam: IFOTT, University of Amsterdam, 60-77.

- (2003) 'Multi-word sequences and their relevance for recent models of Functional Grammar'. *Functions of Language* 10:2, 179-208.

Candlin, C. N. and V. K. Bhatia (1998). 'The Project Report on *Strategies and Competencies in Legal Communication: A Study to Investigate the Communicative Needs of Legal Professionals.* Hong-Kong: The Law Society of Hong-Kong.

Caccchiani, S. (forthcoming). 'Keywords and Key Lexical Bundles as Cuses to Knowledge Construction in RAs in Economics'. In Goźdź-Roszkowski, S. (ed.) *Explorations across Languages and Corpora.* Franfurt: Peter Lang.

Chafe, W. (1985). 'Linguistic differences produced by differences between speaking and writing. In: Olson, D. R., Torrance, N. and Hildyard, A.

Literature, language, and learning: the nature and consequences of reading and writing, Cambridge: Cambridge University Press, 105-23.

Charrow, V. (1982). 'Linguistic theory and the study of legal and bureaucratic language'. In Obler, L. and Menn, L. (eds.) *Exceptional language and linguistics,* New York: Academic Press.

Clear, J. (1993). 'From Firth Principles: Computational Tools for the Study of Collocation.' In Baker et al. (eds.), *Text and Technology: In Honour of John Sinclair,* Amsterdam: John Benjamins, 271-292.

Cohen, B. (1986). *Lexique de cooccurrents; Bourse – conjoncture economique.* Montreal: Linguatech.

Conley, J. M. and W. M. O'Barr (1988). *Just Words. Law, Language and Power.* Chicago and London: The University of Chicago Press.

Conrad, S. and D. Biber (2001). *Variation in English: Multi-Dimensional Studies.* Longman.

Conrad, S. (2001) 'Variation among disciplinary texts: A comparison of textbooks and journal articles in biology and history.' In Conrad and Biber (eds.), 94-107.

Connor, U. and T. Upton 'The genre of grant proposals: A corpus linguistics analysis.' In Connor, U. and Upton, T. (eds.), *Discourse in the Professions,* Amsterdam: John Benjamins, 235-56.

Cortez, V. (2004). 'Lexical Bundles in Published and Student Disciplinary Writing: Examples from History and Biology.' *English for Specific Purposes* 23, 397-423.

Cotterill, J. (ed.) (2002). *Language in the Legal Process.* London: Palgrave.

Coulthard, M. and A. Johnson (2009). *An Introduction to Forensic Linguistics. Language in Evidence.* London: Routledge.

Couture, B. (1986). 'Effective ideation in written text: A functional approach to clarity and exigence.' In Couture, B. (ed.) *Functional Approaches to Writing: Research Perspectives,* Norwood, NJ: Ablex, 69-91.

Crystal, D. and D. Davy (1969). *Investigating English Style.* London: Longman

Culpeber, J. (2009). 'Keyness. Words, parts-of-speech and semantic categories in the character-talk of Shakespeare's *Romeo and Juliet*', *International Journal of Corpus Linguistics* 14:1 (2009), 29-59.

Danet, B. (1980). 'Language in the Courtroom.' In: Giles, Smith and Robinson (eds.), *Language: Social and Psychological Perspectives.* Oxford: Pergamon, 367-376.

- (1985). 'Legal Discourse' In: van Dijk, T. (ed.) *Handbook of Discourse Analysis,* New York: Academic Press, 273-291

de Cock, S. (1998). 'A recurrent word combinations aproach to the study of formulae in the speech of native and non-native speakers of English.' *International Journal of Corpus Linguistics* 3, 59-80.

Devitt, A. (1991). 'Intertextuality in tax accounting'. In: Bazerman, C. and Paradis, J. (eds.), *textual Dynamics of the Professions*. Madison, WI: University of Wisconsin Press.

Dick, R. C. (1985). *Legal Drafting*. Toronto/Calgray/Vancouver: Carswell.

Dumas, B. K. (1990). 'An analysis of the adequacy of federally mandated cigarette package warning.' In: Levi, J. and Walker, A. (eds.) *Language in the Judicial Process*. New York: Plenum, 309-52.

Eckert, P., and J. R. Rickford (ed.) (2001). *Style and sociolinguistic variation*. New York: Cambridge University Press

Ellis, N. (1996). 'Sequencing in SLA: Phonological memory, chunking, and points of order'. *Studies in Second Language Acquisition* 19, 91 -126.

Ferguson, C. A. (1983). 'Dialect, register, and genre: Working assumptions about conventionalization. In: Biber and Finegan (eds.), 15-30.

Finegan, E. (1982) 'Form and function in testament language.' In: Di Pietro, R. J. (ed.) *Linguistics and the professions*, Norwood. N.J.Ablex, 113-120

Foucault, M. (1972). *The Archeology of Knowledge,* (trans. A.M. Sheridan Smith), London: Routledge.

Francis, G. (1994). 'Labelling discourse: an aspect of nominal-group lexical cohesion'. In: Coulthard (ed.), 83-101.

Francis, G. (1986). *Anaphoric nouns,* Discourse Monograph No. 11, University of Birmingham: English Language Research.

Garside, R., Leech, G. and G. Sampson (1987). *The Computational Analysis of English*. London: Longman.

Ghadessy, M. (ed.) (1988) *Registers of Written English. Situational Factors and Linguistic Features*. London and New York: Pinter Publishers

Gibbons, J, (2003), *Forensic Linguistics. An Introduction to Language in the Justice System*. Blackwell Publishing.

- (1994) *Language and the Law*. London: Longman

Gizbert-Studnicki, T. (1986). *Język prawny z perspektywy socjolingwistycznej*. Zeszyty naukowe Uniwersytetu Jagiellońskiego – Prace z nauk politycznych 26.

Gledhill, C. (2000). 'The discourse function of collocation in research article introductions'. *English for Specific Purposes* 19, 115-135.

Goodrich, P. (1987). *Legal Discourse: Studies in Linguistics, Rhetoric and Legal Analysis*. Basingstoke: Macmillan.

Greenbaum, S. and R. Quirk (1990). *A Student's Grammar of the English Language*. London: Longman.

Gries, S. Th. (2009). 'Phraseology and linguistic theory. A brief survey.' In: Granger S. and Meunier, F. *Phraseology. An interdisciplinary perspective*. Amsterdam/Philadelphia: John Benjamins Publishing Company.

Groom, N. (2005). 'Pattern and meaning across genres and disciplines: An exploratory study', *Journal of English for Academic Purposes* 4, 257-277

Gotti, M. (2001). 'Semantic and Pragmatic Values of *Shall* and *Will* in Early Modern English Statutes. In: Gotti and Dossena (eds.) *Modality in Specialized Texts*. Bern: Peter Lang, 89-112.

Gotti, M. (2003) *Specialised Discourse. Linguistic Features and Changing Conventions*. Bern: Peter Lang.

Goźdź-Roszkowski, S. (2006a). 'Recurrent Word Combinations In Judicial Argumentation. A Corpus-Based Study', In: Bartol, D., Duszak, A., Izdebski, H. and Pierrel, J-M. (eds.) *Langue, Droit, Société. Language, Law, Society*. Nancy, 139-152.

- (2006b). 'Frequent phraseology in contractual instruments. A corpus-based study'. In: Gotti, M. And Giannoni, D. (eds.) *New Trends in Specialized Discourse Analysis*. (Linguistics Insights. Studies in Language and Communication), Frankfurt/Mein Peter Lang.

- (2007a). 'Legal terms in context: Phraseological variation across genres'. In Ahmad, K. and Rogers, M. (eds.) *Evidence-based LSP. Translation, Text and Terminology*, Bern: Peter Lang, 455-470.

- (2007b). 'Pattern and meaning in judicial argumentation. An exploratory study'. In Waliński et al (eds.) *Corpora and ICT in Language Studies*. Frankfurt am Main: Peter Lang, 155-165.

- (2008). 'Variation across disciplines and genres. A preliminary multi-dimensional analysis'. In: Lewandowska-Tomaszczyk, B. (ed.) *Corpus Linguistics, Computer Tools, and Applications – State of the Art*. Frankfurt am Main: Peter Lang, 365-380.

- (2009). 'Using co-text to cope with vagueness in legal lexical units. A case study in the Opinions of the United States of Supreme Court', In Sočanac, L., Goddard, C. and Kremer, L. (eds.) (2009). *Curriculum, Multilingualism and the Law*. Zagreb: Nakladni zavod Globus, 193-206.

- (2010). '*Responsibility* and *Welfare*: Keywords and Semantic Categories in Legal Academic Journals', In Giannoni, D. S. and Frade, C. (eds.) *Researching Language and the Law. Textual Features and Translation Issues*. Bern: Peter Lang, 71-87.

Gustafsson, M. (1975). 'Some syntatic properties of English Law Language'. *Publications of the Department of English* 4. Turku: University of Turku.

- (1984) 'The Syntactic Features of Binomial Expressions in Legal English', 4 Text 123, 132.

Hakuta, K. (1974). 'Prefabricated patterns and the emergence of structure in second language acquisition', *Language Learning* 24, 287-297.

Halliday, M. A. K., McIntosh, A. and P. Strevens (1964), *The Linguistic Sciences and Language Teaching*. London: Longman.

Halliday, M. A. K. (1985). *An Introduction to Functional Grammar*. London: Edward Arnold.

- (1988) 'On the language of physical science', In: Ghadessy, M. (ed.), *Registers of Written English*. London: Pinter, 162-78.
Halliday, M. A. K., and H. Ruqaia (1976). *Cohesion in English.* London: Longman.
Harris, P. (1988). *An Introduction to Law.* London: Weidenfeld and Nicolson.
Hatim, B and I. Mason (1990) *Discourse and the translator* Longman: London and New York
Heid, U. (2001). Collocations in Sublanguage Texts: Extraction from Corpora. In: Wright, S. E. And Budin, G. (eds). *Handbook of Terminology Management,* vol.2, Amsterdam/Philadelphia: John Benjamins Publishing.
Herbert, A. J. (1965). *The Structure of Technical English.* London: Longman.
Hiltunen, R. (1990). *Chapters on Legal English. Aspects Past and Present of the Language of the Law,* Helsinki Suomalainen Tiedekatemia
Hoey, M. (2005). *Lexical Priming: A new theory of words and language.* London and New York: Routledge
Hoffmann, L. (1985). *Komunikationsmittel Fachsprache.* Tübingen: Gunter Narr Verlag.
Hollien, H. (2001). *Forensic Voice Identification.* New York: Academic Press.
Howarth, P. (1996). *Phraseology in English academic writing.* Tubingen, Max Niemeyer Verlag.
Howarth, P. (1998a).The phraseology of learners'academic writing. In: Cowie, A. P. (ed.) *Phraseology: theory, analysis, and applications.* Oxford: Oxford University Press, 161-188.
- (1998b). Phraseology and second language proficiency. *Applied Linguistics* 19, 24-44.
Hunston, S. and G. Francis (1998). Verbs Observed: a Corpus-driven Pedagogic Grammar. *Applied Linguistics* 19, 45-72.
- (1999). *Pattern Grammar: a Corpus-driven Approach to the Lexical Grammar of English.* Amsterdam, Benjamins.
Hunston, S. (2002). *Corpora in Applied Linguistics.* Cambridge: Cambridge University Press.
Hyland, K. (2000). *Disciplinary Discourse: Social Interactions in Academic Writing.* Harlow: Pearson Education Ltd.
- (2008). 'As can be seen: lexical bundles and disciplinary variation'. *English for Specific Purposes* 27, 4-21.
- (2009). *Academic Discourse.* London: Continuum.
- (forthcoming). 'Corpora and EAP: Specificity in Disciplinary Discourses'. In Goźdź-Roszkowski, S. Frankfurt: Peter Lang.
Hymes, D. (1974). *Foundations in sociolinguistics: An ethnographic approach.* Philadelphia: University of Pennsylvania Press
- (1984). 'Sociolinguistics: Stability and consolidation'. *International Journal of the Sociology of Language* 45, 39-45

Jackson, B. (1994). *Legal Semiotics and the Sociology of Law.* Onati International Institute for the Sociology of Law.

Jackson, B. (1995). *Making Sense in Law.* Liverpool: Deborah Charles Publication.

Johnson, S., Culpeper, J. and S. Suhr (2003). 'From "politically correct councillors" to "Blairite nonsense": Discourses of political correctness in three British newspapers'. *Discourse and Society,* 14 (1), 28-47.

Jopek-Bosiacka, A. (2006). *Przekład prawny i sądowy.* Warszawa: Wydawnictwo Naukowe PWN.

Karlgrenm, J. (2004). 'The Wheres and Whyfores for Studying Textual Genre Computationally'

Kemmer, S. and M. Barlow (2000). 'Introduction: A usage-based conception of language. In Barlow, M. And Kremmer, S. (eds). *Usage-Based Models of Language,* Stanford CA: CSLI, 7-28

Kennedy, G. (1998). *An Introduction to Corpus Linguistcs,* London and New York: Longman

Kevelson, R. (1988). *The Law as a System of Signs.* Dordrecht: Kluwer/Plenum Press.

- (1989). *The Law and Semiotics.* Dordrecht: Kluwer/Plenum Press.

Kierzkowska, D. (ed.) (1998). *Selection of English Documents.* Warsaw: Tepis.

Kimble, J. (1992). 'The Many Misuses of "Shall".' *Scribes Journal of Legal Writing* 3 61, 65-75.

Kittredge, R. and J. Lehrberger (1982) *Sublanguage. Studies of Language in Restricted Semantic Domain.* Berlin: de Gruyter

Kjaer, A. (1990). 'Phraseology research-state of the art. Methods of describing word combinations in language for specific purposes'. *Terminology Science and Research* vol 1, no.1-2, 3-32.

- (2000). 'On the Structure of Legal Knowledge. The Importance of Knowing Legal Rules for Understanding Legal Texts'. In: *Language, Text and Knowledge.* Berlin, New York : Walter de Gruyter,

Kjellmer, G. (1991). 'A mint of phrases', In: Aijmer, K. and Altenberg, B. (eds) *English corpus linguistics: studies in honour of Jan Svartvik.* London: Longman.

Klinck, D. R. (1992). *The Word of the Law.* Ottawa – Canada: Carleton University Press.

Kurzon, D. (1985). 'Signposts for the reader: A corpus-based study of text-deixis'. *Text* 5/3, 187-200.

- (1994). 'Linguistics and Legal Discourse: An Introduction. *International Journal for the Semiotics of Law* 7 19, 2-10.

- (1997) *Legal Language: Varieties, Genres, Registers, Discourses. International Journal of Applied Linguistics* 7 2, 119-139.

Langacker, R. (2008). *Cognitive Grammar: A Basic Introduction.* Oxford: OUP.

Lauridsen, K. M. (1992). 'The Meaning and Use of the Modals *Can* and *May* in English Contract Law Texts. *Hermes, Journal of Linguistics* 9, 43-64.
Le Cheng and King Kui Sin (2007). 'Contrastive analysis of Chinese and American court judgments'. In: Kredens, K. and Goźdź-Roszkowski, S. (eds.) *Language and the Law: International Outlooks.* Peter Lang. 325-356.
Lee, D. S., Hall, C and M. Hurley (1999). *American Legal English. Using Language in Legal Contexts.* Ann Arbor: The University of Michigan Press.
Leech, G. (1991). 'The state of art in corpus linguistics'. In: Aijmer, K. and Altenberg B. (eds). *English Corpus Linguistics,* London: Longman, 8-29.
Lempert, R. O. and J. Sanders (1989). *An Invitation to Law and Social Science: Desert, Disputes and Distribution.* Philadelphia: University of Pennsylvania Press.
Lewandowska-Tomaszczyk, B. (ed) (2008). *Corpus Linguistics, Computer Tools, and Applications – State of the Art.* Peter Lang.
Levi, J. and A. Walker (eds.) (1990). *Language in the Judicial Process.* New York: Plenum
L'Homme, M. (1998). Characterisation des combinaisons lexicales specialisees par rapport aux collocations de langue generale. In: Fontenelle et al. (Euralex 1998), 513-522.
Maia, B., Silva, R., Barreiro, A. and C. Frois (2008) 'N-grams in search of theories'. In: Lewandowska-Tomaszczyk, B. (ed) *Corpus Linguistics, Computer Tools, and Applications – State of the Art.* Peter Lang, 71-84.
Maley, Y. (1985). 'Judicial Discourse: The Case of t e Legal Judgement', *Beitrage zur Phonetic und Linguistik* 48, 159-173.
- (1987). 'The Language of the Law', In: J. B. Gibbons (ed.) *Language and the Law.* London: Longman, 11-50.
Marckworth, M. and W. Baker (1974). 'A discriminant function analysis of co-variation of a number of syntactic devices in five prose genres', *American Journal of Computational Linguistics, Microfiche 11.*
Martin, J. R. (1985). 'Process and Text: Two aspects of human semiosis. In: Benson, J. D. and Greaves, W. S. (eds). *Systemic Perspectives on Discourse* (Vol.1), Norwood, NJ: Ablex, 248-274.
- (1997). 'Analysing genre: functional parameters', In: Christie and Martin (eds.), 3-39.
- (2001) 'Language, register and genre. In: Burns, A., Coffin, C. (eds). *Analysing English in a global context,* London: Routledge, 149-166.
- (1992). Remarks on Collocations in Sublanguage, In: *TandT 1992,* no. 2/3, pp.157-164.
Mason, T. (1969). 'Judicial Activism: Old and New', *Virginia Law Review* 411.
Matthiessen, C. (1993). 'Register in the round: diversity in a unified theory of register analysis'. In: Ghadessy (ed.) 1993, 221-292.

McEnery, T., Xiao, R. and Y. Tono (2006). *Corpus-based Language Studies. An Advanced Resource Book.* London: Routledge.

McMenamin, G. (1993). *Forensic Stylistics.* Amsterdam: Elsevier.

Mellinkoff, D. (1963). *Language of the Law.* Boston, MA: Little Brown.

Mel'cuk, I. et al. (1994). 'Towards an Efficient Representation of Restricted Lexical Co-occurrence.' In: *Proceedings of EURALEX-94 International Congress.*

Moon, R. (1998). *Fixed Expressions and Idioms in English. A Corpus-based Approach.* Oxford: Clarendon Press.

Nattinger, J. and J. DeCarrico (1992). *Lexical Phrases and Language Teaching.* Oxford: OUP.

Nkwenti-Azeh, B. (2001). 'User-Specific Terminological Data Retrieval'. In: Wright, S. E. and Budin, G. (eds). *Handbook of Terminology Management vol.2 Applications-Oriented Terminology Management.* John Benjamins Publishing Company Amsterdam/Philadelphia, 601-612

Oakey, D. (2002). 'Formulaic language in English academic writing: A corpus-based study of the formal and functional variation of a lexical phrase in different academic disciplines', In" Reppen, R., Fitzmaurice, S. M. and Biber, D. (eds). *Using Corpora to Explore linguistic variation,* Amsterdam: John Benjamins, 111-129.

Olsson, J. (2004) *Forensic Linguistics: An Introduction to Language, Crime and the Law.* New York: The Continuum.

Pavley A. and H. Syder (1983). Two puzzles for linguistic theory: native-like selection and native-like fluency. In: Richards J. and Schmidt R. (eds.) *Language and communication.* London: Longman, 191-226

Partington, A. (1998). *Patterns and Meanings: using corpora for English language research and teaching.* Amsterdam: Benjamins. Partington, and J. Morley 2002. From frequency to ideology: investigating word and cluster/bundle frequency in political debate. *TALC 2002 Conference Proceedings.*

Pavel, S. (1993). Neology and Phraseology as Terminology in the Making. In: Sonneveld H. and Loening K. (eds) *Terminology. Applications in Interdisciplinary Communication,* Amsterdam/Philadelphia: John Benjamins Publishing Company, 21-34.

Pearson, J. (1998). *Terms in Context,* John Benjamins Publishing Company.

Picht, H. (1990). LSP phraseology from the terminological point of view, *Terminology Science and Research* vol 1, no.1-2, 33-48.

Pieńkos, J. (1999). *Podstawy Juryslingwistyki.* Warszawa: Muza SA.

Precht, K. (2000). *Patterns of Stance in English.* Unpublished Ph.D. Dissertation, Northern Arizona University.

Quaglio, P.. (2004). *The Language of NBC's Friends: A Comparison with Face-to-Face Conversation.* Unpublished Ph.D. Dissertation, Northern Arizona University.

Quirk, R., Greenbaum, F., Leech, G. and J. Svartvik (1985). *A comprehensive grammar of the English Language.* London: Longman.

Redeker, G. (1991). Review article: linguistic markers of discourse structure. *Linguistics* 29, 1139-1172.

Renouf, A. and J. Sinclair (1991).' Collocational frameworks in English', In: Aijmer K, Altenberg B. (eds.) *English corpus linguistics: studies in honour of Jan Svartvik.* London: Longman.

Rieber, R. and W. Stewart (eds.) (1990). *The Language Scientist as Expert in the Legal Setting.* New York: New York Academy of Sciences, 606, no.6, 85-105.

Robinson, D. (2006). *Introducing Performative Pragmatics.* New York and London: Routledge.

- (1973). *Drafting: Its applications to conveyancing and commercial documents.* London: Butterworths

Sager, J. C., Dungworth, D. and P. F. McDonald (1980). *English Special Languages.* Wiesbaden: Oscar Brandstetter.

- (1990). *A Practical Course in Terminology Processing.* Amsterdam: John Benjamins Publishing Company.

Šarčević, S. (ed.) (2009). *Legal Language in Action: Translation, Terminology, Drafting and Procedural Issues.* Zagreb: Nakladni zavod Globus.

Schiffrin, D., Tannen, D. and H. E. Hamilton (2003). *The Handbook of Discourse Analysis,* Blackwell Publishing

Schiffrin, D. (1981). 'Tense variation in narrative'. *Language* 57, 45–62.

Schulze, R. and U. Römer (2008). 'Patterns, meaningful units and specialized discourses'. In: *Intenational Journal of Corpus Linguistics* 13:3, 265–270.

- (2009). *Exploring the Lexis-Grammar Interface.* Amsterdam: John Benjamins Publishing Company.

Scott, M. R. (2000). 'Focusing on the Text and Its Key Words. In Lou Burnard, McEnery, Tony (eds.) *Rethinking Language Pedagogy from a Corpus Perspective.* Frankfurt: Peter Lang, 103-122.

- (2008). *WordSmith Tools Help Manual.* Version 5.0 Liverpool: Lexical Analysis Software.

Shei, Chi-Chiang (2005). 'Fixedness in genre specific language and intercultural differences. Comparing English and Chinese fire news corpora', *International Journal of Corpus Linguistics* 10.2, 199-225.

Shuy, R. W. (2001). 'Discourse Analysis in the Legal Context'. In: Schiffrin, D., Tannen, D. and Hamilton, H. E. (eds). *The Handbook of Discourse Analysis,* Blackwell Publishing, 437-452.

Shuy, R. (1994). *Language Crimes.* Oxford: Blackwell.

- (1982). 'Topic as the unit of analysis in a criminal case.' In: Tannen, D. (ed.) *Analyzing Discourse: Text and Talk.* Washington DC: Georgetown University Press, 113-26.

Sinclair, J. (1966) 'Beginning the study of lexis'. In: Bazell, C. E., Cranford, J. C. Halliday, M. A. K. and Robins, R. H. (eds.) *In Memory of J.R. Firth.* London: Longman: 410-430.

- (1987). *Looking Up: An Account of the COBUILD Project in Lexical Computing.* London: Collins.

- (1991). *Corpus, concordance, collocation.* Oxford, Oxford University Press.

Sinclair, J. and R. Daley (2004). *English Collocation Studies: The OSTI report.* London and New York: Continuum.

Sočanac, L., Goddard, C. and L. Kremer (eds.) (2009). *Curriculum, Multilingualism and the Law.* Zagreb: Nakladni zavod Globus

Solan, L. (1993). *The Language of Judges.* Chicago: University of Chicago Press.

Spencer, A. (1975). *Noun-Verb Combinations in Law.* Birmingham: LSU, University of Aston in Birmingham.

Stubbs, M. (2001). *Words and Phrases: Corpus Studies of Lexical Semantics.* Oxford: Blackwell Publishing.

- (2002) 'Two quantitative methods of studying phraseology in English.' *International Journal of Corpus Linguistics* 7:2, 215-244.

- (2004) 'On Very frequent Phrases in English: Distributions, Functions and Structures, Paper given at ICAME 25, Verona, Italy', 19-23 May 2004.

Stubbs, M. and I. Barth (2003). 'Using recurrent phrases as text-type discriminators. A quantitative method and some findings.' *Functions of Language* 10.1, 61-104.

Stygall, Gail (1994). *Trial Language.* Philadelphia: John Benjamins.

- (2002). *Legal texts and Narrative Discourse Analysis.* In Barton E. and Stygall G. (eds.), *Discourse Studies and Composition.* Cresskill, NJ: Hampton Press, 257-82.

Swales, J. (1993) 'Genre and engagement', *Revue Belge de Philologie et d'Histoire,* 71, 3: 687-98

- (1990). *Genre Analysis,* Cambridge: Cambridge University Press.

- (1982). 'The case of cases in academic legal purposes' IRAL 20, 139-48

- (1981). 'Definitions in science and law: a case for subject-specific ESP matters. *Fachsprache* 81/3, 106-12.

- (1988). 'Discourse communities, genres and English as an international language', *World Englishes,* 7, 2, 211-20.

Tabachnick, B. G. and L. S. Fidell (2001). *Using Multivariate Statistics. 4th Ed.* Boston: Allyn and Bacon.

Tannen, D. (ed.) (1982). *Analyzing Discourse: Text and Talk.* Washington DC: Georgetown University Press.

Taniguchi, Y. (1998). 'Is there a growing international arbitration culture? An observation from Asia'. In: van den Berg, A. J. (gen. ed.), *International Dispute Resolution: Towards an International Arbitration Culture*. Dordrecht: Kluwer Law International, 31-40.

Thornton, G. C. (1987). *Legislative Drafting.* London: Butterworths.

Tiersma, P. (1999). *Legal Language.* Chicago: University of Chicago Press.

Tognini-Bonelli (2001). *Corpus Linguistics at Work.* Amsterdam/Philadelphia: John Benjamins.

Tomasello, M. (2003). *Constructing a Language: A Usage-Based Theory of Language Acquisition.* Cambridge MA: Harvard University Press.

Tribble, C. (2000). 'Genres, keywords, teaching: Towards a pedagogic account of the language of project proposals'. In: Burnard, L. and McEnery, T. (eds.), *Rethinking Language Pedagogy from a Corpus Perspective.* Frankfurt: Peter Lang, 75-90.

Trimble, R. M. T. and L. Trimble (1978). 'The Development of EFL Materials for Occupational English: The Technical Manual.' In: Trimble, R. M. T., Trimble, L. and Drobnic, K. (eds.), *English for Specific Purposes. Science and Technology.* English Language Institute, Oregon State University, 74-132.

Trosborg, A. (1995). 'Statutes and Contracts: An Analysis of Legal Speech Acts in the English Language of the Law. *Journal of Pragmatics* 23, 31-53.

- (1997). *Rhetorical Strategies in Legal Language: Discourse Analysis of Statutes and Contracts.* Tubingen: Narr.

- (1997). 'Translating hybrid political texts'. In: Trosborg, A. (ed.) *Text Typology and Translation*. Amsterdam: Benjamins, 145-158.

Trudgill, P. (1983). *Sociolinguistics: An introduction to language and society.* 2nd edition. Harmondsworth: Penguin

Ventola, E. (1984). 'Orientation to social semitics in foreign language teaching'. *Applied Linguistics,* 16, 180-205.

Van Schooten, Hanneke (ed.) (1999). *Semiotics and Legislation, Jurisprudential, Institutional and Sociological Perspectives.* Liverpool: Deborah Charles Publications.

Vermeer, H. (1996). *A Skopos Theory of Translation (Some Arguments For and Against)*. Heidelberg: Textcontext Wissenschaft.

Villavicencio, A., Bond, F., Korhonen, A. and D. McCarthy (2005). 'Introduction to the special issue on multiword expressions: Having a crack at a hard nut'. In: *Computer Speech and Language* 19 (2005), 365-377.

Walter, B. (1988). *The Jury Summation as Speech Genre*, Amsterdam and Philadelphia: John Benjamins

Weinert, R. (1995). 'The role of formulaic language in second language acquisition: a review.' *Applied Linguistics* 16, 180-205.

Weston, M. (1995). 'Translating at the European Court of Human Rights'. *Terminologies et tradition* 3, 121-134.

White, M. (1994). *Language in Job Interviews: Differences Realting to Success and Socioeconomic Variables.* Unpublished Ph.D. Dissertation, Northern Arizona University

Williams, C.(2005). *Tradition and Change in Legal English.* Frankfurt am Main: Peter Lang.

Witczak-Plisiecka, I. (2007). 'Lingusitic aspects of deontic *shall* in the legal contexts.' In: Kredens, K. and Goźdź-Roszkowski *Language and the Law: International Outlooks,* Frankfurt am Mein: Peter Lang, 181-200.

Wray, A. and M. Perkins (2000). 'The functions of formulaic language: an integrated model. *Language and Communication* 20, 1-28.

Wüster, E. (1979). *Einführung in die allgemeine Terminologielehre und die terminologische Lexikographie.* UNESCO ALSED LSP Network.

Xiao, R. and T. McEnery (2005). 'Two approaches to genre analysis: Three genres in Modern American English.' *Journal of English Linguistics,* 33 (1), 62-82.

Yano, Y. (2001). 'World Englishes in 2000 and beyond'. *World Englishes* 20(2), 119-131.

Yorio, C. (1980). 'Conventionalized language forms and the development of communicative competence.' *TESOL Quaterly* 14, 433-442.

APPENDIX A

One hundred KeyWords extracted for each legal genre and grouped according to keyness

Table 1. 100 Positive keywords in academic journals grouped according to keyness

Rank	Keyword	Frequency	KeynessValue	Rank	Keyword	Frequency	KeynessValue
1	Id.	2322	2649,48	51	speech	331	372,12
2	note	1269	2565,99	52	can	902	367,45
3	welfare	757	2486,53	53	firms	171	366,06
4	supra	1172	1816,25	54	social	415	360,17
5	see	2548	1418,98	55	poor	126	357,85
6	school	748	1148,28	56	some	700	343,33
7	citation	343	974,01	57	behaviour	182	332,94
8	death	581	840,44	58	guidelines	265	332,58
9	care	770	828,29	59	penalty	299	331,23
10	these	1061	787,75	60	families	196	328,73
11	self	436	745,17	61	accident	143	328,09
12	are	2955	692,42	62	we	1002	326,91
13	people	457	686,92	63	rhetoric	79	308,61
14	presidential	225	671,05	64	students	242	304,37
15	optimal	157	665,97	65	sovereignty	164	300,15
16	human	325	663,26	66	responsibility	296	292,95
17	model	361	654,84	67	most	498	292,76
18	sentencing	395	638,41	68	more	1089	289,43
19	environmental	460	638,10	69	estimates	115	289,09
20	ethics	207	610,25	70	parents	222	286,22
21	probability	198	584,40	71	however	777	284,30
22	journal	165	577,92	72	also	1018	281,15
23	reform	274	569,60	73	policy	512	276,66
24	president	523	564,29	74	morally	73	274,03
25	their	1502	541,15	75	recollection	65	272,51

26	prosecutors	174	532,73	76	problems	209	271,05
27	they	1178	525,64	77	aid	152	270,21
28	about	633	525,11	78	were	990	269,83
29	child	530	522,67	79	sanctions	131	267,28
30	bias	142	519,35	80	Miranda	97	260,87
31	university	260	510,71	81	results	268	259,12
32	recipients	184	488,60	82	beliefs	92	251,88
33	many	442	476,07	83	lawyers	174	251,12
34	economics	135	475,57	84	theory	197	251,10
35	defense	524	470,93	85	politics	83	247,14
36	ethical	141	463,36	86	article	574	246,83
37	none	281	458,63	87	society	160	246,37
38	supreme	500	434,41	88	governor	106	239,32
39	level	343	432,87	89	represented	183	238,06
40	crimes	237	419,27	90	patient	158	237,67
41	education	496	407,03	91	American	321	235,78
42	while	515	398,39	92	values	132	235,44
43	country	364	396,82	93	treaty	144	234,82
44	higher	277	386,45	94	harm	169	227,93
45	moral	167	394,40	95	voluntary	199	227,62
46	risk	394	394,01	96	literature	91	226,71
47	discovery	250	388,06	97	dependent	125	226,54
48	victim	182	388,04	98	powers	254	225,87
49	children	468	379,56	99	jobs	115	224,72
50	at	4436	374,34	100	legislation	214	220,55

Table 2. Positive keywords in bills grouped according to keyness

Rank	Keyword	Frequency	KeynessValue	Rank	Keyword	Frequency	KeynessValue
1	sec.	6313	15166,86	51	administrator	707	1303,67
2	section	14289	15071,91	52	commodity	537	1301,09
3	subsection	5883	13536,53	53	research	924	1293,42
4	secretary	4998	10867,95	54	works	747	1251,56

5	paragraph	4850	10460,52	55	organization	941	1250,03
6	under	13224	10224,29	56	commission	1832	1218,96
7	inserting	2942	8321,38	57	disabilities	570	1217,42
8	subparagraph	2962	8023,84	58	futures	456	1200,56
9	title	4534	6661,25	59	beginning	815	1182,85
10	plan	5669	6314,87	60	this	11309	1163,54
11	striking	2420	6296,11	61	assistance	1083	1141,00
12	amended	3391	5361,08	62	conservation	490	1130,12
13	year	4198	5278,03	63	housing	576	1107,09
14	shall	12570	4590,15	64	appropriated	486	1106,18
15	date	5593	4106,17	65	service	1802	1093,87
16	Act	6277	3642,09	66	years	1613	1049,69
17	described	2298	3031,55	67	services	1973	1042,41
18	document	1708	2772,22	68	period	2147	1028,95
19	enactment	1405	2758,25	69	apply	1529	1009,85
20	of	68670	2750,78	70	taxable	720	998,83
21	end	2056	2668,17	71	and	35151	964,10
22	adding	1134	2597,38	72	individual	1470	931,09
23	such	11776	2583,06	73	coverage	679	890,30
24	after	4238	2546,41	74	report	1229	886,71
25	program	2046	2526,63	75	facility	704	879,09
26	fiscal	1334	2517,00	76	development	915	858,52
27	security	2262	2470,70	77	subclause	315	857,75
28	for	19115	2415,69	78	education	1022	855,15
29	following	2701	2375,89	79	demonstration	370	845,52
30	term	2831	2285,21	80	projects	415	845,42
31	chapter	1217	2072,85	81	means	1819	815,13
32	national	2112	2061,61	82	programs	790	812,42
33	eligible	1303	1967,01	83	determined	1200	805,61
34	health	1750	1892,50	84	relating	1136	800,90
35	agency	1690	1816,02	85	sections	733	784,44
36	requirements	1836	1745,53	86	work	1500	782,76
37	by	16342	1743,55	87	entity	1010	774,19

38	subtitle	621	1697,84	88	reference	968	772,77
39	effective	2192	1649,08	89	appropriate	1263	761,49
40	purposes	2165	1604,74	90	amount	2236	747,75
41	general	3192	1456,35	91	paragraphs	436	744,86
42	qualified	1212	1443,98	92	subparagraphs	288	734,58
43	amendments	1088	1439,84	93	agencies	573	732,85
44	percent	1247	1405,44	94	redesignating	250	719,48
45	educational	904	1357,97	95	activities	935	715,50
46	transmission	878	1352,66	96	study	588	712,32
47	code	1831	1339,73	97	subchapter	348	706,68
48	funding	846	1332,47	98	subsections	373	691,51
49	or	24239	1319,62	99	referred	797	670,83
50	project	762	1310,19	100	carry	603	651,68

Table 3. Positive keywords in legal briefs grouped according to keyness

Rank	Keyword	Frequency	KeynessValue	Rank	Keyword	Frequency	KeynessValue
1	court	6348	3898,25	51	access	518	413,32
2	pet.	1134	3045,27	52	advocacy	144	411,82
3	that	14631	2577,45	53	content	327	409,32
4	v.	3930	1869,55	54	federal	1983	396,61
5	district	1504	1501,49	55	government	955	390,11
6	conspiracy	540	1334,43	56	united	1811	389,81
7	sex	422	1125,51	57	drug	414	385,04
8	see	2852	1097,70	58	fee	456	366,33
9	appeals	1229	1031,65	59	plea	253	355,80
10	id.	1970	1008,69	60	cert.	269	352,73
11	admissions	250	877,82	61	explained	294	349,97
12	at	6278	867,81	62	was	2960	348,85
13	minors	385	801,99	63	record	488	346,26
14	petitioners	625	793,35	64	adult	234	339,81
15	solicitor	311	788,32	65	seizure	133	338,88
16	search	342	749,98	66	testimony	303	333,67

17	error	438	717,73	67	prison	230	331,54
18	community	594	693,68	68	ibid.	416	327,81
19	race	307	686,92	69	those	1100	327,48
20	acquittal	194	675,97	70	inmates	124	317,73
21	harmful	301	675,29	71	did	808	312,97
22	defendant	909	626,25	72	statute	816	310,58
23	probation	205	623,99	73	rehearing	160	295,07
24	facto	214	603,28	74	decision	800	291,51
25	respondent	515	588,06	75	concluded	345	291,46
26	political	537	573,10	76	speech	350	286,94
27	Congress's	222	558,93	77	double	142	278,80
28	also	1444	539,07	78	banc	149	277,26
29	jeopardy	162	534,87	79	hearing	317	272,14
30	because	1314	527,59	80	minority	161	258,24
31	plaintiffs	511	525,10	81	moreover	290	242,28
32	constitutional	638	509,05	82	amicus	143	239,07
33	denied	435	508,46	83	officials	245	232,71
34	sexual	254	504,83	84	count	136	232,15
35	circuit	693	499,00	85	criminal	498	231,75
36	trial	956	481,57	86	amendment	804	227,54
37	petitioner	536	479,54	87	offenses	173	226,46
38	racial	211	472,51	88	punitive	154	225,53
39	offenders	242	471,94	89	applicants	114	224,23
40	suspicion	149	466,34	90	testified	131	220,77
41	offender	246	464,42	91	unconstitutional	186	220,34
42	states	2343	463,84	92	prosecution	213	216,64
43	respondent's	265	454,94	93	presented	281	213,71
44	guilty	299	451,02	94	motive	97	212,00
45	congress	1159	441,18	95	plain	152	208,53
46	counsel	641	440,65	96	indeed	314	207,47
47	compelling	250	436,04	97	rejected	248	207,45
48	evidence	1030	432,59	98	cong.	162	207,17
49	corporations	278	418,81	99	found	459	205,12

50	assistant	216	415,76	100	challenge	247	205,00

Table 4. Positive keywords in contracts grouped according to keyness

Rank	Keyword	Frequency	KeynessValue	Rank	Keyword	Frequency	KeynessValue
1	or	37482	27296,69	51	provided	2464	1537,52
2	any	22461	25940,10	52	to	39069	1497,07
3	shall	16203	16625,95	53	notice	1964	1492,47
4	company	7151	16100,61	54	affiliates	530	1490,27
5	agreement	8851	16045,88	55	of	55974	1497,92
6	such	13727	8460,17	56	contemplated	635	1461,61
7	shares	2365	6057,02	57	default	749	1455,09
8	all	6656	5913,96	58	company's	606	1400,83
9	stock	2352	4981,14	59	foregoing	638	1376,53
10	and	35791	4848,55	60	thereto	594	1376,03
11	other	7727	4534,46	61	group	1236	1359,47
12	partner	1644	4200,28	62	purchase	1153	1343,82
13	subsidiaries	1326	3985,29	63	premises	688	1339,89
14	hereof	1245	3978,79	64	connection	1145	1339,43
15	business	2778	3530,28	65	agent	1050	1338,08
16	borrower	1320	3511,82	66	respect	2382	1307,54
17	hereunder	1087	3447,78	67	upon	2138	1270,37
18	partnership	1577	3314,15	68	set	1625	1259,90
19	buyer	1415	3224,85	69	payable	777	1228,33
20	herein	1097	3080,09	70	day	1303	1213,64
21	closing	1255	3074,23	71	taxes	812	1199,88
22	hereto	995	3055,00	72	parties	2085	1195,57
23	seller	1420	3048,31	73	days	1399	1193,65
24	directors	1258	2956,57	74	borrowing	439	1187,71
25	be	14022	2811,38	75	respective	614	1179,92
26	party	3672	2723,53	76	employee	1349	1179,43
27	thereof	1492	2684,15	77	deemed	858	1177,18
28	each	3337	2590,29	78	indemnification	419	1176,60

29	forth	1522	2435,43	79	confidential	560	1174,93
30	hereby	981	2430,54	80	units	554	1172,27
31	event	1550	2413,39	81	except	1436	1171,80
32	lender	966	2405,22	82	expenses	902	1169,82
33	subsidiary	883	2391,06	83	amount	2214	1165,77
34	securities	1895	2204,10	84	payment	1590	1144,71
35	pursuant	2013	2192,30	85	merger	625	1143,95
36	date	4207	2154,42	86	meeting	746	1064,30
37	corporation	1613	2031,31	87	stockholders	384	1057,38
38	time	3337	1953,25	88	rights	1958	1055,68
39	assets	1363	1939,72	89	writing	773	1052,54
40	its	4869	1900,68	90	cash	714	1052,35
41	obligations	1362	1864,89	91	tax	1670	1034,93
42	agrees	806	1834,59	92	parent	719	1034,79
43	written	1381	1799,61	93	accordance	1132	1022,24
44	exhibit	683	1787,55	94	indemnified	332	1021,89
45	outstanding	691	1667,35	95	duly	437	1017,41
46	prior	1707	1660,78	96	including	2071	1013,81
47	liabilities	793	1651,16	97	employees	1055	1013,49
48	termination	1161	1602,05	98	holder	574	1013,44
49	by	13952	1569,43	99	material	1237	1012,26
50	otherwise	1724	1549,57	100	lenders	398	985,68

Table 5. Positive keywords in professional articles grouped according to keyness

Rank	Keyword	Frequency	KeynessValue	Rank	Keyword	Frequency	KeynessValue
1	class	896	3,343,86	51	the	15417	147,28
2	you	605	1,992,70	52	issue	234	143,88
3	your	391	1,648,40	53	exercise	178	139,53
4	option	420	1,024,44	54	courts	269	137,51
5	representation	269	853,41	55	plaintiff	156	136,85
6	trial	493	695,90	56	injury	95	135,44
7	lawyer	182	670,76	57	rule	351	135,01

8	summary	219	667,46	58	lawyers	76	129,09
9	appellate	232	666,19	59	a	4974	126,28
10	client	208	641,96	60	motions	47	123,77
11	certification	209	588,30	61	Inc.	192	123,63
12	court	1431	548,63	62	proposed	128	123,59
13	appeal	286	541,76	63	important	113	123,06
14	options	211	531,75	64	usually	56	121,20
15	issues	231	523,56	65	purchase	175	117,79
16	attorney	294	521,84	66	Cir.	135	116,78
17	lease	279	486,62	67	appellant	42	115,13
18	will	738	397,22	68	if	820	112,47
19	litigation	195	387,92	69	most	180	111,09
20	merger	178	375,98	70	conflict	104	108,34
21	plaintiffs	221	374,11	71	filed	158	108,30
22	evidence	396	339,11	72	fact	199	105,44
23	should	415	338,54	73	companies	117	105,15
24	must	419	311,54	74	represent	61	103,25
25	loans	109	310,06	75	rules	234	102,64
26	joint	176	308,36	76	corporate	94	100,01
27	judgment	303	305,82	77	market	153	97,95
28	clients	90	296,95	78	often	93	96,43
29	stock	305	284,44	79	Superior	50	94,32
30	can	394	264,75	80	lawsuits	31	92,70
31	mortgage	120	261,41	81	recent	73	91,12
32	motion	180	257,46	82	sure	40	90,45
33	bank	234	256,47	83	when	329	89,76
34	members	218	232,76	84	multiple	56	88,58
35	lawsuit	83	222,47	85	risk	119	88,04
36	defendants	162	216,20	86	conflicts	53	87,45
37	claims	288	210,89	87	many	124	87,12
38	settlement	131	204,22	88	example	131	85,68
39	loan	146	192,46	89	also	340	83,64
40	firm	114	189,93	90	some	220	81,89

41	estate	119	183,83	91	actually	82	81,58
42	compensation	184	182,64	92	financial	143	80,43
43	decision	278	182,63	93	value	168	80,30
44	Co.	186	180,54	94	counsel	155	80,01
45	Supreme	190	179,81	95	App.	197	79,44
46	questions	114	178,37	96	potential	96	76,19
47	attorneys	114	168,52	97	analysis	119	74,87
48	are	946	166,21	98	objections	35	74,46
49	an	1284	157,35	99	recently	44	73,17
50	action	363	155,72	100	defense	141	73,05

Table 6. Positive keywords in opinions grouped according to keyness

Rank	Keyword	Frequency	KeynessValue	Rank	Keyword	Frequency	KeynessValue
1	court	8866	4840,81	51	sovereign	473	742,69
2	footnote	1643	4638,14	52	government	1504	739,01
3	that	22293	4144,10	53	religion	377	722,40
4	we	3199	3737,17	54	constitutional	911	711,95
5	ante	1275	3689,90	55	states	3511	682,99
6	at	11235	3353,56	56	rule	1890	677,84
7	see	5092	3313,10	57	respondent	663	636,03
8	v.	6005	3162,78	58	judge	896	623,19
9	opinion	1534	2080,20	59	writ	497	617,81
10	justice	1575	2012,09	60	immunity	662	617,58
11	dissenting	783	1694,86	61	jurisdiction	1211	616,45
12	our	1419	1689,64	62	not	9688	612,62
13	it	7441	1658,97	63	had	2143	612,25
14	appeals	1815	1616,69	64	does	1923	612,05
15	concurring	685	1496,17	65	constitution	622	604,91
16	Court's	1485	1453,23	66	reading	392	584,03
17	habeas	573	1326,28	67	even	1382	582,95
18	respondents	844	1312,81	68	text	516	578,53
19	war	762	1297,26	69	joined	316	563,39

20	here	1114	1290,93	70	but	2936	530,84
21	ibid.	813	1169,04	71	us	465	502,23
22	statute	1543	1142,02	72	emphasis	436	495,87
23	brief	733	1061,01	73	footnotes	204	485,62
24	certiorari	702	1057,72	74	argument	655	472,06
25	petitioner	880	1036,90	75	plurality	250	462,52
26	state	4756	1022,79	76	suit	591	458,84
27	congress	1898	973,59	77	interpretation	534	453,92
28	courts	1560	972,70	78	history	509	441,24
29	jury	877	911,76	79	statutory	747	432,90
30	circuit	1074	901,10	80	his	2462	421,20
31	police	564	896,59	81	claim	1439	411,69
32	Scalia	363	890,71	82	sentencing	476	411,47
33	Id.	2553	883,10	83	ordinance	306	406,40
34	Breyer	308	881,05	84	remand	218	405,44
35	was	4835	862,81	85	ninth	401	399,04
36	judgment	1255	860,57	86	commerce	509	390,35
37	because	1992	858,94	87	when	1746	379,38
38	supra	1296	852,16	88	post	600	377,28
39	Stevens	359	840,83	89	process	1445	374,95
40	trial	1472	840,05	90	could	1341	363,84
41	question	1201	837,04	91	quoting	392	361,07
42	J.	1632	835,55	92	criminal	744	359,32
43	would	3470	826,23	93	claims	1119	357,82
44	dissent	396	822,28	94	no	3501	356,69
45	district	1609	821,20	95	whether	1904	353,41
46	petitioners	778	797,15	96	he	2204	348,90
47	federal	3146	793,49	97	issue	1015	346,61
48	did	1372	789,05	98	says	210	331,83
49	Thomas	425	772,87	99	simply	478	328,44
50	evidence	1585	748,98	100	only	2023	318,49

Table 7. Positive keywords in textbooks grouped according to keyness

Rank	Keyword	Frequency	KeynessValue	Rank	Keyword	Frequency	KeynessValue
1	contract	4632	13566,67	51	peform	428	697,35
2	it	5812	5,516,47	52	an	3524	695,29
3	he	2624	4112,70	53	one	1385	679,84
4	was	3998	3846,50	54	debt	426	658,93
5	is	9256	3834,39	55	implied	270	655,21
6	his	2352	2793,02	56	land	520	649,73
7	breach	975	2627,60	57	though	422	644,98
8	the	44133	2458,94	58	doctrine	361	640,75
9	performance	1162	2372,26	59	himself	297	635,88
10	where	1398	2147,25	60	favor	151	632,48
11	goods	679	2118,30	61	clauses	311	625,85
12	be	6938	1981,67	62	frustration	139	625,82
13	promise	521	1974,74	63	they	1097	607,02
14	contracts	882	1936,96	64	loss	452	606,23
15	contractual	576	1871,51	65	vendor	198	603,52
16	but	2190	1766,14	66	would	1699	591,34
17	Ltd.	512	1705,47	67	mistake	185	576,64
18	been	1899	1616,54	68	some	727	545,95
19	damages	864	1434,07	69	reliance	282	542,94
20	if	2901	1385,82	70	rescission	130	542,92
21	there	1509	1308,32	71	seems	244	530,36
22	had	1500	1305,69	72	A's	116	521,34
23	him	729	1183,87	73	terms	848	519,31
24	can	1155	1111,74	74	equitable	254	506,84
25	promisee	226	1106,85	75	what	602	504,42
26	to	18074	1095,97	76	said	460	502,46
27	which	3373	1077,02	77	cannot	504	502,01
28	has	2365	1041,23	78	contracting	211	490,13
29	a	13933	1033,99	79	assignee	271	489,20
30	intention	357	1017,73	80	have	2150	430,12

31	plaintiff	589	999,99	81	were	1015	479,59
32	law	2015	944,71	82	misrepresent ation	162	479,30
33	money	532	914,91	83	words	295	472,59
34	repudiation	206	901,95	84	specific	467	469,97
35	should	1016	864,01	85	sue	194	460,88
36	not	4896	837,52	86	obligation	451	458,56
37	cases	986	834,09	87	done	259	456,78
38	so	1198	830,73	88	innocent	184	453,50
39	will	1690	788,73	89	could	775	449,75
40	parties	1090	783,78	90	circumstance s	444	442,26
41	acceptance	320	760,08	91	liable	307	441,44
42	discharge	335	754,70	92	debtor	392	439,41
43	must	1006	747,49	93	assignment	360	434,25
44	recover	299	743,24	94	void	167	432,80
45	creditor	310	732,00	95	bound	236	426,39
46	party	1462	728,77	96	may	2299	426,31
47	consideration	556	726,40	97	executory	93	405,99
48	arbitration	368	720,77	98	secondly	94	405,71
49	that	8371	719,39	99	liability	594	401,98
50	principle	401	705,54	100	sum	312	399,84

APPENDIX B

Mean scores and the results of statistical procedures and tests for the legal genres along the 1988 dimensions

The SAS System

--- genre=Academic ---

The MEANS Procedure

Variable	N	Mean	Std Dev	Minimum	Maximum
dim1	71	-17.5870423	4.8892361	-24.1900000	6.5900000
dim2	71	-3.1280282	0.7716950	-4.9700000	-1.1700000
dim3	71	2.6822535	2.7915516	-1.4900000	8.9800000
dim4	71	-1.5271831	1.5677830	-3.9500000	4.1100000
dim5	71	3.9169014	1.9827921	0.0600000	10.9300000

--- genre=Bills ---

Variable	N	Mean	Std Dev	Minimum	Maximum
dim1	60	-23.9590000	2.5427455	-30.6200000	-13.0500000
dim2	60	-4.9410000	0.3418975	-5.7300000	-3.8900000
dim3	60	10.4653333	2.4230444	4.0700000	14.8900000
dim4	60	-1.5976667	1.4165551	-5.7200000	2.3000000
dim5	60	6.4856667	2.2806685	1.5400000	12.4000000

--- genre=Briefs ---

Variable	N	Mean	Std Dev	Minimum	Maximum
dim1	63	-18.0701587	2.1291953	-22.6500000	-10.8500000
dim2	63	-2.7790476	0.8477974	-4.2700000	0.4900000
dim3	63	6.7865079	1.4563456	2.5300000	9.6300000
dim4	63	-1.9042857	1.2104208	-4.0300000	0.3200000
dim5	63	4.7238095	1.5025274	1.9200000	9.9500000

--- genre=Contract ---

Variable	N	Mean	Std Dev	Minimum	Maximum
dim1	177	-19.2581921	2.9662279	-26.5100000	-8.5500000
dim2	177	-4.2226554	0.8436348	-5.7300000	0.1400000
dim3	177	9.6989266	3.1045300	0.2200000	27.2200000
dim4	177	0.6636158	2.5489390	-6.6100000	8.6200000
dim5	177	8.1707910	4.2286643	-1.4300000	43.8600000

The SAS System

-- genre=Professional article --

The MEANS Procedure

Variable	N	Mean	Std Dev	Minimum	Maximum
dim1	100	-16.1892000	6.7801927	31.4500000	4.9700000
dim2	100	-2.8639000	1.4409228	-5.2000000	1.8000000
dim3	100	6.8347000	2.7816551	-2.0700000	14.0000000
dim4	100	1.2100000	3.9749130	-5.0500000	17.6400000
dim5	100	5.0477000	2.7538116	-0.8000000	14.8600000

-- genre=Opinions --

Variable	N	Mean	Std Dev	Minimum	Maximum
dim1	114	-15.4167544	2.5860098	-24.0400000	-9.1900000
dim2	114	-2.4772807	1.0255387	-4.3900000	1.1300000
dim3	114	5.9362281	1.7703009	-3.6100000	10.1400000
dim4	114	-1.6057018	1.4469687	-4.6000000	6.5600000
dim5	114	4.1335965	1.4475204	-3.6300000	7.7200000

-- genre=Textbook --

Variable	N	Mean	Std Dev	Minimum	Maximum
dim1	101	-10.7461386	3.3376333	-22.5000000	-3.7500000
dim2	101	-1.8679208	1.2144680	-4.4700000	2.7100000
dim3	101	8.0047525	2.1614641	3.0400000	16.1500000
dim4	101	2.2004950	2.4604676	-2.5800000	11.4800000

dim5 101 7.8112871 2.2854171 3.2700000 14.3300000
ƒƒƒ

The SAS System

The GLM Procedure

Class Level Information

Class	Levels	Values
Genre	7	Academic Bills Briefs Contract Professional Articles Opinions Textbook

Number of Observations Read 686
Number of Observations Used 686

The SAS System

The GLM Procedure

Dependent Variable: dim1

Source	DF	Sum of Squares	Mean Square	F Value	Pr > F
Model	6	8204.96694	1367.49449	**90.10**	<.0001
Error	679	10305.19597	15.17702		
Corrected Total	685	18510.16290			

R-Square	Coeff Var	Root MSE	dim1 Mean
0.443268	-22.85137	3.895769	-17.04829

Source	DF	Type I SS	Mean Square	F Value	Pr > F
Genre	6	8204.966937	1367.494489	90.10	<.0001

Source	DF	Type III SS	Mean Square	F Value	Pr > F
Genre	6	8204.966937	1367.494489	90.10	<.0001

The SAS System 15:51 Tuesday, June 19, 2007 5

The GLM Procedure

Dependent Variable: dim2

Source	DF	Sum of Squares	Mean Square	F Value	Pr > F
Model	6	628.550367	104.758395	103.04	<.0001
Error	679	690.296758	1.016637		
Corrected Total	685	1318.847125			

R-Square	Coeff Var	Root MSE	dim2 Mean
0.476591	-31.46159	1.008284	-3.204810

Source	DF	Type I SS	Mean Square	F Value	Pr > F
Genre	6	628.5503672	104.7583945	103.04	<.0001

Source	DF	Type III SS	Mean Square	F Value	Pr > F
Genre	6	628.5503672	104.7583945	103.04	<.0001

The SAS System

The GLM Procedure

Dependent Variable: dim3

Source	DF	Sum of Squares	Mean Square	F Value	Pr > F
Model	6	3411.960851	568.660142	89.65	<.0001
Error	679	4307.049548	6.343225		
Corrected Total	685	7719.010399			

R-Square	Coeff Var	Root MSE	dim3 Mean
0.442021	33.67067	2.518576	7.480029

Source	DF	Type I SS	Mean Square	F Value	Pr > F
Genre	6	3411.960851	568.660142	89.65	<.0001

Source	DF	Type III SS	Mean Square	F Value	Pr > F
Genre	6	3411.960851	568.660142	89.65	<.0001

The SAS System

The GLM Procedure

Dependent Variable: dim4

Source	DF	Sum of Squares	Mean Square	F Value	Pr > F
Model	6	1551.378453	258.563075	44.66	<.0001
Error	679	3930.946008	5.789317		
Corrected Total	685	5482.324461			

R-Square	Coeff Var	Root MSE	dim4 Mean
0.282978	-3542.027	2.406100	-0.067930

Source	DF	Type I SS	Mean Square	F Value	Pr > F
genre	6	1551.378453	258.563075	44.66	<.0001

Source	DF	Type III SS	Mean Square	F Value	Pr > F
genre	6	1551.378453	258.563075	44.66	<.0001

The SAS System

The GLM Procedure

Dependent Variable: dim5

Source	DF	Sum of Squares	Mean Square	F Value	Pr > F
Model	6	2072.840841	345.473474	43.61	<.0001
Error	679	5379.068496	7.922045		
Corrected Total	685	7451.909337			

R-Square	Coeff Var	Root MSE	dim5 Mean
0.278162	46.23610	2.814613	6.087478

Source	DF	Type I SS	Mean Square	F Value	Pr > F
Genre	6	2072.840841	345.473474	43.61	<.0001

Source	DF	Type III SS	Mean Square	F Value	Pr > F
Genre	6	2072.840841	345.473474	43.61	<.0001

The SAS System 15:51 Tuesday, June 19, 2007 9

The GLM Procedure

Duncan's Multiple Range Test for dim1

NOTE: This test controls the Type I comparisonwise error rate, not the experimentwise error rate.

Alpha 0.05
Error Degrees of Freedom 679
Error Mean Square 15.17702
Harmonic Mean of Cell Sizes 86.47652

NOTE: Cell sizes are not equal.

Number of Means	2	3	4	5	6	7
Critical Range	1.163	1.225	1.266	1.296	1.320	1.339

Means with the same letter are not significantly different.

Duncan Grouping	Mean	N	genre
A	-10.7461	101	Textbook
B	-15.4168	114	Opinions
B			
B	-16.1892	100	Professional articles
C	-17.5870	71	Academic
C			
C	-18.0702	63	Briefs
D	-19.2582	177	Contract
E	-23.9590	60	Bills

The SAS System

The GLM Procedure

Scheffe's Test for dim1

NOTE: This test controls the Type I experimentwise error rate.

Alpha	0.05
Error Degrees of Freedom	679
Error Mean Square	15.17702
Critical Value of F	2.11191
Minimum Significant Difference	2.109
Harmonic Mean of Cell Sizes	86.47652

NOTE: Cell sizes are not equal.

Means with the same letter are not significantly different.

Scheffe Grouping	Mean	N	genre
A	-10.7461	101	Textbook
B	-15.4168	114	Opinions
B			
C B	-16.1892	100	Law firm
C			
C D	-17.5870	71	Academic
C D			
C D	-18.0702	63	Briefs
D	-19.2582	177	Contract
E	-23.9590	60	Bills

The SAS System

The GLM Procedure

Duncan's Multiple Range Test for dim2

NOTE: This test controls the Type I comparisonwise error rate, not the experimentwise error rate.

Alpha	0.05
Error Degrees of Freedom	679
Error Mean Square	1.016637
Harmonic Mean of Cell Sizes	86.47652

NOTE: Cell sizes are not equal.

Number of Means	2	3	4	5	6	7
Critical Range	.3011	.3170	.3276	.3355	.3416	.3466

Means with the same letter are not significantly different.

Duncan Grouping	Mean	N	genre
A	-1.8679	101	Textbook
B	-2.4773	114	Opinions
C	-2.7790	63	Briefs
C			
D C	-2.8639	100	Professional article
D			
D	-3.1280	71	Academic
E	-4.2227	177	Contract
F	-4.9410	60	Bills

The SAS System

The GLM Procedure

Scheffe's Test for dim2

NOTE: This test controls the Type I experimentwise error rate.

Alpha	0.05
Error Degrees of Freedom	679
Error Mean Square	1.016637
Critical Value of F	2.11191
Minimum Significant Difference	0.5458
Harmonic Mean of Cell Sizes	86.47652

NOTE: Cell sizes are not equal.

Means with the same letter are not significantly different.

Scheffe Grouping	Mean	N	genre
A	-1.8679	101	Textbook
B	-2.4773	114	Opinions
B			
C B	-2.7790	63	Briefs
C B			

C B -2.8639 100 Professional articles
C
C -3.1280 71 Academic

D -4.2227 177 Contract

E -4.9410 60 Bills

The SAS System

The GLM Procedure

Duncan's Multiple Range Test for dim3

NOTE: This test controls the Type I comparisonwise error rate, not the experimentwise error rate.

Alpha	0.05
Error Degrees of Freedom	679
Error Mean Square	6.343225
Harmonic Mean of Cell Sizes	86.47652

NOTE: Cell sizes are not equal.

Number of Means	2	3	4	5	6	7
Critical Range	.7520	.7918	.8183	.8380	.8534	.8659

Means with the same letter are not significantly different.

Duncan Grouping	Mean	N	genre
A	10.4653	60	Bills
B	9.6989	177	Contract
C	8.0048	101	Textbook
D	6.8347	100	Professional article
D			
D	6.7865	63	Briefs
E	5.9362	114	Opinions
F	2.6823	71	Academic

The SAS System

The GLM Procedure

Scheffe's Test for dim3

NOTE: This test controls the Type I experimentwise error rate.

Alpha	0.05
Error Degrees of Freedom	679
Error Mean Square	6.343225
Critical Value of F	2.11191
Minimum Significant Difference	1.3634
Harmonic Mean of Cell Sizes	86.47652

NOTE: Cell sizes are not equal.

Means with the same letter are not significantly different.

Scheffe Grouping	Mean	N	genre
A	10.4653	60	Bills
A			
A	9.6989	177	Contract
B	8.0048	101	Textbook
B			
C B	6.8347	100	Professional article
C B			
C B	6.7865	63	Briefs
C			
C	5.9362	114	Opinions
D	2.6823	71	Academic

The SAS System

The GLM Procedure

Duncan's Multiple Range Test for dim4

NOTE: This test controls the Type I comparisonwise error rate, not the experimentwise error rate.

Alpha	0.05
Error Degrees of Freedom	679

Error Mean Square 5.789317
Harmonic Mean of Cell Sizes 86.47652

NOTE: Cell sizes are not equal.

Number of Means	2	3	4	5	6	7
Critical Range	.7185	.7564	.7818	.8006	.8153	.8272

Means with the same letter are not significantly different.

Duncan Grouping	Mean	N	genre
A	2.2005	101	Textbook
B	1.2100	100	Professional articles
B			
B	0.6636	177	Contract
C	-1.5272	71	Academic
C			
C	-1.5977	60	Bills
C			
C	-1.6057	114	Opinions
C			
C	-1.9043	63	Briefs

The SAS System

The GLM Procedure

Scheffe's Test for dim4

NOTE: This test controls the Type I experimentwise error rate.

Alpha 0.05
Error Degrees of Freedom 679
Error Mean Square 5.789317
Critical Value of F 2.11191
Minimum Significant Difference 1.3025
Harmonic Mean of Cell Sizes 86.47652

NOTE: Cell sizes are not equal.

Means with the same letter are not significantly different.

Scheffe Grouping Mean N genre

A 2.2005 101 Textbook

A

B A 1.2100 100 Professional articles

B

B 0.6636 177 Contract

C -1.5272 71 Academic

C

C -1.5977 60 Bills

C

C -1.6057 114 Opinions

C

C -1.9043 63 Briefs

The SAS System

The GLM Procedure

Duncan's Multiple Range Test for dim5

NOTE: This test controls the Type I comparisonwise error rate, not the experimentwise error rate.

Alpha 0.05
Error Degrees of Freedom 679
Error Mean Square 7.922045
Harmonic Mean of Cell Sizes 86.47652

NOTE: Cell sizes are not equal.

Number of Means	2	3	4	5	6	7
Critical Range	.8404	.8848	.9145	.9365	.9537	.9677

Means with the same letter are not significantly different.

Duncan Grouping Mean N genre

A 8.1708 177 Contract

A

A 7.8113 101 Textbook

B 6.4857 60 Bills

C	5.0477	100	Professionalarticles
C			
D C	4.7238	63	Briefs
D			
D	4.1336	114	Opinions
D			
D	3.9169	71	Academic

The SAS System

The GLM Procedure

Scheffe's Test for dim5

NOTE: This test controls the Type I experimentwise error rate.

Alpha	0.05
Error Degrees of Freedom	679
Error Mean Square	7.922045
Critical Value of F	2.11191
Minimum Significant Difference	1.5237
Harmonic Mean of Cell Sizes	86.47652

NOTE: Cell sizes are not equal.

Means with the same letter are not significantly different.

Scheffe Grouping	Mean	N	genre
A	8.1708	177	Contract
A			
B A	7.8113	101	Textbook
B			
B C	6.4857	60	Bills
C			
D C	5.0477	100	Professionalarticles
D			
D	4.7238	63	Briefs
D			
D	4.1336	114	Opinions
D			
D	3.9169	71	Academic

INDEX

ŁÓDŹ
Studies in Language

Vol. 1 Barbara Lewandowska-Tomaszczyk / Patrick James Melia (eds.): PALC'99: Practical Applications in Language Corpora. Papers from the International Conference at the Universtiy of Łódź, 15–18 April 1999. 2000.

Vol. 2 Lou Burnard / Tony McEnery (eds.): Rethinking Language Pedagogy from a Corpus Perspective. Papers from the third international conference on Teaching and Language Corpora. 2000.

Vol. 3 Barbara Lewandowska-Tomaszczyk / John Osborne / Frits Schulte: Foreign Language Teaching and Information and Communication Technology. 2001.

Vol. 4 Piotr Cap: Explorations in Political Discourse. Methodological and Critical Perspectives. 2002.

Vol. 5 Ewa Waniek-Klimczak / Patrick James Melia (eds.): Accents and Speech in Teaching English Phonetics and Phonology. EFL perspective. 2002.

Vol. 6 Barbara Lewandowska-Tomaszczyk / Kamila Turewicz (eds.): Cognitive Linguistics Today. 2002.

Vol. 7 Barbara Lewandowska-Tomaszczyk (ed.): PALC 2001: Practical Applications in Language Corpora. 2003.

Vol. 8 Corpus Linguistics by the Lune. A Festschrift for Geoffrey Leech. Edited by Andrew Wilson, Paul Rayson and Tony McEnery. 2003.

Vol. 9 Barbara Lewandowska-Tomaszczyk (ed.): Practical Applications in Language and Computers. PALC 2003. 2004.

Vol. 10 Imagery in Language. Festschrift in Honour of Professor Ronald W. Langacker. Edited by Barbara Lewandowska-Tomaszczyk and Alina Kwiatkowska. 2004.

Vol. 11 Seana Coulson / Barbara Lewandowska-Tomaszczyk (eds.): The Literal and Nonliteral in Language and Thought. 2005.

Vol. 12 Piotr Cap (ed.): Pragmatics Today. 2005.

Vol. 13 Jacek Waliñski / Krzysztof Kredens / Stanisław Goźdź-Roszkowski (eds.): Corpora and ICT in Language Studies. PALC 2005. 2007.

Vol 14 Krzysztof Kosecki (ed.): Perspectives on Metonymy. Proceedings of the International Conference "Perspectives on Metonymy", held in Łódź, Poland, May 6–7, 2005. 2007.

Vol. 15 Barbara Lewandowska-Tomaszczyk / Tomasz Płudowski / Dolores Valencia Tanno (eds.): The Media and International Communication. 2007.

Vol. 16 Krzysztof Kredens / Stanisław Goźdź-Roszkowski (eds.): Language and the Law: International Outlooks. 2007.

Vol. 17 Barbara Lewandowska-Tomaszczyk (ed.): Corpus Linguistics, Computer Tools, and Applications – State of the Art. PALC 2007. 2008.

Vol. 18 Barbara Lewandowska-Tomaszczyk / Katarzyna Dziwirek (eds.): Studies in Cognitive Corpus Linguistics. 2009.

Vol. 19 Barbara Lewandowska-Tomaszczyk / Marcel Thelen (eds.): Meaning in Translation. 2010.

Vol. 20 Łukasz Bogucki / Krzysztof Kredens (eds.): Perspectives on Audiovisual Translation. 2010.

Vol. 21 Piotr Stalmaszczyk (ed.): Turning Points in the Philosophy of Language and Linguistics. 2011.

Vol. 22 Stanisław Goźdź-Roszkowski: Patterns of Linguistic Variation in American Legal English. A Corpus-Based Study. 2011.

www.peterlang.de